London Higher

London Higher

The Establishment of
Higher Education in London

Edited by

RODERICK FLOUD and SEAN GLYNN

THE ATHLONE PRESS
London & Atlantic Highlands, NJ

First published in 1998 by
THE ATHLONE PRESS
1 Park Drive, London, NW11 7SG
and 165 First Avenue,
Atlantic Highlands, NJ 07716

© Roderick Floud and Sean Glynn 1998

British Library Cataloguing in Publication Data
A catalogue record for this book is available from the British Library

ISBN 0 485 11524 7

Library of Congress Cataloging in Publication Data

London Higher .: the establishment of higher education in London /
edited by Roderick Floud and Sean Glynn.
    p.   cm.
Includes index.
ISBN 0–485–11524–7 (hc)
    1. Education, Higher—England—London—History. 2. Higher
education and state—England—London—History. 3. London (England)—
History. I. Floud, Roderick. II. Glynn, Sean.
LA639.L8L67   1998
378.421'2—dc21   97–47007
                                                                      CIP

Typeset by Ensystems, Saffron Walden

Printed and bound in Great Britain by
Cambridge University Press

Contents

Preface

This book celebrates over 150 years of higher education for the people of London. The occasion for its publication is the sesqui-centennial of the institution which began in 1848 as the Metropolitan Evening Classes for Young Men and which was transformed, through many changes of name and amalgamations, into London Guildhall University. But the book is not primarily a history of that university; instead, it considers the whole confusing array of higher education which has been provided, since the first half of the nineteenth century, for Londoners and those who work in that great city and it has benefitted from the contributions of many who work in those other universities and colleges.

The current mission of London Guildhall University, 'Serving London, a World City' seeks to encapsulate in a modern form the aims of those many men and women who founded, worked for and studied in the schools, colleges and universities whose history is described in this book. The higher education in which they took part was local, serving London's economy and society, but it was also national and international in the sense that London institutions attracted students from throughout Britain and indeed the world and sought to provide for them an education of the highest standard. But the bedrock was the local community, large and diverse although it has always been.

Paradoxically, this is a history of higher education in London in which the University of London takes a back seat. This is partly because the University already has an excellent history of its own,[1] mainly because the institutions which are described in this book

[1] N. Harte, 1986, *The University of London 1836–1986* London: The Athlone Press.

have never been considered as a whole before. It is also because, in the latter part of the twentieth century, some have seen a great international university, such as the University of London, to be serving an international community of scholars rather than the local community. This has led some parts of the University of London away from their roots and allowed them largely to neglect the communities in which they are physically located. By contrast, the colleges, polytechnics and universities described here have always sought to serve those diverse groups of people.

The supposed opposition between a local or regional and a national or international university seems to be a peculiarly English phenomenon, born perhaps from the dominance of Oxford and Cambridge within English universities or from the tradition among the English upper and middle classes of sending their children away from home. Thus was created the opposition of 'town and gown', in which young undergraduates imported into various English cities looked down upon 'townies', who themselves reacted badly, sometimes violently, to the usurpation of their social space. The creation of the new generation of rural campus universities in the 1960s, following the Robbins Report, reinforced this image of English universities as being apart from the community. The creation soon afterwards of the 'binary line' between universities and polytechnics, with the latter established firmly in city centres, was a further confirmation.

The phenomenon is very much an English one, though it might be fancifully traced back to the 'wandering scholars' of the middle ages. Scotland has long had a tradition of universities with strong local roots, not least because the vast majority of students have continued to live at home. In France and Germany, once again, local residence links university to community. Even in the United States of America, where the large distances often enforce residence at universities away from home, the strength of the state university systems has ensured that many of the leading universities have a strong connection with local industry and agriculture.

There are, in 1998, many signs that change is underway. The rapid expansion of the British university system in the late 1980s and early 1990s was accomplished only because many students continued to live at home and to study at their local university, rather than travelling across the country to live in halls of residence; financial pressures were partly responsible, but it was also because so many of the new students were older than 18 or 19, mature students with family ties and their roots in the community. There seems no doubt that these pressures will continue and that, more and more, universities will draw their students from their local communities.

In addition, however, many universities have realized not only that they have responsibilities to their local communities but also that they depend on a thriving local community. In many British cities, universities are now among the leading employers and play a major role in urban regeneration projects. They advise local industry, as they often did when they were founded in the late nineteenth century, but they have also become local centres for the arts and for a wide range of vocational and leisure courses. In all these ways, they are returning to their roots.

In London, the role of universities in the local economy is less obvious because of the sheer size and complexity of the city, but nevertheless still vital. London's universities are directly responsible for generating 2 per cent of London's gross domestic product, but indirectly responsible for training much of the labour force on which the rest of GDP depends. London remains, as it was in the late nineteenth century, the British city with the highest proportion of part-time students, heirs to the great tradition of the Mechanics' Institutes which inspired many of the institutions described in this book. As London becomes increasingly an economy based on the service sector and what are now known as the 'knowledge' industries, the importance of the development of skills for these new trades will grow still further and the contribution of the local universities will become even greater.

This book has sought, therefore, to explore the myriad ways by which higher education has emerged from and contributed to the life of London. I am personally grateful to all the authors, for accepting my invitation initially to consider the project and then for their continued interest and enthusiasm even as deadlines beckoned. My co-editor, Sean Glynn, has done most of the work of editing as well as making his own substantial contribution to the chapters. Athlone Press have been supportive and patient.

Last, London Guildhall University has underwritten the production of this book. As Provost of the University since 1988, I am naturally biased in its favour, but I am convinced that the strengths of the University, rooted in its history since 1848, have shone through in its steadfast concern for its students and for the academic values which underpin all its courses, from the conventionally academic to the wholly vocational. It has been a delight to lead an institution which educates impartially Ph.D. students in econometrics as well as apprentice silversmiths and which values all its students for what they can do and for how much they can improve. That, I believe, has been the tradition and the faith of all the institutions whose work this book describes.

Roderick Floud

Contributors

Roderick Floud Provost of London Guildhall University

Sean Glynn Senior Research Fellow, London Guildhall University

John Pratt Director of the Centre for Institutional Studies, University of East London

Nick Richards Research Fellow, Centre for Institutional Studies, University of East London

Anne Kershen Director of the Centre for the Study of Migration, Queen Mary and Westfield College

Miriam David Director of the Social Sciences Research Centre, South Bank University

Brenda Weeden University Archivist, Information Resource Services, University of Westminster

Arthur Chandler University Archivist, University of Surrey

John Izbicki Former Head of Public Affairs, University of North London

Ricahrd Aldrich Professor of History, University of London Institute of Education

Richard Williams Librarian, Lewis Walpole Library, Yale University

William Vaughan Professor of History of Art, Birkbeck College

CHAPTER ONE

The establishment of higher education in London: a survey

Sean Glynn

Higher education reflects the society it serves.[1] It is also a moulding influence on the social future, operating at the interface of social change and, as a result, is frequently controversial. Higher education patterns and policies reflect efforts and ideas which aim at both social and cultural continuity, and change. This paradox, and potential conflict, lies behind much of the ongoing polemic.[2] Recent years have seen dramatic developments and rapid growth in British higher education. These changes are based upon and have been made possible by building on a system which first began to develop in recognizable form in the years before 1914.

This book seeks to examine and highlight the establishment of a higher education system in London during the period 1830–1914, examining the main outcomes and the unique circumstances which produced them. Much was achieved in these years and it was certainly possible to refer to a distinctive and different London 'system' of higher education by the late nineteenth century. Indeed, Sidney Webb did so in his magisterial survey published in 1904.[3] However, the 'system', such as it was, had arisen as much by accident as design, and its adequacy and effectiveness was very much open to question. Many years later, and speaking essentially about the then-designated universities, the Robbins Report commented appropriately:

> today it would be a misnomer to speak of a system of higher education in this country, if by system is meant a consciously co-ordinated organisation. . . . Higher education has not been planned as a whole or developed within a framework consciously devised to promote harmonious evolution. What system there is has come about as the result of a series of particular initiatives, concerned

with particular needs and situations, and there is no way of dealing conveniently with all the problems common to higher education as a whole.[4]

It is immediately aparent that there are serious complexities in clearly defining both higher education and London. In what follows it is not the intention to attempt close definitions of either, nor do we intend to confine ourselves exclusively to the period specified above. The essential concern is with the *establishment* of the modern system of higher education in the London urban agglomeration. It is clear that there were important developments before 1830 and after 1914 and these will be examined where it is considered appropriate. The main developments came in the last quarter of the nineteenth century, spilling over into the twentieth. They commence with the establishment of the City and Guilds of London Institute in 1878 and culminate in the reform of the University of London in the late 1890s and the establishment of the London County Council as the main education authority for London in 1903. As a result of these late Victorian changes it can be argued that more was being done in terms of further and higher education for the majority of Londoners at the end of the nineteenth century than at the end of the twentieth.

During the main period under consideration metropolitan London experienced dramatic change both in character and scale.[5] The eighteenth century city of aristocratic elegance, palladian terraces and garden squares – with its counterpart of the 'mob' and 'Gin Lane' – gave way to the world metropolis: the political, commercial and financial capital and major port of the first industrial nation and the centre of the greatest empire in history. Historians have been confronted with great difficulties in attempting to comprehend, describe and analyse the vast complexities of modern London and there has been heavy reliance on images.[6] The nineteenth century city was increasingly described as a 'Metropolis' from the 1830s onwards but clear definitions of metropolitan London only began to emerge in the second half of the century. Young and Garside refer to the: 'sheer difficulty of comprehending London not just as a place in space but as a drama in time. Issues change, disappear, re-emerge. The continuities and discontinuities seem to defy the broad sweep of analysis'.[7] Londoners and, in particular, their myriad of public institutions and agencies, struggled to comprehend the scale and impact of a unique and unprecedented era of metropolitan growth and historians also have been daunted by these complexities. In consequence, we are left with a plethora of detailed and local studies which remain only ambiguously related to metroplitan development as a whole.[8] Insofar as the latter has been dealt with, the results tend to be heavily generalized and, inevitably, simplistic. Higher education is no exception to this; the rich legacy of individual institutional and personal record has been extensively mined, but the general picture remains unclear and is frequently confused. The latter day attention to corporate image has promoted a good deal of hyperbole which has gone largely unchallenged by historians. In this situation, it is difficult to evaluate the role and significance of individual developments and institutions in education and other spheres. There have been exaggerations in some cases while, at the same time, important developments and issues have been overlooked.

THE CHANGING PATTERN AND PROVISION OF HIGHER EDUCATION
In dealing with the development of higher education we need, inevitably, to examine the nature and dynamic of London's phenomenal growth during the nineteenth and early twentieth centuries. Demographic change and spatial re-arrangement was simply the most obvious manifestation of important economic and social developments, both within and beyond the metropolis. These, together with attendant political changes will also need to be considered in order to attempt to reach an understanding of the demand for and supply of higher education. It is clear at the outset that the evidence relating to supply is more readily obtainable than that relating to demand. While we know reasonably well what was actually provided in the way of higher education, it is rather less clear what was being demanded. Nevertheless, in the chapters which follow both sides of the equation will be examined.

In Victorian and Edwardian Britain higher education served a complex, highly segmented and differentiated society which was evolving rapidly. In London the social situation was probably even more complex than in the nation as a whole and the rural and new industrial stereotypes simply did not fit. In terms of higher education it may be said, as a simplification, that there were four main agencies and avenues of provision. First, and most important, was a highly variegated myriad of voluntarist institutions and instruments which was rapidly augmented during the nineteenth century. This *voluntarist* provision varied enormously and was subjected to frequent change. Institutional failure was much more likely than long- or even medium-term success and the record is littered with casualities.[9] From the middle of the century the beginnings of systematization began to emerge as *central* and later *local government*, augmented by professional and *other authorities*, began to intervene and have an impact. This intervention was promoted primarily through two activities: funding and regulation. When the history of individual institutions of higher education is examined the above agencies are invariably represented at different stages and, at most times, operate simultaneously.

Education was expensive to provide and higher education was the most expensive form. Also, it was not self-financing, although students were usually required to pay some contribution. Apart from staff and operating expenditures, there were major fixed costs in order to secure premises and property was relatively expensive in London. Leasing arrangements were rarely satisfactory on a long-term basis and most institutions sought to own their own buildings. Without exception, educational institutions encountered financial problems which were frequently life threatening and often terminal. Finance was a crucial factor affecting development and a major conditioning influence. The need to secure funds determined the nature of higher educational provision, both in general and in particular, affecting the nature of institutions established and prevailing and determining who studied, who taught and what courses were available. The funding of higher education is examined in detail in Chapter seven below.

British education history has often been approached in terms of what might be called a 'Whig' interpretation which sees development as a progression from patchy, piecemeal and experimental provision on a voluntarist basis to the eventual establishment of a public and systematized order. What follows will lend some credence to this approach while, at the same time, providing a good deal of evidence for a possible 'postmodernist' interpretation of historical developments. It is certainly the case that British government seemed slow to act and, in the nineteenth century at least, preferred to leave things to voluntary effort. However, government action, both local and central, had to confront a gross inadequacy of voluntary effort and government was often the innovator.[10] Also, government and private effort was often closely linked through the activities of important intermediaries. There was also some reciprocity between public and private activity, not least where the latter involved the City of London.

In the early voluntarist stage of institutional development there was almost always a major individual benefactor, giving generously in terms of funds or effort, and in some cases both. Alongside important individual benefactors such as Hogg, Cass, Beaumont, Bancroft, Morley, Holloway, and many others, there was also, almost inevitably, a Society or institutional input of some kind. Few educational institutions were founded without a conscious Christian involvement and even the 'Godless' institution of Gower Street, which became University College, was initially seen by some as a national academy for dissenting Christians.[11] The Established Church played an important role, mainly through members of the clergy, and other religious denominations also had an important involvement. The role of the Livery Companies of the City of London is examined in Chapter five. From the middle years of the nineteenth century central government began to intervene directly and systematically through two agencies. The Science and Art Department and the Board of Education. Later still, local government became involved with the creation of the School Board for London (1870) and the Technical Education Committee of the London County Council which was established in 1893. These government agencies operated independently and simultaneously and, to some extent, in rivalry with each other. Such rivalries were, on occasion, bitter and had a significant influence on development. Another central agency, the Charity Commissioners, also assumed an important and independent role which was especially relevant to London after the creation of the London Parochial Charities Commission in 1884. Much of the work of these various bodies began to be brought together and co-ordinated under the 1903 Education Act which made the LCC the principal education authority for London. However, important areas continued to remain outside the control of the new authority including the University and a range of voluntary but important institutions. Finally, one should also mention the important contribution from the City and Guilds of London Institute. The Corporation of the City of London, together with many of the Livery Companies, became heavily involved in the funding, regulation and management of several educational institutions and in the organization of technical and vocational education.

Commencing his survey of adult education, published in 1851, J.W. Hudson commented in an effusive and patronizing manner:

> The unexampled efforts now making in every part of the Kingdom for the intellectual and physical improvement of the lower classes of the community, distinguish the present, as the age of phil-anthropy and good-will to all men. The middle classes vie with the rich in promoting the great and good-work of education.[12]

There is ample evidence that an influential minority of the Victorian elite was well-disposed towards further provision of education and this is perhaps not surprising in a society dedicated to 'self-help' and individual improvement. An important example was set at the social pinnacle by Prince Albert who bestowed not only patronage and encouragement but also personal financial donations on a wide range of educational activities. Victorian providers of education constitute an almost endless list which includes many bodies and organizations primarily concerned with other matters. The Chartists, the YMCA, Co-operative Societies, for example, made significant provisions for education beyond the elementary level.[13] The role of the Church, which dated from medieval times, has already been mentioned. This was mainly in elementary instruction but the need to train priests and teachers had given rise to an interest in higher education and this was augmented after 1830.[14] Victorian radicals, utilitarians and reform-ers challenged the traditional view that education beyond the elementary level was not for the masses and could, indeed, be dangerous in giving the lower orders ideas above their station. Higher education began to be seen as a route to enlightenment and personal fulfilment for more than a narrow elite. At a later stage, the perceived need to improve scientific knowledge and technical training became an important influence on educational provision. By the second half of the nineteenth century education could be justified, even to the most conservative opinion, on grounds of social cohesion. Powerful utilitarian arguments also began to emerge in terms of 'national efficiency' and the needs of the economy. These arguments did not come from industrialists and business leaders, but from educationalists. They were shrewdly deployed by an influential lobby for science education led by Lyon Playfair and Thomas Huxley. This was succeeded by attempts to promote technical and commercial education and education for the masses. These pressures, together with the resulting experiments, were largely deployed in London with a consequent enrichment of the educational pattern.

If the list of educational providers is long and varied it can also be said that the same is true of the instruments. In the conventional view, higher education was provided by the ancient universities at Oxford and Cambridge and their Scottish and Irish counterparts. The nineteenth century saw the creation of new universities in London and elsewhere, and these were augmented by the Polytechnics, Colleges and Technical Institutes. In fact, the picture is much more varied than this and it is possible to make a very long list of the instruments of further education. This would include, *inter alia*, the atheneums and literary institutes, literary and scientific associations, libraries which made books, quality newspapers and journals available, museums and galleries, mechanics' institutes, reading rooms, discussion groups and lectures, evening classes and university extension.[15] This represents a complex institutional history which cannot be fully comprehended, even in relation to London, in what follows. Our concern rather is to survey and highlight some of the main developments which are relevant to the establishment of the modern higher education system.

The Census of 1851, which was almost certainly incomplete, listed 1,017 'literary and scientific' institutions in England and Wales. It also listed 1,545 evening schools for adults with 39,783 pupils.[16] Most of this activity would not fit any modern definition of higher education. However, clear definitions are difficult and it might be wrong to attempt to impose twentieth century definitions on the nineteenth when the majority achieved nothing beyond the most rudimentary instruction and only a very small minority experienced secondary education in any recognizable form. Free elementary education for all was not established until the 1890s. Much of the early teaching carried out by London University, for example, is most accurately characterized as 'secondary' and this was probably essential in order to ensure a supply of pupils for higher courses.[17] On the other hand, some of the institutions and activities mentioned above were operating in areas and at levels which are nowadays part of the higher education curriculum.

Over time a particularly English concept of university and higher education has prevailed against repeated challenges which continue at present. The ideal is based essentially on Oxford and Cambridge. It involved an elitist approach whereby a very small minority was selected on economic, social and cultural as well as academic criteria. Instruction was linked with scholarship and research and administered to post-18 year olds on a full-time basis in collegiate and semi-cloistered circumstances, in a single or narrow range of subjects which could be studied to intensive levels. Collegiate and gentlemanly values predominated and semi-rural or small-town seclusion provided what was seen as the ideal mileaux.[18] In Scotland and other European countries there were different approaches. The Scottish academies were operated on a post-16 basis with much broader subject approach and in less cloistered situations. In the early nineteenth century Oxford and Cambridge began to be attacked on a number of grounds. In particular, for religious, gender and socio-economic exclusions and narrow curricula activity. New universities and colleges, including London, were founded to cater for non-Anglicans, women and other excluded groups and to provide higher education which was more affordable, accessible and flexible in terms of subject cover-age.[19] In its early years London University borrowed more from the Scottish examples than from Oxford and was in the tradition of the Dissenting Academies while also borrowing from German example (see below). However, over time the Oxford model proved to be adaptable and capable of modest reform, thereby retaining its position as the higher education pinnacle, but more importantly, as the *ideal* institutional and pedagogical form. Reform in British higher education has repeatedly confronted the problem that the Oxford model is expensive and difficult, if not impossible, to replicate on a wider basis. Repeatedly efforts have been made and ways found to avoid these difficulties, at least in part, and the ideal has been upheld and has endured. The Oxford system survived from a pre-industrial age when only a small aristocratic elite aspired to university education, largely for social and religious reasons, and were economically able to participate. Late in the nineteenth century changing employment patterns and the advent of what has sometimes been called the 'second industrial revolution' provided the basis for an argument that an expanded and broadened system of higher education, giving attention to science, technology and commerce, was necessary.[20] This argument was put in Britain by a small group of professional educationalists and reformers, such as Sidney Webb and Thomas Huxley, who happened to be concentrated in the capital. As a result, these developments had a particular prominence and greater resonance in London. Meeting these newly perceived needs was carried out in a patchy, piecemeal and uncertain manner and older concepts and traditions endured and had an important influence.

British institutions of higher education, at all levels, have tended to be 'upwardly mobile' in both social and academic terms and where this has been resisted the result has usually been long-term failure. These dynamic tendencies probably reflect social, cultural and financial realities, as well as values, and it should also be said that the enduring Oxford ideal can easily be defended in objective educational terms and particularly from the point of view of scholarship and academic freedom. Ironically, perhaps, the fact remains that virtually all the higher educational endeavour in London before 1914 was prefaced on the assumption that the Oxford model was inadequate and inappropriate. Quite apart from the excluded middle-class elements, which London University was established to provide for, many London institutions were aimed, quite specifically, at the working classes. Without exception, these were rapidly taken over by higher socio-economic groups with consequent changes in organization, aspirations and curriculum. The London Mechanics' Institute, founded in the 1820s, eventually became Birkbeck College and, in 1907, joined London University. Most Mechanics' Institutes, including several in London, had ceased to exist by 1870. The 'Peoples' Palace' founded in the 1880s for the poor of East London followed a similar route to Birkbeck as Queen Mary College (see Chapter three). The City and Guilds College, founded in 1890 to educate teachers of technology and 'superior workmen' became part of Imperial College (see Chapter five). The London Polytechnics, founded between 1880 and 1914, specifically for the 'poorer classes of London', also became part of the university sector in the long run. Attempts to provide education for the majority beyond elementary level were a failure. This failure reflected a lack of demand for what was provided. Most people did not begin to receive even an elementary education until late in the nineteenth century. Secondary education was very limited, to a small number of endowed and private schools, and often of poor quality. University and King's Colleges were obliged to establish schools to ensure a supply of students, and to commence degree work at low levels. Much of the education for people over 14 was intended to make good the deficiencies in elementary and second-ary education. In particular, this was the main aim of part-time and evening instruction which burgeoned in London after 1890. The main demand for higher education came from the upwardly mobile and aspirant middle classes. These demands were often for 'liberal' education which came to include languages and literature as well as the classics. However, in the later nineteenth century vocational demands began to make a major impact and the hope of occupational reward became the main incentive to attend college. At the same time, occupation became the main determinant of attendance and the manual working class remained heavily under-represented. Working-class demands for vocational education were not met, in general, because this was left to employers, the apprenticeship system and to training on the job. Genuinely vocational education was both expensive and difficult to provide, but there was an attempt to improve working class knowledge of scientific principles and technologies. Upward mobility in this provision was driven by financial and professional considerations. Administrators, students and teaching staff aspired to higher intellectual and professional status and this influenced curricula. More important was the fact that funding patterns were pressured and eventually determined by these supply and demand conditions, influencing heavily institutional survival and character.

THE CHANGING METROPOLIS

Victorian London inspired the awe and amazement of many visitors but also acquired a sinister and menacing image by virtue of its burgeoning and apparent absence of cohesion and control. This ran from Cobbett's 'infernal wen' through the novels of Dickens to the 'outcast' London of 'Jack the Ripper' in the later part of the century.[21] London increased its population by approximately 10,000 each year, or almost 20 per cent each decade, rising from about 1 million at the beginning of the nineteenth century to 5 million at the end.[22] Growth in metropolitan population was substantially augmented by in-migration mainly from the adjacent rural and relatively poor Counties of Essex, Kent, Hertfordshire, Surrey and Middlesex.[23] There was also significant longer distance migration from all parts of the British Isles. Irish migration rose to high levels after the Great Famine of 1846 and, in the final decades of the century, Jewish migration from Russia and Eastern Europe made an impact.[24] In-migration was contained and counterbalanced by suburbanization as London spilled into the Home Counties and the commuter network spread ever wider as transport improved and became cheaper.[25] London, unlike some of its European counterparts, was surrounded by land which was relatively easily made available and was suitable for development. This seems to have acted as a physical, social and political safety valve. It was also a conditioning influence on community. By the third quarter of the nineteenth century the middle classes had largely fled central London for the more salubrious atmosphere of suburban villas. Few people of any standing and importance in the City actually lived there and the civic institutions of the Square Mile were overwhelmingly dominated by tradesmen and small shopkeepers (see Chapter five).

London remained an agglomeration of neighbourhoods spreading from the original deographic foci of the eponymous City of London, which was well-established as the national financial and commercial centre, and the Royal and political capital at Westminster. Growth spread from these nodes into neighbouring villages which were rapidly absorbed into the urban mass. In the middle decades of the nineteenth century London became the focus of a national rail network.[26] The railways, and, more importantly, trams and omnibuses, began to provide a means of population redistribution in the metropolis itself. The middle classes began to move out of the central areas to new suburbs, while, for a time, the lower socio-economic groups remained immobile. This reflected the high cost of Victorian transport in relation to working-class incomes. As a result, some more central areas such as Spitalfields, which in the eighteenth and early nineteenth centuries had contained substantial middle class populations, gradually drifted down the social scale. By the

1880s Spitalfields had become the notorious slum associated with 'Jack the Ripper' murders. Several inner city areas followed a similar if less precipitous fate as the better-off became increasingly mobile. However, in the final decades of the century, large sections of the manual working class also began to migrate to new suburban areas especially on the eastern and northern margins.[27]

The economy and labour market of nineteenth century London have been insufficiently researched and understood by historians. London's role in British industrialization has perhaps been underestimated and a fundamental explanation for the phenomenal growth and prowess of Victorian London has yet to be supplied, but these issues are examined in Chapter two. In the eighteenth century the economy of London was largely geared to services and personal consumption with burgeoning foreign trade and imperial expansion supplying an essential dynamic. London companies in most activities tended to be small scale and the extensive range of manufacturing activity was organized largely on a craft and bespoke basis. The industrial revolution occurred outside London, mainly in the coalfield areas.[28] Many traditional London manufacturing activities were destroyed or damaged by cheaper production elsewhere and falling transport costs. Other activities were damaged by increasing site and labour costs in London after 1815. Shipbuilding, for example, left the Thames in the mid-nineteenth century.[29] Many trades and industries only survived by moving out of London or by moving up-market, often leaving substantial working-class populations bereft of regular employment. Manufacturing production which remained in central London concentrated increasingly on domestic consumption and luxury items for the better-off, together with furniture and clothing, which survived by becoming 'sweated trades'. In traditional working-class areas of east and north London homework, small workshops and 'sweating' became endemic. These trades were volatile with heavy reliance on cheap, casualized, often immigrant, female and child labour.[30] As a result, nineteenth century London became a notorious centre for poor and degraded workers. This disturbing and threatening 'undermass' was distinguishable from the nineteenth century British working-class stereotype.[31] There is a good deal of evidence that London workers were more difficult to organize, for example, into trade unions or co-operatives, and, while the lack of even basic education was palpable, there was greater resistance and indifference in London than elsewhere.[32] Hudson states that London organizations for education and improvement 'had a shorter career than others owing rather to the apathy evinced by the labouring population than to their superior intelligence'.[33]

While 'outcast' London has received a good deal of attention, both from contemporaries and historians, this tends to convey a rather distorted picture. Nineteenth century London also had a large, relatively prosperous and upwardly mobile working class which merged into newly-emergent lower middle-class elements. Indeed, London's social structure below the professional middle-class level was highly complex and relatively fluid. Social mobility was much higher in London than elsewhere. The pattern of artisan and lower middle-class occupations varied enormously, with the result that clear social categorizations are difficult. Nevertheless, the scale of inward migration and population growth is evidence that the Metropolis provided ample opportunities for social and economic advancement and this has to be set against the historiographical emphasis on poverty and deprivation. While declining industries and 'sweated' trades undoubtedly blighted many lives, burgeoning commerce, retailing, finance and services created growing employment opportunities. As did the growth in land transport, navigation and the Port of London. In particular, London had large numbers of young men anxious to make their way in life at differing levels and well aware of available opportunities in the metropolitan economy. Such people figure prominently in the pages of Victorian and Edwardian novels, from Dickens to Wells, and they were the main customers and consumers of higher education.

London's rapid growth overwhelmed the existing bounderies and local authorities and the rationalization and reform of metropolitan institutions became a major concern of progressive opinion.[34] The Metropolitan Police Authority was established in 1829, operating in a radius of four to seven miles from Charing Cross, but excluding the City of London. However, local government reform in the 1830s failed to have any impact on London and, prior to 1847, there were over 300 administrative units operating in the London area deriving powers from approximately 250 local Acts of Parliament.[35] These included eight Sewer Commissions, statutory trusts for paving and other amenities, turnpike trusts and local vestries, varying greatly in size and structure.[36] What has been termed the 'Struggle for London' commenced seriously in the 1840s with Edwin Chadwick's campaign for public health reforms. The Metropolitan Commission for Sewers, established in 1847, was the first London-wide authority, other than the Police, and its boundaries were adopted by the LCC in 1888.

London's complex route towards administrative reform has been characterized as a long struggle between progressive opinion and powerful vested interests in the form, particularly, of local vestries and the City of London. A contest between 'English' localism and 'French' centralism, between utilitarianism and conservatism, and, eventually, between socialism and market forces. It has been suggested that the Corporation of the City of London 'could rival, pre-empt or subvert any metropolitan movement'.[37] The City had salvaged and consolidated its autonomy, ancient rights and privileges during the 'Silent Revolution' of 1688 and these continued to be strenously guarded.[38] City influence, rights and jursidiction extended well beyond the famous Square Mile and represented a powerful barrier to centralizing tendencies. Where these managed to succeed, the City was invariably excluded. Perhaps ironically, the City's continuing determination to preserve its autonomy was a main influence in giving rise to its eventual assumption of a quite prominent and extraordinary role in the provision, funding, administration and regulation of higher education. This included extensive benefactions from longstanding City Charities which were consolidated and made available 'To promote the education of the poorer inhabitants of the Metropolis' under the London Parochial Charities Act of 1883. Further substantial allocations of funds to a range of specific educational activities by the City Corporation and the Livery Companies; and the establishment of the City and Guilds Institution in 1878. Attacks upon the privileged position of the City became particularly intense during the 1870s at a time when there was growing awareness of the need to improve technical education. Largely as a result, the City's efforts were directed particulary towards technical education. The important role of the City in promoting higher education in London and elsewhere is examined in Chapter five.

THE BEGINNINGS OF HIGHER EDUCATION IN LONDON

Higher education in London has a very long history despite the fact that there was no formally designated university until 1828. While Oxford and Cambridge may have served the needs of the aristocracy and the Established Church well enough, the capital city made demands for higher learning in more practical and vocational ways. Training in medicine, surgery and law was established during the Middle Ages and the London teaching hospitals and the Inns of Court have long histories. In its role as political capital and major port and commercial centre London also demanded higher skills in a number of other areas and there is a lengthy but incomplete record of formal instruction in mathematics, languages, scrivening, navigation, book-keeping, naval and army training and many other subjects which are now an important part of the higher education curriculum. Most of this instruction was supplied by small, *ad hoc*, and usually ephemeral, privately operated establishments.[39] However, naval and military training was organized by government and notable efforts were made by religious, professional and social organizations and societies. In 1615 London was described as 'The Third Universitie of England' when Sir George Buck claimed that 'Within and about the Most Famous Cittie of London' instruction was offered in law, medicine, theology, mathematics, sciences, modern and ancient languages, courtly exercises, useful arts and skills.[40] During the Tudor period the City established a network of Grammar Schools and also gave generously to higher education. Between 1480 and 1660 City charities gave £92,000 towards fellowships and scholarships at Oxford and Cambridge and this represented 4.89 per cent of London charitable dispensations.[41] In 1579 Sir Thomas Gresham, founder of the Royal Exchange, had bequeathed his house in Bishopsgate plus rents from the Royal Exchange to be held by the City Corporation and the Mercer's Company. A College with seven professors in specified subjects was founded and lectures were given on an occasional basis at Bishopsgate from 1579 to 1768 and thereafter in the Royal Exchange until 1843. Gresham College did not develop as an important centre for teaching and learning and failed to fulfill the hopes of its founder despite a more or less continuous existence to the present time. Attempts to link the college with City and Guilds and to establish a university were made in the late nineteenth century but these failed.

Post restoration London became a centre for the aristocracy and this entrenched London's position as the national capital. From the late eighteenth century London became the location for learned societies and similar institutions, many of which reflected the growing interest in science and literature. In the words of F.M.L. Thompson, 'London was to play a prominent part in the reorganisation of the branches of knowledge as they subdivided and multiplied, calling out for systematic classification and arrangement so that teaching could be well-ordered, and further advances in defined disciplines made possible'.[42] The Society of Arts, which became the Royal Society in 1810, was founded in 1755. In the early nineteenth century a wave of institutions followed. These included the London Institution, 1809, the Philomathic Institution, 1807, the Russell Institution, 1808, the Geological Society, 1807, the Astronomical Society, 1820, the Zoological Society, 1826, the Geographical Society, 1830, the Botanical Society, 1839, the Chemical Society, 1841. The Philomathic Institution was one of the earliest of a flood of literary and scientific associations for the social elite. Founded under the patronage of the Duke of Sussex it aimed at 'the general cultivation and exercise of the intellectual powers, and the promotion of art, science and literature, by means of lectures, library, reading room, essay and discussion classes, and the publication of a journal containing original essays, poems and other compositions by the members'. In 1835 the Whittington Club was established on the model of the Manchester Athenaeum. Institutes were founded in Marylebone, in 1832, and Islington in 1833. These institutions spread downwards socially to some extent and also geographically to the 'out-boroughs' of Southwark, Chelsea, Greenwich, Lambeth and Limehouse. Some, at least, established evening classes in languages and music. By 1838 there were more than 20 literary and mutual improvement societies in the metropolis.

Such institutions catered mainly for the well-off and were not primarily dedicated to formal instruction. In the first half of the nineteenth century it seems probable that education in London may have fallen behind that available in some provincial towns and cities, particularly in the industrializing North. In 1837 Brougham had made the controversial claim that 'education was less provided for in the large towns than in country districts'.[43] London's rapid growth left the Established Church and other educational providers struggling to keep pace.

In 1823 a Mechanic's Institute was established in the City of London by a group which included J.C. Robertson, Thomas Hodgkin, Francis Place, Jeremy Bentham and James Mill and was chaired by George Birkbeck. Others followed in the London area and there were 28 in 1850, out of a national total of 610.[44] The Institute failed to live up to its original intention of instructing working-class men in the principles of science. According to Hudson, 'The Institution has been for some years little more than an association of shopkeepers and their apprentices, law copyists and attorney's clerks'. Even so, there were cash problems.[45] A City of London Mechanic's Institute was established in 1836 as the Tower Street Mutual Improvement Association. This involved classes, lectures and a library. Members paid 2/6 per quarter (12.5p) subscription. Almost by definition, these 'institutes' or 'mutual improvement societies' were for the upwardly mobile and they were often accused of being 'middle class and middle aged'.[46] The Mechanic's Institutes were not the first or the last educational institution aimed at meeting the needs of the working class and failing to do so. Manual workers lacked the energy, time and resources to study, even in the evening. While workers were interested in genuinely vocational education this was rarely on offer, largely for cost reasons. Courses which might have been suitable for working-class students were either not on offer or were crowded out of the curriculum by financial pressures or the predilictions of professional educators. Nevertheless, efforts to reach the masses continued to be made.

The Young Men's Christian Association was founded in the City of London in 1844 by George Williams, a draper's assistant.[47] A reading room and library was established in Gresham Street where lectures and classes were held in a wide range of subjects.[48] From 1849 classes were held in Exeter Hall which became YMCA headquarters in 1881. There were eight London YMCAs by 1851 out of a national total of 16. In 1836 the London Working Men's Association had initiated the 'Peoples' Charter' which was adopted by the Chartist Movement. National Hall in Holborn became a centre for meetings, lectures and classes and day and Sunday schools were established from 1848.[49] Christian and socialist members of the Chartist movement were especially active in education and the establishment of the London Working Mens' College in 1854, by F.D. Maurice, Tom Hughes and others, can be traced to this influence.[50] The College commenced in Red Lion Square, but moved to Great Ormonde Street in 1857. Initially about half the students, who were all over 16, were drawn from the manual working class, but this tended to diminish over time. In 1864 a Working Womens' College was established in Queen Square.

Central government first began to become directly involved in education in the 1830s. However, this involved the support of existing, voluntary activities rather than new initiatives. The motivations were a mixture of utilitarian and moral imperatives, reflecting the views and activities of minority groups and individuals. Under the Education Act of 1833 an annual sum of £20,000 was distributed on the advice of the National Society for Educating the Poor in the Principles of the Established Church and the British and Foreign Schools Society. In 1840 two inspectors were appointed by the Committee of the Privy Council on Education. One of these, the Rev. W.J. Kennedy, in his report of 1848, was critical of the widespread use of child labour and school-leaving at an early age. He urged the development of evening classes. In 1848 the Ten Hours Act limited the daily duration of juvenile labour. This placed a new emphasis on evening instruction. Also in 1848 Bishop Blomfield, the Bishop of London, called upon the clergy to offer evening instruction and this was taken up by the Rev. William Mackenzie who established the Metropolitan Evening Classes for Young Men. These developed into the City of London College, established at Crosbie Hall, Bishopsgate in 1861. From 1851 grants were given for evening instruction by the central government. These were to match the fees charged and to be used to pay for additional teachers.[51] Evening instruction developed in a number of new and existing institutions such as Mechanic's Institutes and became the norm for post-elementary education.

As a result of Ewart's Select Committee on Arts and Manufactures, which reported in 1835, central government sponsored the establishment and expansion of special schools of Design and Technology in London and other centres.[52] The Normal School of Design later became the Royal College of Art. From this beginning we can trace the Science and Art Department which was formally established in 1853 under the Board of Trade. From the 1850s the Science and Art Department was only one of three central government agencies with extensive responsibilities for education. The other two were the Education Department, in Whitehall, and the Charity Commissioners. The Education Department (Whitehall) and the Science and Arts Department (South Kensington) were organized under the Committee on Education of the Privy Council. The former was mainly concerned with elementary education, but did extend to higher levels, albeit on a questionable legal basis. The Science and Arts Department aimed to encourage the teaching of applied sciences and arts through the encouragement of schools and museums. It also became an important examining and regulatory body. Payment was invariably supplementary and on the basis of results obtained in examinations or on presentation of scientific examples.[53] Grants were given to existing voluntary institutions and were undoubtedly an important conditioning influence on the development of higher education. In 1859, under a new scheme, any institution could apply for recognition by the Department. Teachers had to be certificated and their salaries were grant-augmented. The Department matched sums raised from fees and local grants in approved situations and additional payments were made to teachers on the basis of results. Under these arrangements Mechanic's Institutes and other voluntary institutions were able to apply for grants although, in many cases, this involved the establishment of suitable teaching and hiring appropriate staff in line with Departmental requirements. As a result, there was increasing emphasis on academic, rather than vocational or recreational, requirements and examinations became more important. In 1856 the Science and Art Department of the Board of Trade and the Committee on Education of the Privy Council were officially merged into the Department of Education. However, each retained a separate existence, the former in Kensington and the latter in Whitehall.

After the Great Exhibition of 1851 the Commissioners and others, including Prince Albert, developed initiatives whereby some of the surplus funds from the Exhibition would be used in the furtherance of 'industrial education'.[54] Funds amounting to £186,436 were available from the profits of the Exhibition and these were augmented by a central government grant of £150,000. Land was purchased in South Kensington and this eventually became a nucleus for institutions connected with higher education and science and technology. Learned societies, colleges, museums gathered in South Kensington and it also became the location of the Science and Art Department and the City and Guilds of London Central Institution. By the early twentieth century South Kensington had an impressive cluster of science institutions and several of these were combined to form Imperial College in 1907. In this process, however, the original purpose of developing 'industrial education' may have been given less attention than it deserved.[55]

In 1851 the Education Department offered aid to evening schools connected with day schools currently under inspection. By 1858 there were 2,036 schools holding evening classes with 54,571 male and 26,395 female pupils.[56] Under these arrangements the main provisions were for elementary education, but upward drift and provisions for specialist institutions ensured that there was some input into higher education. Three-quarters of the schools aided under these arrangements were run by the Established Church.[57] In the 1860s there seems to have been rapid growth in grant-aided evening schools although the revised regulations of 1862 defined elementary education as the main function. From 1871 scholars over 18 became ineligible for grants, but in 1876 the age limit was raised to 21. Many evening schools were eventually absorbed into the London and national systems of technical and higher education.

Under the Forster Education Act of 1870 local School Boards were established on the basis of direct elections with the power to raise funds for education through precepts on local authorities. This Act was not originally intended to apply to London but an amendment proposed by W.M. Torrens led to its inclusion. The School Board for London was established on the basis of ten electoral divisions covering the 114 square miles of the Metropolitan Board of Works area. The first Board met in the Guildhall in December, 1870. The main concern was with elementary education and evening and adult education received little attention in the early years. In 1872 a Departmental Coding limited grants to those under 18. However, in 1882 there was a School Board initiative which led to the opening of 83 evening schools in London, enrolling 9,000 pupils. Many of these schools also involved teaching under Science and Arts Department regulations and subsidies, as well as voluntary teaching activity.

Some of this related to further and higher education, especially in science and modern languages.[58] Essentially, however, the initiatives in higher education were still being left to voluntary and unofficial efforts. Government at local and national level preferred to allow these to proceed before intervening with assistance and regulation.

In the history of London higher education the 1880s stands out as a crucial decade. Between the late 1870s and the early 1890s a series of initiatives had the effect of transforming educational provision in the capital. These initiatives arose from a complex blend of public and private activity. Three important new agencies, in particular, were responsible for this transformation. These were the City and Guilds of London Institution, the City Parochial Charities Foundation and the Technical Education Board of the London County Council. These three bodies were dominated by a small group of influential individuals and there were important inter-connections. All three set out to build upon and co-operate with existing provision and to extend it through voluntarist institutions and individual benefaction. At the same time, each also had access to new and substantial resources for education. The way in which they chose to disburse these resources had an important influence. By the closing years of the nineteenth century what can be referred to as a 'system' of further and higher education was being established in London. Features of this system became a model for the English regions and elsewhere.[59]

THE CITY AND GUILDS OF LONDON INSTITUTE

The City and Guilds of London Institute (CGLI) resulted from a long series of discussions involving the Corporation of London and the leading Livery Companies. These are examined in more detail in Chapter five. A few leading individuals, including Sir Sydney Waterlow and Lord Selbourne played a prominent role in overcoming both indifference and obstruction from City interests. Developments leading to the establishment of City and Guilds were assisted by, and in part resulted from, the fact that the City was under attack from reformers and this came to include leading members of the Liberal Party including W.E. Gladstone and Sir

William Harcourt. City interests were a major barrier to municipal reform in London and the Livery Companies or Guilds, which were an integral part of governance in the City, became a target. The City Companies had largely lost their original functions, involving the supervision and representation of a particular trade or 'misterie', but continued to exist for social and political reasons.[60] They also continued to control substantial resources, usually in the form of trust monies or property, left by former members. Critics argued that these funds were being misappropriated and spent on lavish dinners and stipends by a corrupt few. In most cases Company control had fallen into the hands of people who had no connection with the defining trade or craft and entry was effectively purchased and controlled by oligarchies. Resources which had once been more or less communal had fallen into the hands of small, unrepresentative and possibly suspect coteries. There were demands that the Guilds be disbanded and their resources devoted to public purposes and, in 1880, a Royal Commission was established by Sir William Harcourt, the Liberal Home Secretary, to enquire into their situation and activities.[61] Before this came about it was being suggested that, since the Guilds had had a traditional responsibility for training and the control of apprenticeship, it was appropriate that they should devote resources to education and to technical and vocational education in particular. The eventual result was the City and Guilds of London Institute, established in 1878 on the basis of reports drawn up by six eminent men including Thomas Huxley, Henry Truman Wood, Sir John Donnelly, Douglas Galton, George Bartley and Sir William Armstrong. On the basis of these reports a blueprint was prepared and the new Institute was devoted to the dissemination of scientific principles with application to industry. A small group of influential figures had a major say in what was actually done.

The establishment of the Institute owed much to a few of the 'big twelve' Livery Companies and many smaller ones were indifferent or hostile. Ironically, most of the larger Companies subsequently went their own way in the 1880s, as a result of disappointment and disagreements, and gave their main attention to particular educational institutions elsewhere. The Goldsmiths established their own Technical Institute, in what had been a private school premises, at New Cross. This became Goldsmiths'

College and was later handed over to the University of London. The Drapers' turned their attention to and became major benefactors of the Peoples' Palace, later Queen Mary College. The Skinners' were generous to Northampton College, later City University, and the Clothworkers had a commitment to what eventually developed into the University of Leeds.

The CGLI established two very important educational institutions as well as several lesser foundations. Finsbury Technical College, opened in 1883, became a model for technical institutes throughout the country. In 1884, CGLI opened its Central Institution in Exhibition Road, South Kensington, for the training of teachers and managers in science and technology 'relating to industry'. This became part of Imperial College in 1907 through amalgamation with the Royal College of Science and the Royal School of Mines.[62] CGLI took over from the Society of Arts the supervision of examinations in technical subjects, holding its first examinations in 1879. These were extended and local committees were established to examine and supervise the work of existing teaching establishments in technical subjects. In 1880 Phillip Magnus was appointed Director and CGLI became an important influence in British vocational and technical education. Its role is considered more fully in Chapter five.

THE CITY OF LONDON PAROCHIAL CHARITIES FOUNDATION

The enormous resources of the Livery Companies were, of course, only a small part of the City of London's wealth. There were other funds to which the London community could lay claim on a moral if not legal basis in the form of the City parochial charities. In the medieval period the City had been divided into more than 100 small parishes, each with its own church and vestry. By the late nineteenth century most of the churches had gone and the City was de-populated but the administrative arrangements and boundaries endured. While most of the City parishes were archaic they often continued to hold assets in trust which were usually devoted to ecclesiastical or charitable causes. These assets were, in aggregate, substantial and tending to increase in value in line with City property and real estate values.[63] Since the poor had long since been driven out of the City by high rents, and there was little demand for new churches, the funds were largely surplus to requirements and, in some cases, subjected to corrupt or questionable administration by individuals and small groups. As a result, from the early part of the nineteenth century the Charity Commissioners were called upon, from time to time, to intervene in City parochial affairs. From the 1860s some members of the Anglican Clergy began to press for reform and urged that the funds be devoted to middle-class education. In 1878 a Royal Commission was established by Disraeli to consider the City parochial charities and legislation followed in 1883.[64]

Under the City of London Parochial Charities Act of 1883, which was strenuously resisted by City interests, the Charity Commissioners were given the task of preparing a scheme for the re-application of City parochial charity funds. This was a task which took the Commissioners several years to complete and we can learn a great deal about the development of higher education in Victorian Britain through an examination of this process.[65] The Commissioners, the Clergy and others who supported them, were heavily committed to education and had a lengthy record of directing charitable funds accordingly. However, this commitment was quite clearly to middle-class education, often beyond the elementary level. Redirecting the City parochial funds was no easy matter in the face of strong resistance from the City and strongly competing claims from different causes. There were ecclesiatical demands and the campaign for 'open spaces', such as Victoria Park, had strong popular support as did the need for municipal improvements. It was agreed at the outset that, under the main scheme covering the majority of City parochial charities, the funds should be devoted to the whole of London, rather than the City, and that the poor should benefit.

In the circumstances, it is perhaps not surprising that the Charity Commissioners found their answer in Technical Education which was being being advocated, most strenuously, by influential opinion in the 1880s.[66] CGLI had already made a move in this direction, but much more was needed, particulary in terms of instuction. In the early 1880s the Samuelson Commission was reporting on technical instruction and its findings provided strong support. One of the Charity Commissioners, Henry Cunynghame, argued in 1886 for a focus on technical education using the Regent Street Polytechnic and the Peoples' Palace as models.[67] Since the latter was hardly established in 1886 it is clear that Regent Street was the main model. It offered evening instruction in vocational subjects for young men and women while also providing some recreational and social facilities. During the late 1880s the Charity Commissioners embarked upon a scheme to establish a network of Polytechnics, on the Regent Street model, throughout London, using the City parochial charity funds supplemented by voluntary donations. In the process, public opinion and effort was managed and manipulated in the desired direction and some of the complexities and dangers of the operation are revealed in Chapter eight. Committees were established on a regional basis with the intention of promoting district colleges and the Commissioners let it be known, on an informal basis, that they would match funds raised from the public through voluntary contibutions. From these beginnings London acquired a network of Polytechnics, institutes and colleges although, in each case, the story was different and there were major variations in gestation.

The term 'polytechnic' was taken from Regent Street but related originally to the Royal Polytechnic Institute which had been founded by Sir George Cayley in 1838 as a 'Gallery of Arts and Science'. This had featured demonstrations including the famous 'Pepper's Ghost' but had also involved some instruction. Trade and other evening classes were already operating there when Quintin Hogg purchased the building in 1882, moving his 'Institute' from Covent Garden. By 1894 Hogg had established nearly 100 classes with 5,000 student enrolments.

South London was particularly quick off the mark in raising money for three proposed polytechnics south of the Thames. In part this may have been because of the influence and energy of a City entrepreneur, Evan Spicer, who chaired the steering committee (see Chapter seven). Borough and Battersea Polytechnics were established in the early 1890s. A third was planned for Deptford but the Goldsmith's Company offered to fund this from their own resources and this gave London south of the river another advantage. Progress elsewhere, and especially in North London, was slower and the Northern and Northwestern Polytechnics came later. The reasons for this are examined below in Chapter eight. By 1891, when the City Parochial Charities Foundation became formally established and operational, the Charity Commissioners had committed most of the City parochial funds to the London polytechnics leaving the new Foundation with a somewhat limited range of options in terms of future expenditure.[68]

It was, of course, quite clear from the outset that the ambitions of the Charity Commissioners were grandiose in relation to the CPC funds available and that other sources would have to be called upon if London was to get its polytechnics. The appeal for voluntary contributions did not go unheeded. There were donations by leading Livery Companies and aristocratic donations including the site for Northampton College in Clerkenwell. However, the voluntary response was quite inadequate on a general basis and agitation followed in parts of the metropolitan area which appeared to be missing out on CPC funds. The agitation in North London is illustrated in Chapter eight. In the event, it was the public revenues which came to the rescue in the rather bizarre form of the 'whisky money'.

THE TECHNICAL EDUCATION BOARD OF THE LONDON COUNTY COUNCIL

Under the first Technical Instruction Act, passed in 1889, County Councils were empowered to introduce a penny rate for the support of technical education. This power was not used in London by the London County County (LCC), established in 1888, but its influence, nevertheless, was considerable in promoting the cause of education. The whisky money arose, by accident rather than design, from the Local Taxation (Customs and Excise) Act of 1890 which imposed an additional duty on beer and spirits sold in public houses; the intention being to use the proceeds to compensate publicans made redundant by a proposed reduction in the number of public houses and taverns. This was opposed by the Temperance lobby which was highly influential in the Liberal Party and it became clear that distressed publicans engendered little public sympathy. In the circumstances, the Government was embarrassed by a surplus of funds and Arthur Acland, M.P., a leading supporter and lobbyist for technical education, seized the opportunity to propose, successfully, that the available revenues be made available to County Councils to defray the rates, or to pay for technical education, so that the rate increases under the Technical Instruction Act of 1889 need not take place. In this rather opportunistic manner an implicit connection was established between the whisky money and technical education. In the 1890s in London the whisky money, which was substantial, became the mainstay of further and higher education and the most potent influence in sustaining the ambitions of the Charity Commissioners.

The LCC first met in 1889 but showed little interest in education in its early years (see Chapter six). The School Board for London, established in 1870, was responsible for elementary education and the new Council took the view that City funds, rather than the rates, should be devoted to technical education. London's share of the whisky money was entirely devoted to reducing the rates. The second Council, elected in 1892, included Sidney Webb and Quintin Hogg and it was the latter who successfully moved that the LCC should assume responsibilities for technical education. This led to the establishment, in 1892, of a special committee under the chairmanship of Webb who commenced by calling upon H. Llewellyn Smith to investigate and report upon the whole question of technical education in London. Llewellyn Smith was Secretary of the National Association for the Promotion of Technical Education, an influential and well-connected lobby organization.

The importance of Llewellyn Smith's Report is difficult to exaggerate. Not only did it gather a wide range of information, it effectively defined technical education and prepared a programme of action to deal with what was described as a woeful inadequacy of provision in relation to needs and in comparison with elsewhere. This is discussed more fully in Chapters two and six. Technical education was defined to include the whole field of general education, apart from ancient languages and literature and, while elementary education was a matter for the London School Board (LSB), there was to be no higher age limit for technical education. Smith considered the needs of industries in London on a district basis and suggested co-operation between educational providers. His blueprint for TEB activity, which was subsequently adopted, proposed a controlled policy of working through existing institutions to meet local needs. Where these were inadequate or non-existent new provision would have to be made. On the demand side, Smith proposed a system of pre-employment scholarships from the post-elementary school stage and beyond up to University level, so that parents could be induced to keep their children

at school beyond the normal leaving age. The TEB was established
by the LCC on the basis of the Report in 1893.[69]

Llewellyn Smith's Report was the third instance of a detailed
blueprint for initiative in higher education being provided by a
committed expert, adopted, and closely followed. Expert advice in
the establishment of CGLI had come from the six eminent figures
consulted and, in the case of the CPCF, William Cunynghame had
provided closely argued written advice which was also closely
followed. By the early 1890s London had acquired three new
bodies with important responsibilities for post-elementary education and with the ability to call upon and deploy substantial
financial resources. The bodies became both co-operative partners
and bitter rivals. Their aims and functions were both complimen-
tary and competing and they had important implications for each
other. These three bodies were dominated by a small group of
individuals and there was a good deal of overlapping membership
and cross-representation. The three bodies came together over the
London Polytechnics in 1893 and established the London Polytechnic Council in 1894. The Council was made up of members of
the TEB who were also members of the CPCF Governing Body
or the CGLI Council, plus the TEB Chairman and two members
from each of these three constituent bodies.

Over time the TEB gradually increased its relative importance,
reflecting its legal status and access to financial resources. It
continued to rely on the whisky money, absorbing an increasing
share of London's allocation, but the rating potential remained in
abeyance. The 'Progressive' majority which dominated the LCC
in its early years had a preponderance of Liberals who believed in
keeping taxation to a minimum. The same people also held that
City of London and other private sector sources should be called
upon first for education funding.[70] The counterpart of these
attitutes was to be found in City institutions which took the
opportunity to withdraw funding in the face of increasing LCC
involvement.[71]

The TEB was an important pioneering experiment which had
major long term implications for London and beyond. However,
in relation to the needs and problems which Llewellyn Smith had
identified and detailed in his 1892 Report, its efforts were mainly
directed at the secondary level and were, inevitably, inadequate.
The higher level scholarships extended only to very small num-

bers. Apart from scholarships, the TEB also made grants to a wide range and mumber of existing institutions at secondary level and above (including London University) and sought to raise standards in schools and colleges. This led to the assumption of an inspecting role with information gathering and co-ordinating functions. Gradually the TEB began to move towards a degree of control over the institutions it assisted as well as the new ones it founded. Llewellyn Smith had given particular attention to the industrial needs of London, reviewing employment patterns and prospects on an area basis. In the 1890s a number of vocational and training centres, with specific craft and industry applications, were established[72] as well as the Central School of Arts and Crafts (1896).

The work of the TEB brought it into conflict with the London School Board (LSB) which, since its establishment in 1870, had been responsible for elementary education. This conflict became highly politicized and absorbed a great deal of wasted energy. Conflict arose because the activities of the LSB extended beyond the elementary level, into higher grade schools and especially into evening teaching and related activities. This involved competition with other providers and the control of secondary education became a polemical issue with the TEB and the LSB effectively in direct competition. This issue was not resolved by the Cockerton decision of 1899, which held that the LSB was acting illegally in providing and funding education beyond its elementary remit, but the matter did come to an end in 1902 as a result of the (Balfour) Education Act. A special Act to cover London was introduced in 1903 and, from 1904, the LCC became the supreme education authority for London, replacing the LSB and the TEB and having responsibility for all London's education outside the voluntary and University sectors.[73]

THE QUESTION OF UNIVERSITY EDUCATION IN LONDON

In the 1890s there was a period of open debate about education in London at the highest level and specifically about the need for university education. It is clear that this debate reflected a certain amount of disappointment in relation to the University of London which had been founded in 1836 but existed only as an examining body. This debate is easily misunderstood in retrospect, clouded as it was by different concepts of what a university was and should

London Higher

be. There are widely differing views as to why and on what example the University of London was established in the first place in the form of what was to become University College (1828). Religious and other rivalries with King's College (1831) were important in leading to Government intervention and the establishment of a University examining body, but teaching and other matters remained the responsibility of the constituent colleges.[74] These catered for small numbers of students drawn from middle class families. Both UCL and Kings established their own schools and commenced higher education at low levels of attainment in the early decades of their existence.[75] They were staffed largely with graduates of Oxford and Cambridge and, not surprisingly, tended to follow the traditions of those institutions in supplying a liberal education to day students on a marginally broader curriculum. While the original models for London University may have been German, Scottish or American, the fact remains that these did not endure and the essential aim soon became the provision of a cheaper and uncloistered version of what was available at Oxford and Cambridge. Women were not allowed to graduate until 1880 and there was little in terms of vocational education outside medicine.

The growth of London University was slow and clearly constrained by a lack of demand for the kind of higher education its colleges provided from the burgeoning London middle classes. It is equally clear that there was strong demand for alternative forms of higher education and, in particular, for evening instruction in vocational subjects. This had to be supplied by non-University institutions which students found attractive and could attend and afford. In particular, Hogg's Regent Street Polytechnic proved to be highly popular and could be seen as a first step towards higher education on a large scale. The popularity of Regent's Street in the 1880s is partially attributable to the fact that it provided evening instruction with a vocational emphasis, but the provision of social and recreational facilities may have been more important.

London University was in London but not of it in the sense that it tended to see itself as a national rather than a civic institution. It commenced at a time when several national learned societies were emerging in London and it was founded by national government. In the Victorian period London University saw itself as being there to serve the nation and the Empire rather than the metropolis. It held no particular brief for the population of London, as such, or particular sections of that population, or regions of the capital. Academic considerations came first and, while there was an emphasis on research, no obligation was accepted to research the needs of London. Technology gave way to science and applied science gave ground to pure science. As Sanderson has shown, some of London's industries did benefit from University research, but there was some conspicuous neglect of major areas of the metropolitan economy.[76] In Chapter three Anne Kerschen shows how the People's Palace, through its gradual transformation into Queen Mary College, and part of London University, failed and ceased to serve the people of East London in social, recreational or even educational terms. By the 1920s most of the non-academic activities had been dropped and hardly any students of the College were drawn from the local community. When Goldsmith's College was given to London University (rather than the LCC) by the Goldsmith's Company in 1904 demands for a community college to serve the south east of London were ignored by the University Senate, over many years, even though the College was not formally integrated into the University.[77] The University of London followed its own agenda, for perfectly justifiable reasons, and the needs of London were not a high priority. As a result there were other initiatives. Leading members of the Catholic Church sought to serve the Catholic community by establishing a Catholic University in 1875 but this quickly collapsed as a result of internal dissention and inadequate financial support.[78]

In the early 1890s there were moves to found a new university in London based on Gresham College and named after Prince Albert.[79] No Gresham or Albert University emerged from these efforts. Available City resources were already heavily committed to the CGLI and the Polytechnics and supporters of the existing University made strenuous efforts to avoid its eclipse and preserve the monopoly. Almost inevitably, the reform and expansion of the University followed. The University of London Act of 1898 made a number of important changes which involved the formal establishment of a teaching university. Also, staff in non-affiliated colleges could be recognized as eligible to teach for the internal degrees of the University. In effect, this Act gave the University a potential measure of control over higher education in

London. By 1903 there were 2,000 internal students attending the University and a further 500 students studying for internal degrees at non-affiliated colleges.[80] Most of the London Polytechnics began to offer University degrees and being 'recognized' by the University became a matter of status for their staff. By 1904 six Polytechnics were providing complete degree courses for internal degrees of the University of London. There were 50 'recognized' teachers and 500 University of London undergraduates in the Polytechnics.

There was disagreement between leading figures in higher education over the University connection. Sidney Webb was keen to see the London School of Economics, founded in 1895, become a school of the University at the earliest opportunity.[81] Hogg at Regent Street and Millis at Borough took a different view, believing that the University influence would destroy the original purpose of their institutions. As a result of such differences of opinion, different colleges took different paths. Webb clearly believed that the University could relate to 'the limitations, the needs and the opportunities of London life'[82] and cater for those from 'households of limited means and strenuous lives'.[83] In fact, the University did little to provide practical and vocational courses or professional training. Students were recruited nationally and internationally with a strong bias towards males from higher income backgrounds. As a result, an important role remained for non-University institutions, which continued to provide the main part of further and higher education, and part-time evening instruction remained the main form. Statistics of student enrolment have to be treated with caution but in Chapter two an attempt is made to indicate the extent of higher education in London at the end of the nineteenth century.

The Universities did attempt to reach a wider population through 'extension'. This had commenced from Oxford and Cambridge in the 1850s and the University of London had also become involved.[84] A London Society for the Extension of University Teaching was established in 1876 and was operating from 63 centres by the 1890s. The Oxford Delegacy was established in 1892 and the WEA in 1903. By the early 1890s there were 60,000 attendances at 450 courses, as well as numerous occasional lectures, classes and weekend schools.[85] While efforts emanating from Oxford have received the main attention, the University of London played the leading role in the capital and increasingly so over time. Toynbee Hall, opened in 1885 by Samuel Barnett, is known more for its illustrious social and political connections than its work in higher education, but its founder saw it as the nucleus for a university of East London.[86] This did not happen and Toynbee Hall eventually ceased its teaching activity altogether. University extension together with the increasing activities of the LCC and a range of voluntary bodies ensured that London was in the vanguard of adult education by 1914 and went on in the inter-war years to establish a system which was held up as an example elsewhere.

At the turn of the century London had a complex variety of educational providers including the University, the TEB, the LSB, the CGLI, the CPCF, the City Guilds, and an enormous range of other voluntary bodies funded by a mixture of public and private sources. This system was simplified a little through the 1903 Education Act but the major changes did not come until after 1912 when the Authority embarked upon a radical re-organization of evening teaching. As a result of the 1913 re-organization 242 Evening Institutes were opened in September, 1914.[87]

London had nine Polytechnic institutions by 1897 with 26,000 students, by 1905 three more had been added. These included the Sir John Cass Institute, opened in 1902, and the Goldsmith's Institute which in its early years was maintained almost entirely by the Goldsmith's Company. The TEB also assisted Hackney Technical Institute in Cassland Road and Hackney Institute in Dalston Lane, but these did not become recognized as polytechnics although the People's Palace was. The main London Polytechnics were Battersea, City of London, Borough, South Western (Chelsea), Regent Street, Woolwich and Northern (North Western came much later). The City of London Polytechnic was a token alliance of Birkbeck College, Northampton Institute and City of London College to meet CPCF requirements. The individual colleges were held to be too small and to have too few social and recreational facilities to match the model of a polytechnic. It was also the case that their students were probably, in the main, not from the 'poorer classes'. In 1896 these polytechnic institutions drew their income from the following sources:[88]

Sources of income London Polytechnics 1896–7

CPCF	22.8
TEB	19.9
City Companies	17.3
Private sources	9.4
Government grants	7.1
Student fees	23.5
TOTAL	100.0

In subsequent years the LCC through the TEB became relatively more important as a source and began to exert an important influence on policy which continued after the TEB was terminated and replaced in 1904. Trade classes were an important feature of the new Polytechnics. By 1901 there were over 200 classes covering more than 50 trades as well as a number of special schools for particular trades. These classes were restricted to people in the trade in order to minimize potential disruption to employment patterns. In Sidney Webb's view, in 1904, 'This kind of evening instruction for the intelligent workman is unique in the world. No other city has anything to equal it' . However, this was only part of their activity. Webb also pointed out that instruction 'ranges from the Higher Grade Day School for boys and girls of fourteen, up to high University instruction and post graduate research'.[89] Various aspects of the London Polytechnics and their development are examined in the book which follows. Each institution took a unique path until all became part of the formally designated university sector in 1992.

Many different aspects of the development of higher education in London are considered from different viewpoints in the chapters to follow. Readers will be left to draw their own conclusions and there is ample scope for differing interpretations. By 1914 London had developed a complex range of post-elementary educational outlets which are broadly recognizable from a present-day perspective. Attempts had been made to cater for both sexes and across the entire range of society, albeit in segregated, stereotyped and differentiated ways. In the inter-war period some aspects of the system expanded and consolidated, notably adult education, but the general picture was one of relative stagnation with some decline in the more vocational areas in the face of mass unemployment. After the second world war there was another period of rapid expansion building on the developments which had taken place mainly in the last 20 years of the nineteenth century. It is on those developments, in particular, that the contributions which follow will focus.

CHAPTER TWO

Higher education and the London economy 1830–1914

John Pratt and Nick Richards

It is not possible to offer an unchallenged account of the relationship between higher education and the London economy. Economists and economic historians are not themselves agreed about the relationship between education and economic growth. There is a literature, for example Schultz,[1] arguing that investment in human capital, through education (and other social provision), contributed to the economic growth of industrialized countries. Harbison and Myers[2] found correlations between educational spending and per capita income in different countries. However, according to Mace[3] they assumed causality without justification either theoretically or empirically. Denison[4] took a 'production-function' approach which assumes that output is a function of inputs of labour and capital. He showed that two-thirds of America's economic growth between 1929 and 1957 could not be explained by these two variables. But he (too) simply assumed that a large part of the residual was due to education. Psacharopoulos[5] calculated rates of return to education (based on the extra earnings of educated people and the costs of their education), but these also rely on the assumption that the enhanced earnings are attributable to education. There are alternative explanations for all these findings. Education may simply be acting as a 'filter', screening for people with high innate ability, and not in itself adding to productivity or growth. Or education may be consumption rather than investment (rich people and rich countries want and can afford more education), so that it is a result – not a cause – of economic growth.

There is controversy, too, about conventional views of British economic history. Some evidence raises questions about the relationship between higher education and economic growth, both in the UK as a whole and in London. A perennial issue in British economic history is the question of Britain's economic predominance and decline. Britain was the birthplace of the industrial revolution. As the pioneering industrial economy, it became dominant, only to be challenged by its rivals (chiefly USA and Germany) by the end of the nineteenth century. Analyses of this period, rather than confirming the contribution of education to economic growth, have raised the question whether Britain's education system (or lack of it) – particularly as it related to science and technology – contributed to the country's relative decline. Nor is there agreement about the nature of the London economy in this period. But it is clear that links were being made at this time between education, particularly technical and, later, higher education and the growth of the economy.[6] The arguments for improvement in technical education, especially, were made on economic grounds, and, as Roderick and Stephens note,[7] were particularly voiced after the Great Exhibition of 1851, which took place in London. The argument was not exclusively economic, as later chapters show, but it had its response in the growth of a wide range of educational institutions which set much of the pattern for the system of higher education in London today. This chapter discusses salient features of the London economy in this period, and charts the responses to the emerging demands for higher education to meet economic needs.

LONDON IN THE NINETEENTH CENTURY

London in the 1830s was already a rapidly growing city. At the beginning of the nineteenth century, the population of what is now the Greater London area was about 1 million.[8] By 1831 it had doubled, and by the time of the First World War had reached a size comparable with that today, around 7 million. In 1914, London's 7 million people constituted 16 per cent of the national population.[9] Half of the growth over this period took place in outer London, in what later became the outer London boroughs, though at that time was part of the home counties of Kent, Surrey, Middlesex, Hertfordshire and Essex. What had once been market towns became part of the conurbation.[10] Even in the area that became the administrative county of London in 1889, most of the growth occurred in the outer ring of boroughs, rather than those of the old core around the City.

Economic activity in London, as in many cities, had developed concentrically. The old core in and around the City of London was, in the early nineteenth century as now, the main commercial and financial area. Around this was an irregular ring which contained the bulk of manufacturing employment. Areas such as Finsbury, Shoreditch and Bethnal Green to the north and east, and Southwark to the south, all had more than 50 per cent of the work force in manufacturing in the 1851 census (Figure 2.1). There was more than 40 per cent in manufacturing in Stepney and further east in Poplar and in radial bands in Lambeth to the south, running along the river Wandle, and to the north in St Pancras, following the line of the river Fleet and several main railways. The ring was extended in some instances further outwards, to the areas of West Ham in the east for example. In the east, there was a particularly high proportion of the working population engaged in shoemaking, clothing and furniture, and in transport (many concerned with the docks).

Beyond this ring were the outer suburbs, to which the wealthier residents had already begun to move by the 1850s, though their main growth came later in the century and in the next. This ring included many of the western boroughs, such as Kensington, Chelsea, Wandsworth, Lewisham and Greenwich to the south and Hampstead, Islington and Hackney to the north. In these areas, there were high levels of employment in the professions and commerce and service industries. By the end of the nineteenth century the development of the suburbs – assisted by the growth of transport infrastructure and the LCC policy of cheap workmen's fares further encouraged this economic pattern. This in turn stimulated demand, for example for food, transport distribution and leisure services, as well as for education and other public amenities. Later in the inter-war period, argues Green,[11] suburbanization helped to sustain high growth rates in new industries, and this too saw its response in the pattern of higher education provision.

THE LONDON ECONOMY

Traditionally, accounts of the industrial revolution have emphasized the role of large-scale manufacturing industry (e.g. factory as opposed to workshop production) in Britain's rise to pre-eminence as the 'workshop of the world'. The industrial revolution

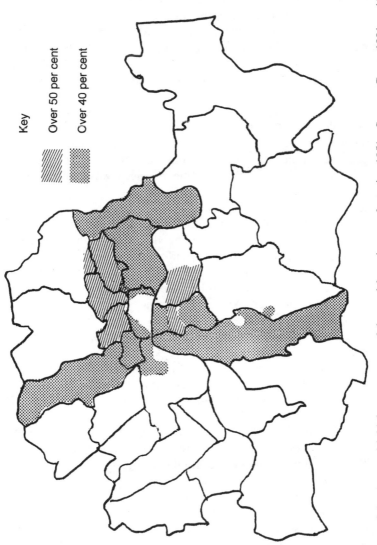

Key

▨ Over 50 per cent

▦ Over 40 per cent

Figure 2.1   Areas with high percentages of the workforce in manufacturing 1851   Source: Green 1991, p. 18

was also seen to gather most momentum outside of London, in cities such as Liverpool, Manchester, Leeds and Birmingham. The industrial revolution was 'like a storm that passed over London and broke elsewhere'.[12] London was 'backward' compared to the dynamism of industrial change in the Midlands and the North, remaining rooted in 'low-productivity service provision'. Thus these interpretations of London's industrial history tend to be associated with accounts of sweated labour and large-scale social deprivation.[13]

However, this conventional view has been challenged. First, small-scale manufacturing production using simple technology remained important in London throughout the nineteenth century – specific examples include shoemaking and the rag trade. Survival for these often did mean adoption of piece work and sweated labour and the de-skilling of trades.

Second, the growth of the service sector (e.g. transport, finance and commerce), contributed more overall to London's economic growth than manufacturing.[14] In the first half of the nineteenth century, London's economy was, unlike some of the other major cities in Britain, led as much by service and transport industries as by manufacturing. Services and transport accounted for over half of the recorded employment. Service sector employment accounted for more than half of all new jobs nationally between 1841 and 1911, and one-fifth of these were in London and Middlesex. Hall's analysis of 1861 Census data[15] shows that manufacturing accounted for barely a third of employment (32 per cent) in Greater London, whilst services provided 61 per cent (with transport and distributive services each accounting for 10 per cent of all jobs) (Table 2.1).

Green[16] argues that London's growth since the sixteenth century had depended on trade and commerce, and that British expansion in the eighteenth century led to the growth of overseas trade, 'much of which was organised and financed by London merchants and routed through the port'. As a result, the wealth generated by this trade was 'in turn ... often expended in the capital'. London was a vast consumer market, and this affected the nature of the manufacturing industry within the capital by laying the basis for the development of 'a variety of high quality manufacturing trades'.

Thus, manufacturing in London in the first half of the nineteenth

Table 2.1   *Employment in Greater London 1861*

	Number (000)	Per cent
Services	903.0	61.0
of which		
Transport	*138.2*	*9.4*
Distributive trades	*138.5*	*9.4*
Building	*98.1*	*6.6*
Manufacturing	468.8	31.7
Other	107.0	7.3
Total	1478.8	100.0

Source: Hall (1962)

century was characterized by 'high value in relation to bulk' and it was 'dependent on close contact with the final consumer'.[17] Such craft industries as clothing, shoemaking, furniture, printing, metals and engineering were conspicuous. The 1851 Census data show that clothing, boot and shoe manufacture accounted for 10 per cent of male employment in the county of London, and 27 per cent of female employment (Table 2.2). A further 5 per cent of males were employed in metals and engineering industries and a similar percentage in wood and furniture. By contrast, London at this time had few industries heavily reliant on raw materials and concerned with the production of semi-finished goods. Heavy engineering was uncommon, and what there was tended to leave London. Although London was at one stage the national centre for shipbuilding, this too declined rapidly in mid-century. Industries such as chemicals moved to the outer areas, particularly down-river.

It was as a result of this pattern of manufacturing industry in the records of the time that London has been seen as unusual in the absence of a large-scale factory system; smaller workshops and domestic industry tended to be dominant. The 1851 Census showed that 86 per cent of employers had fewer than ten workers. Large employers did exist, but they tended to be clustered around the river and the docks, where there was access to raw materials and transport, on the south side of the river, for example in Bermondsey, and north of it in Poplar and, further out, West Ham. These two phenomena – of widespread small-scale industry

Table 2.2   *Occupational structure of the county of London 1851–1931*

Males	1851		1901		1931	
	Number	Per cent	Number	Per cent	Number	Per cent
Construction	61,319	10.2	149,962	1.7	101,384	7.9
Conveyance	59,998	10.0	243,924	17.4	158,424	12.3
Food & drink manufacture	59,844	10.0	138,762	9.9	46,240	3.6
Clothing, boot & shoe making	59,235	9.9	81,187	5.8	58,874	4.6
General labour	57,248	9.6	75,010	5.4	N/A	N/A
Professional	38,519	6.4	65,407	4.7	47,643	3.7
Metal & Engineering	31,392	5.2	95,503	6.8	123,270	9.6
Wood & Furniture	29,214	4.9	61,891	4.4	42,704	3.3
Domestic service	25,660	4.3	53,525	3.8	105,123	8.2*
Commerce, finance	22,198	3.7	134,261	9.6	298,218	23.1
Local & central gov	18,960	3.2	46,638	3.3	124,520	9.7
Printing & paper	18,746	3.1	63,566	4.5	62,245	4.7
Others	116,442	19.5	190,333	13.6	123,224	9.6
Total	598,775	100.0	1399,969	100.0	1289,859	100.0

Females	1851		1901		1931	
	Number	Per cent	Number	Per cent	Number	Per cent
Domestic service	171,123	52.0	328,337	45.6	250,792	31.6*
Clothing boot and shoe making	89,908	27.3	156,050	21.7	113,996	14.4
Professional	18,212	5.5	52,962	7.4	10,194	1.3
Food and drink manufacture	14,819	4.5	49,492	6.9	39,568	5.0
Commerce, finance	3,233	1.0	20,285	2.8	143,606	18.1
Printing and paper	3,164	1.0	33,369	4.6	36,703	4.6
Local & central government	724	0.2	5,796	0.8	51,196	6.5
Metals and engineering	494	0.2	3,932	0.6	29,564	3.7
Others	27,194	8.3	69,108	9.6	118,571	14.9
Total	328,871	100.0	719,331	100.0	794,109	100.1

Source: Green 1991, using Census for England and Wales, 1851, 1901, 1931
Note: * includes employment in hotels and lodging houses

and the importance of the service sector – have been seen as particularly relevant to the success of London's economy, and as helping London to remain relatively unaffected by cyclical economic fluctuations to maintain high growth.[18] The service sector was held to be more resilient to the cyclical depression that affected heavy industry.

Another key factor in London's economic growth in the nineteenth century was the development of the railways. By 1843 there were nearly 2,000 miles of railway in Britain and by 1848, 5,000 miles. They altered the London economy as well as the nation's. By reducing transport costs they helped to increase the total market, especially the export market, and so increased London's importance as a port. London, too, no longer needed to rely on local producers for its food. The immense financial cost and scale of operation also helped to make London more important as a financial centre. The wealth of the London market also ensured that local demand for products (and services) was high.[19] It was the largest city in Europe in 1800 and its growth during the next century was substantial. It was the political and administrative centre of the nation. The importance of the demand side of London's economy in the nineteenth century has not been closely examined, but evidence from the 1920s and 1930s suggests that the demands of London and the Southeast aided recovery from the slump.

Recent commentators have developed some of the ideas implicit in this view. Johnson argues that what set London's economy apart from the rest of the country was not so much its employment structure, but its mode of operation.[20] It was a 'modern' economy, in that it was large scale, had good communication infrastructure and was fully 'monetized' from an early date. (It is interesting that he does not mention education as part of this 'modern' economy!)[21] Small workshop production methods requiring unskilled labour enabled great flexibility in clothing and other trades. Flexibility was also a dominant characteristic of the labour market, in that workers were able to move between different types of employment when the need arose. This 'unrestricted competition in the London labour market', amongst other things, had a profound impact upon London working class politics. Others have interpreted the lower than national average church attendance, trade union, co-op and friendly society membership as a withdrawal from the realities of economic power in Victorian London – a negative 'culture of consolation'.[22] Johnson disagrees: the London economy, he says, generated 'a positive culture of competitive achievement built on the foundations of a dynamic and thriving small-scale manufacturing economy'.[23]

Green[24] also presents a revised interpretation of London's economy. Drawing on data on housebuilding, bankruptcies and tonnage entering London's port, he suggests that peaks and troughs of economic activity were more pronounced in the capital, particularly in the first half of the nineteenth century, than elsewhere. Rapid growth was not a guarantee that progress was smooth.

Green challenges the common emphasis on London's predominance of 'small masters'. The 1851 Census seems to strongly support the notion that a very large proportion of firms employed less than ten men. He argues that the Census underestimated the true number of firms in London by half and the true size of the workforce in trades where large numbers of women were employed. Nor did the Census take into account wholesalers who sub-contracted on a large scale. The spread of subcontracting allowed the growth of large firms, whilst the greater concentration of capital was achieved through more efficient production. 'In both cases large firms gained prominence over small.'[25]

The conventional view of London workers as 'relatively passive bystanders' compared to those in industrial districts or regions in Lancashire, Yorkshire or the Midlands is also questioned. Green cites evidence which shows at least 294 labour disputes in London between 1790–1870. He also suggests that large firms tended to be at the forefront of transformation in the labour process, specifically the de-skilling of the labour process and opposition to apprenticeship laws. Thus he concludes: 'London as a hotbed of industrial militancy, the focus of large capital and the scene of economic instability may offend those for whom the traditional image still holds true'.[26]

Notwithstanding the complexity – and controversialness – of these analyses of the London economy, by the early twentiethth century its structure was similar to that of half a century or more earlier. The service sector was still the largest, with in 1911, 50 per cent of the workforce (41 per cent of male workers and 66 per cent of females were engaged in this sector) (Table 2.3). 42 per

Table 2.3   *Workforce distribution (Per cent) London 1911*

	Male	Female	All
Adults 15+ engaged in workforce	93	43	66
Workers engaged in productive sector	42	34	39
Workers engaged in service sector	41	66	50
Workers engaged in transport and communication	18	0.6	12
Workers engaged in engineering and metals	9	2	6
Industrial workers in firms with fewer than 100 staff			63
Industrial firms with fewer than 20 employees			66
Average annual unemployment 1910–14	6.0		
Unemployed July 1914	4.6		

Source: Lawrence et al., pp. 566–7

cent of male workers, and 34 per cent of females, were engaged in the productive sector and 18 and 0.6 per cent in transport. There was 6 per cent average male unemployment 1910–14. These patterns were sustained even after the First World War: almost 50 per cent of employment was in the service sector in 1921 (compared with 45 per cent in 1861). Manufacturing accounted for 33 per cent of employment in 1921 compared with 32 per cent in 1861.[27]

But this development was in the context of relative national decline[28] and this had affected the structure of the London economy. Although the broad balance between service and manufacturing sectors was maintained, there were changes within these sectors. Some traditional industries and – particularly – trades declined and were replaced by more modern consumer industries, such as electrical engineering and vehicle manufacture. Clothing and shoe making were challenged by cheaper production elsewhere, which lead to the expansion of sweated labour.

Silk weaving was an example of a light industry which sharply declined and had virtually disappeared by the turn of the century. It flourished in Spitalfields from the middle of the seventeenth century, and later spread to Bethnal Green. It was at its peak between 1800 and 1825. However, wages fixed by the 'Spitalfields Acts' encouraged some sections of the industry to migrate, and the reduction of a complete ban on foreign wrought silks to one of heavy import duty in 1826 increased competition from abroad.

The weavers and their families became increasingly impoverished. The industry was dealt a further blow by the repeal of duty on French wrought silks in 1860.[29] An investigation into the struggling English silk industry for the Royal Commission on Technical Instruction, reported that numbers of loom operators in London had declined from 60,000 in 1825 to less than 4,000 in 1884.[30] The four main causes of its decline in London were attributed by a local informant to competition from power looms in Manchester, the removal of duties on foreign products, and reasons which implied a lack of education in the industry:

> The absence of sound practical knowledge on the part of the employers, and their inability to produce goods of the highest class, in which only hand looms can be employed.
>
> The fact that, until recently, most persons, who had for the previous 40 years been engaged in the trade, did not appear to recognise that silk manufacturing was a business requiring great taste, study, and experience'.[31]

By 1914 there were only 114 workers still employed in weaving in London.[32]

The example of the shipbuilding industry illustrates many of the problems encountered by large-scale manufacturing in London. London had been the country's centre for shipbuilding: in the 1850s, the Thames launched more than a quarter of the entire UK tonnage of merchant shipping. In 1866 it was estimated as less than 5 per cent,[33] though the Thames Iron Works continued as a producer until 1912. Employment in the industry fell correspondingly. In 1865 27,000 men were employed in Thames shipbuilding and marine engineering. By 1871 the number was 9,000 and still falling. Factors in the decline of the industry included increased competition from Northern yards with their closer access to raw materials of iron and coal, and cheaper labour.

There were changes in the service sector, too. Commerce and finance provided 4 per cent of male employment in 1851, but 10 per cent in 1901 and 23 per cent in 1931 (Table 2.2). For women the changes were often more extreme, with domestic service falling from 52 to 32 per cent of female employment from 1851 to 1931. With the experience of the First World War, many more women went into jobs in assembly as well as clerical jobs and the teaching and caring professions.

Whatever the extent to which the London economy in the nineteenth century had been reliant upon large or small scale firms, it is clear that as that century ended and London developed in the twentieth century, large-scale production became more important. In 1851, the Census recorded that 86 per cent of firms in London had fewer than ten male employees. In 1911, 66 per cent of industrial firms had fewer than 20 male and female staff, and 63 per cent of industrial workers were in firms with fewer than 100 staff (Table 2.3). This was a long-term trend. By 1930, only 33 per cent of firms in Greater London had fewer than ten employees; 8 per cent had more than 100 employees, a further 9 per cent had 50–99 employees and 50 per cent had 10–49. In 1851, the recorded figures were 0.6, 1 and 12 per cent respectively (Table 2.4). A surge of foreign investment after the First World War also led to the establishment of large companies in and more often around London, affecting its economy and ultimately its higher education. For example, the Ford Motor Company settled at Dagenham to the east of London in 1931,[34] while other American companies such as Firestone Tyres, Gillette and Hoover settled along the Great West Road – 'the golden mile' – after its opening in 1925.[35]

Table 2.4   *Size of employment units in London 1851 and Greater London 1930*

	1851		1930	
	Number	Per cent	Number	Per cent
Less than 10	11,807	86.0	10,859	33.4
10–49	1,705	12.4	16,205	49.8
50–99	137	1.0	2,934	9.0
100+	80	0.6	2,537	7.8
Total	13,729		32,535	

Source: Green 1991, p. 30

HIGHER EDUCATION AND THE LONDON ECONOMY

The industrial revolution changed the pattern of economic activity so that education, and eventually higher education, became increasingly important to the economy. The main difference in the 1830s from the 1730s was a shift from a 'largely self subsistent family unit of production' to 'the capitalistic market-oriented forms of enterprise employing specialised labour and costly capital

equipment'.[36] Both the specialized labour and those who planned
and managed the capital investment were held to need education,
though it was some time before this was widely recognized. As
Deane puts it, until at least the middle of the nineteenth century,
'the typical British working man was either a casual labourer on
the roads, railways, building sites or docks, or an artisan or
mechanic in a small workshop'. Most factory operatives were
women or children and many factory trades employed more
outworkers than factory workers. And there was no shortage of
labour as the rural population fled from agriculture (in this sense,
victims of its success) into the cities, London amongst them, for
industrial and service sector employment.

The demands of the British economy for educated labour
developed as the system of mass production began to emerge in
the late nineteenth century. This developed first in the USA[37]
where conditions favoured it – abundant natural resources, a vast
market and a supply of generally unskilled immigrant labour.
Whilst European countries like Britain adopted these methods,
their circumstances differed; they had fewer natural resources but
a stock – and (restrictive) tradition – of skilled labour. Mass
production resulted in the substitution of unskilled for skilled
labour but increased off-shop floor human capital (for management and research and development). Britain and other European
countries tended to pursue a craft production strategy, maintaining
the use of skilled labour, using standard machinery to produce
customized products.[38] Although the British government sent a
commission to the USA as early as the 1850s to examine American
machinery, American technology was only slowly adopted, even
in Edwardian Britain.[39] One result of this was that manufacturing
output per person in Britain was only half that of the USA from
at least the mid nineteenth century.[40] (Comparisons with Germany
over the same period are interesting; British manufacturing output
per person in 1913 was 19 per cent higher than Germany's, having
been roughly similar since the 1870s.)

Against this background, it is not surprising that shop floor
training figured larger in the preparation of the workforce in
Britain than the USA. In 1914, about 15 per cent of the British
engineering workforce consisted of apprentices, compared with
about 1 per cent of employees in engineering (the only data
available) in the USA.[41] In the USA, over 30 per cent of managers

had degrees in 1928, a level not reached in Britain until the 1950s. Moreover, and presaging current concerns, accountants appear to have played a significant role in British management before the First World War. In research and development Britain appeared to devote only half the resources (as a percentage of manufacturing output) of the USA in the 1930s (the earliest available data) – less than 0.5 per cent compared with 1.0 per cent.

The technical training system in Britain tended to place greater emphasis on part-time training than in the USA, often with the explicit intention of encouraging vertical mobility.[42] It was thus somewhat less specialized, with a greater concern for general training, though less than in Germany. Part-time training flourished in Britain because, argues Floud, it was rewarded by occupational and (often social) mobility. Floud[43] cites an employer's view in the 1884 Report of the Royal Commission on Technical Instruction that 'generally the studious and most intelligent of workmen and apprentices' took evening classes, and from these 'foremen, leading workmen and sometimes draughtsmen' were selected. It was from these evening classes that much of the current provision for higher education in London developed.

In these words, too, are evident the distinctions of social class that significantly affected the pattern of development of higher education in the nineteenth century and which are still visible in the system today (see Chapter four). Much of the provision that developed in the nineteenth century was technical education (or in the terms of the time technical instruction) for aspirant workers, particularly artisans and supervisors in the manufacturing sector, or lower middle-class clerks in the service sector. This provision had social (or socializing?) as well as economic objectives, inspired, for example, by ideals of muscular Christianity as in the foundation of the Regent Street Polytechnic (see Chapter eight). The wealthier upper classes, if they sought higher education at all, did so in the universities and few did so with directly economic aims in mind. There was another social divide, too. Most technical and university education was for men. Only in teacher education, as it developed around the turn of the century, did a major route into higher education open for women (see Chapter nine). Although women could theoretically attend lectures at King's and University Colleges from 1828, they were not admitted to London University degrees on the same terms as men until 1878.[44] Pollard's analysis of education and the economy[45] omits the education of women since it 'has been omitted in most of the relevant literature'!

The origin of many of the 'new' universities in London today and some of the constituent colleges of London University was in nineteenth century technical education. One of the earliest developments was the foundation of the mechanics' institutes in the 1820s. These were intended to serve the educational needs of artisans, by providing instruction in scientific principles and useful knowledge. Self-improvement was their watchword. At least two higher education institutions in London (Birkbeck College and the University of East London) can trace their origins to a mechanics' institute, though it is interesting that the idea first developed not in London, or even in England, but in Glasgow as far back as 1800. Nevertheless, in 1851, J. W. Hudson was able to record that there were at least 610 literary and mechanics' institutes in England, with 102,050 members and 691,500 books in their libraries.[46] Later estimates give an even higher figure for enrolments.[47] Within an area defined as London, which was not much larger than the old central core, there were 17 institutions including the London Mechanics' Institute founded by George Birkbeck and others in 1823. Their combined membership was in the region of 7,430. In addition, nationally there were 90 smaller mutual improvement societies, evening adult schools, Church of England and other Christian institutions with nearly 5,000 members.[48] The Young Men's Christian Association was one example of the latter. Founded in London in 1844 on the initiative of a draper's assistant 'for the improvement of the spiritual condition of young men', its aims were quickly expanded to include self improvement through education.[49] The growth of the metropolis encouraged mechanics' institutes to be founded in adjoining districts such as Hackney, Hampstead, Tottenham and Poplar in Middlesex; Blackheath Woolwich and Greenwich in Kent; Bermondsey, Southwark, and Camberwell in Surrey. At least two were established in connection with large manufacturing employers: the Eastern Counties Railway founded a mechanics institute primarily for its workers at Stratford, then in Essex, and the Royal Arsenal at Woolwich also had its own institute.[50] The growth of the institutes is an indicator of their popularity, but the outcomes were not always those intended. The institutes were widely criticized, as the artisans were replaced by the middle classes, and for their curriculum, which more closely resembled liberal adult education than technical education. The socialist, Engels, found that the education was 'tame, flabby and subservient to the ruling politics and religion'.[51] The London Mechanics' Institute was amongst those criticized. In 1845, the editor of the *Mechanics' Magazine* wrote that 'the mechanics of London, as a body, have long ceased to identify themselves in any way with the institution'.[52] Working class dissatisfaction occasionally resulted in new initiatives. In south London, for example, resentment of domination by middle-class elements led artisans to break away from the Greenwich Society for the Diffusion of Knowledge in 1852 and form a rival East Greenwich Institution. In 1857, similar frustrations with the new organization prompted the establishment of the Greenwich Mutual Improvement Society.[53] Nevertheless, the mechanics' institutes were the most widespread means of educating adults in England and their numbers increased through the 1860s. Eventually they declined as state provision for technical education emerged, and many were absorbed by local authority institutions, though the London Mechanics' Institute developed into Birkbeck College.

Hudson's history of adult education, published in the year of the Great Exhibition, compared the provision of mechanics' institutes in Britain with its chief industrial competitors. In France they represented a political threat and had been suppressed by successive governments since 1823. In Germany the extensive elementary system made them 'scarcely necessary'. In America provision 'far excelled Great Britain'.[54] Technical education at this time faced a number of problems. First, technology was thought to be for the lower classes and though it related to the development of the economy it was provided fitfully and cautiously. As one contemporary complained: 'we find in the country and town schools little preparation for occupations, still less for the future agriculturist or mechanic'.[55] There were fears of raising workers above their station. The Royal Institution, for example, had abandoned residential classes for young mechanics in 1801 because it was thought to have 'a dangerous political tendency', since science for the working classes was associated with radicalism and the French Revolution.[56] Industrialists were also afraid of revealing commercial secrets to competitors. State provision, as in education generally, was minimal. The first state grants to voluntary societies for education were not made until 1833. Efforts such as the mechanics' institutes failed in part because of the failings of general education. More than a third of those marrying in 1841 signed the register with a mark. The national attitude towards education for the economy was largely one of complacency. Victorian England did not detect a pressing need to improve the education of its workforce; labour was plentiful and the demands of the technology of the time could be mastered by the employees; Britain was industrially pre-eminent and higher education was not widely seen as necessary to innovate and change to meet competition. This situation pertained for most of the century. England 'entered the fierce economic competition after 1870 with artisans the least trained and a middle class the worst educated in Europe',[57] and 'During the closing years of the nineteenth century it was widely held that Great Britain was falling behind her industrial competitors abroad and that their advance was largely due to superior technical education'.[58]

So far as universities were concerned the situation in London at the beginning of the nineteenth century was parlous. There were no universities in London. Higher education in England in the period displayed the class divide that affected technical education. The two established universities, Oxford and Cambridge, applied religious tests, and eschewed subjects of practical relevance. Higher education in England resided in 'two outmoded universities and the Royal Institution' with an 'inefficient Royal Society and a multiplicity of scientific and learned societies'. The organization of science was 'fitful, uncoordinated and haphazard'.[59] Although the main scientific societies were in London, their contribution was lambasted by Babbage, as early as 1831 in his *Reflections on the Decline of Science*, as amateurish and self serving – ' a party or coterie' whose object was 'to maintain itself in power, and divide, so far as it could, all the good things amongst its members'.[60] So far as the universities were concerned, 'the intellectual life of England was not to be found inside the walls of Oxford and Cambridge but in the Dissenting Academies and in the various societies beginning to appear throughout the country'.[61] It was from this tradition that much education relevant to industrial development and the service industries of London's economy would emerge. But this higher education relied on individual effort and private benefaction. It was inadequate to meet the demands of the industrial age, and partly in response to these, new institutions were established. The first in London was University College, founded in 1826.

University College was designed on the model of the recently opened University of Berlin. It offered a route for middle-class students unable to enter Oxford and Cambridge (having no religious tests for admission) and explicitly studied the sciences. Chairs of Chemistry and Engineering were among the first to be established. University College was, of course, as much a national institution as a London one, but in 1845 part-time evening classes were opened in practical chemistry, designed for people working in manufacturing, and serving a local clientele. As the century went on, University College pioneered higher education in London in other branches of the sciences and engineering – establishing chairs in, for example, Physics in 1867 (the first in England) and Civil Engineering in 1874.

There were other similar developments. Aspiring chemists in the early nineteenth century tended to study abroad and it was not until the 1840s that the Royal College of Chemistry was founded in London, originally as the Davy College of Practical Chemistry. Its aims were significant in the context of the topic of this chapter – education and economic growth. Whilst it was 'mainly devoted to pure science', there was explicit – though condescending – consideration of the needs of the economy: 'to meet the exigencies of this country . . . an appendage (sic.) will be provided devoted to the Economic Arts'.[62] The economic relevance of the Society's classes was evident in the composition of its student body, which reflects the wealth of small-scale, but broadly scientifically-based trades in the capital: 'gentlemen following chemistry as a profession, or as an object of scientific taste, chemists and druggists, medical students . . . agriculturalists, manufacturers in almost all branches of the chemical arts, copper smelters, dyers, painters, varnish makers, soap boilers, brewers and sugarmakers'.[63] After running into financial difficulties, the Royal College became the chemistry department of the Metropolitan School of Science in 1853, a precursor institution of today's Imperial College.

A broadly similar development was that of the School of Mines, which also became part of Imperial College. It started life in 1839 as an institution with a directly economic purpose – the Museum of Economic Geology. After a report of a Committee of the House of Commons in 1849 detected a need for facilities for mining education – again 'such as are provided by the mining schools and colleges ... in the principal mining districts of the Continent'[64] – the Museum became the School of Mines and of Science Applied to the Arts in 1851. In 1853 it joined with the Royal College of Chemistry and eventually became the Royal School of Mines in 1890. Its orientation remained practical 'to enable the student to enter with advantage upon the actual process of mining, or of the Arts'[65] though its direct contribution to the London economy was necessarily limited by the absence of a mining industry.

It took the growth of Victorian state provision in the later part of the nineteenth century to begin to develop technical and higher education relevant to the needs of the economy. In the 1850s, the arguments of 'savants' like Playfair and Huxley helped to promote technical and scientific education. In London, Playfair was active in purchasing the land in South Kensington on which Imperial College, the Royal College of Art and the Science and Natural History Museums now stand. Playfair became Secretary of The Science and Art Department established by the government in 1853 to encourage the teaching of the applied sciences, and which promoted secondary and technical education. In this role, Playfair was active in developing the School of Mines in South Kensington. The Science and Art Department was also effective in promoting technical education through its grants for science classes, initiated in 1859 and which included an element of payment by results, and through its examinations in the sciences, the full scheme for which began in 1860.

Other bodies – and individuals – became active. The Society of Arts started examinations in 1856 for artisans, expanding into specific trades and industries in 1873. In 1854, the Working Men's College was established, offering trade classes as well as more liberal adult education and inspired by Christian Socialism.[66] A similar ideal underpinned the foundation in 1882 of the Polytechnic in Regent Street by Quintin Hogg, a City merchant. Hogg was dismayed by finding that only about 2 per cent of young people between 16 and 25 in 1880 were attending any sort of educational institution.[67] He explicitly set out to offer social recreational and educational facilities, an ideal furthered by the publication in the same year of Besant's novel *All sorts and conditions of men*, which envisaged a 'Palace of Delight' for working people in the East End of London. The People's Palace (later Queen Mary College) was a further manifestation of Besant's dream. Christian idealism – not to say 'colonisation'[68] – also underlay the University Settlement movement which reached its climax in the 1880s, which in addition to its intentions to bring together socially the 'two nations', offered educational classes such as those at Toynbee Hall, though as with other initiatives before, they were criticized for their domination by middle classes rather than the working classes.[69] But as the Appendix shows, technical instruction at Toynbee Hall and the Bermondsey Settlement was supported by LCC grants in the 1890s.

In 1876, one of the major developments in technical education in London – and the rest of the country – took place when the City of London Livery Companies decided to promote education, especially technical education for 'young artisans and others in the scientific and artistic branches of their trades'.[70] The City and Guilds of London Institute (CGLI) was incorporated in 1880 and started its system of examinations which focused for the first time on genuine trades, both the traditional – such as plumbing, goldsmithing and cabinet making – and the new areas emerging in industrial production – such as telegraphy, heating and ventilation and mechanical engineering.[71] Responsibility for much of the policy for technical education was shared between these two central examining bodies – the Science and Art Department and CGLI – and 'the scope of the courses was narrow and highly theoretical and the needs of many industries were entirely neglected'.[72] At least one programme (mechanical engineering) was dominated by professors of the Institute's own colleges and King's College London.[73]

For London, however, the CGLI was particularly important as it founded the City and Guilds' Institute at Finsbury in 1881, the first English technical college. It was a development of previous trade classes started under the name of the Artisans' Institute[74] and situated in one of the areas of manufacturing industry. It offered day and evening classes in mechanical and electrical engineering, technical chemistry, applied art and trade classes. Though it continued in existence, some of its impetus was lost as the city companies 'dissipated their energies in uncoordinated ventures'.[75] The Drapers Company, 'the original mainstay' of Finsbury transferred its support to the People's Palace (precursor of Queen Mary College) in 1888. However, in 1884, the CGLI also opened the Central Institution in South Kensington, now part of Imperial College, intended to educate technical teachers, engineers, architects and works managers (see Chapter five).

Despite the City of London's economic importance and the significance of technical and commercial education for it, this activity, as Saint describes it, 'was practically the extent of City disbursement towards London's technical education'.[76] However, other funds were becoming available from City sources. The City Parochial Charities Act of 1883 made available £50,000 a year for the development of further education in the metropolis.[77] The City Parochial Foundation established in 1891, after much discussion about the use of funds in ancient parochial charities, assisted the promotion of technical education in London by proposing the creation of a ring of seven polytechnics on the lines of the Regent Street Polytechnic already established by Quintin Hogg. Some of these were founded in expectation of the 1891 scheme and with help from city foundations and became major higher education institutions for the capital. They included polytechnics at Woolwich (now Greenwich University), Borough (now part of South Bank University), Battersea (now Surrey University after moving to Guildford in the 1960s) and Chelsea (now Chelsea College part of London University). The Goldsmiths' Company founded a polytechnic (now Goldsmiths' College) at New Cross (see Chapter five).

These developments reflected the concern that continued to be expressed about the inadequacy of Britain's education system for the industrial system on which its economy depended. Playfair commented in 1867, after a visit to the Paris Exhibition, on the low standard of British exhibits, which reflected the fact that 'France, Prussia, Austria, Belgium and Switzerland possess good systems of industrial education for the masters and managers of factories and workshops and that England possesses none'.[78] The Taunton Commission to whom Playfair addressed these comments found that most British industrialists agreed. The concern continued and further government enquiries, such as the Devonshire Commission of 1870–75, pressed the case for greater investment in scientific and technical education. In 1881, a Royal Commission on Technical Instruction was set up and its report in 1884 argued again for science and art classes and more science education in teacher training. It was reports like these which set the stage for the major advances in the development of technical and higher education at the end of the nineteenth century. Government recognition of the need to act in technical education paved the way for the development of many of the higher education institutions in London today.

The development was facilitated by the reform of local government in 1888, creating competent, elected, multipurpose county authorities able to offer a comprehensive range of public services. Hitherto, many London-wide services (such as drainage and sewage) had been the responsibility of the Metropolitan Board of Works. Others were the responsibility of local vestries and boards. The Local Government Act of 1888 had particular importance for London, since it created the London County Council (LCC), bringing under the responsibility of a single authority areas which had previously been in the counties of Middlesex, Surrey and Kent. The LCC covered much of the built up area of London, though significant areas – West Ham and Willesden for example were excluded, the importance of the former however recognized by its county borough status. Other areas now in the Greater London area remained the responsibility of the county authorities.

Whilst responsibility for elementary education still resided with school boards, the new local authorities were soon empowered to act in technical education. The 1889 Technical Instruction Act enabled them to raise a penny rate for technical and manual instruction – their first educational responsibility. From 1890 to the First World War, education accounted for half of the UK's expenditure on social services and absorbed a third of the rates raised in 1913.[79] The LCC took no action on the permissive powers given under the Technical Instruction Act until 1892, when a new council was elected and Sidney Webb and Quintin Hogg took the lead in proposing a special committee of inquiry to draw up a technical education scheme for London.[80] Webb became chair. Herbert Llewellyn Smith was engaged to survey the resources for technical education in London. The report included analysis of London employment, showing how manufacturing industry was distributed, with certain trades associated with particular localities

– building with south and west London and Hackney, metal trades with Poplar and Greenwich, wood and furniture with Shoreditch and Bethnal Green, printing and bookbinding with Holborn and Southwark, chemical trades with Southwark, clothing with City, Shoreditch and Bethnal Green. But Llewellyn Smith found a dismal picture of education to meet the needs of this sector of the London economy. London was 'not only far behind Germany and France in quantity and quality, but also far behind our chief provincial towns'.[81] Manchester had 14,000 in evening classes; to be equivalent London needed 140,000 – not the 24,000 found by the survey. Llewellyn Smith also recorded evidence of the abiding mistrust of education amongst both workers and management: 'The chief obstacle to the scientific training of the managers of the numerous small chemical and colour works in East London and the tanneries in Bermondsey is their rooted disbelief in the value of such training'.[82]

Among the LCC's responses to the report was the establishment of a Technical Education Board (chaired by Webb) which aided existing institutions, such as the Regent Street Polytechnic, and promoted the foundation of others, many of them (such as the London Day College, now the University of London Institute of Education)) precursors of current higher education institutions (see Chapter six). The LCC was also able to use 'whisky money' – acquired through the 1890 Local Taxation (Customs and Excise) Act – to build new institutions and use funds under the Technical Instruction Act to support these and existing ones. Twelve polytechnics or technical institutions were built in London with the aid of 'whisky money'.[83] The 1890 Act was repealed by the 1902 Education Act but funds continued to be earmarked for technical education. The aim in the 1890s was to provide provision for the industries and workers in the locality. Indeed, the Ministry of Education in 1950 concluded that the 'new financial power flowing from local rates and "whisky money" led to local initiative in the suggestion of subjects for courses suitable to local needs'.[84]

The pattern of provision thus reflected the economic and social geography of the capital, rather than a rational distribution on a London-wide framework. Many of the new institutions were monotechnic technical institutes, built on existing classes. Examples are legion – the Shoreditch Technical Institute served the local furniture industry, Hammersmith School of Art the aspiring middle classes of west London, the Leathersellers College the tanning industry in Bermondsey; the Bolt Court school of Photo-Engraving and Lithography was a few yards off the Fleet Street home of the Press. The LCC also supported trade classes at the Working Men's College. Figure 2.2 shows the location of the major institutions in 1895–96. Their relationship to the historic prevalence of manufacturing employment in Figure 2.1 is worth noting. Over half were in the areas with greater than 40 per cent of the workforce in manufacturing in 1851.

By 1912, the LCC Education Officer was able to claim that there were in London 'few institutions of importance which could not show that in original research, in technical advice, in offering or criticizing designs or in undertaking tests, they have not been of much direct assistance to some local trade or industry'.[85] His report however gives an impression of some struggle to find extensive examples. Those cited include investigations into tanning undertaken by the Leathersellers' College and the work of the LCC School of Photo-Engraving and Lithography which 'had a direct influence on general practice in photo-engraving'. However, there were also examples of co-operation between technical institutions and industry, such as the annual contribution to Borough Polytechnic from the National Association of Master Bakers and Confectioners to support the baking school. The Midland Railway and Gas Light and Coke Company both sent apprentices to two half-days at Northern Polytechnic and Westminster Technical Institute respectively. Consultative committees between the LCC and associations of employers and workers had been formed to some effect in some industries. That for bookbinding led to the establishment of a day trade school in the Central School of Arts and Crafts in 1909, whilst classes in diamond mounting and setting were established at the Central School and Sir John Cass Technical Institute on recommendations from a similar committee for goldsmithing, silversmithing and jewellery.

Outside of the County of London the reorganization of local government and the implementation of the technical instruction acts enabled a certain amount of civic enterprise. As the metropolis spread beyond LCC boundaries, adjacent counties responded with a range of 'polytechnics', technical institutes and classes of their own. Developments in the new suburbs varied in the size

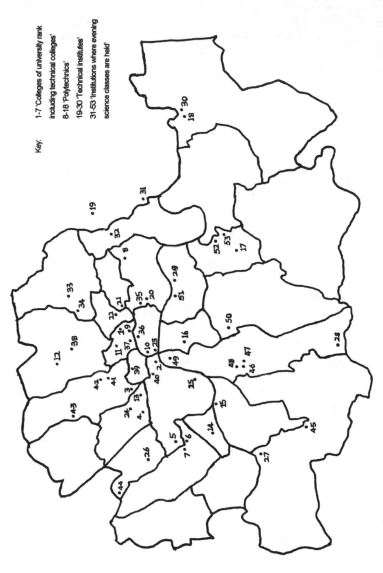

Figure 2.2   'Institutions where instruction is given in science and technology' 1895–96   Source: See Appendix

and scope of their provision, reflecting local concentrations of population. In Middlesex, the county's largest institutions fringed the LCC boundary: for example, Acton and Chiswick Polytechnic enrolled 1,725 students in 1911, and taught a range of courses as diverse as motor car engineering, Botany, French and land surveying; Tottenham Polytechnic (with 1,186 students), and Willesden (with 1,653 students) were also well attended.[86] Similarly, in the burgeoning Essex suburbs technical institutes were established at Leyton (1896), Walthamstow (1897), West Ham (1898) and East Ham (1905).[87] Others were established in Surrey and Kent.

To begin with local authorities often utilized existing buildings for technical instruction: schools, public libraries and local halls were used in this way. Occasionally, municipal provision superseded earlier initiatives. For example, Croydon council took over Pitlake Technical Institute (founded by the parish curate) to establish Croydon Polytechnic in 1891, and soon opened branches at South Norwood, Thornton Heath and Purley.[88] Whilst the Edison Institute at Ponders End, established by the Edison Swan Electric Company to provide evening classes and social activities for its workers, was taken over by Middlesex and turned into a technical institute, where: 'The classes in electrical wiring and engineering and the trade classes for the lads at the [Enfield] small arms factory are noticeable features of the work'.[89]

Complaints of overcrowding were not uncommon since premises were often shared: In Willesden the Polytechnic was being used for day and evening technical classes, an art school and girls trade school in 1912.[90] In Leyton, where similar circumstances prevailed, local children were forced to attend Walthamstow schools instead.[91]

The highest concentration of industry in these extra-metropolitan areas could be found in the Essex County Borough of West Ham, which provides a case study of the development of higher education and industry in late nineteenth century London beyond jurisdiction of the LCC.

West Ham, which was a largely agricultural parish in the 1820s, became the industrial heartland of southeast England and London's 'gateway to the world'[92] by the end of the nineteenth century. Davis described West Ham as 'Victorian London's Silicon Valley'.[93] Milling had been a local industry since Doomsday, and paper making, distilling and textiles grew up along the river Lea.

In 1839 a transformation began with the arrival of the Easter
Counties Railway linking London and Norwich, and within a few
years Stratford was a major railway depot and locomotive works.
The contractors building the line in the south of the borough also
bought up a large area of grazing land running down to the
Thames, which became the site of Victoria Dock in 1855. Heavy
industry soon moved in to take advantage of the wharfage facilities
on the Thames and lower Lea. The Gas Light and Coke Company's works were the largest in the world when it opened in
neighbouring East Ham in 1870, drawing much of its workforce
from Canning Town in West Ham. The opening of the Albert
Dock in 1880 completed a two and a half mile system running
through the whole southern promontory, to which the King
George V Dock was added in 1921. West Ham became the ninth
most populous town in England in 1901 with 267,000 people.

A patchwork of voluntary educational provision emerged. The
earliest provider of technical instruction in West Ham was probably the Eastern Counties (later Great Eastern) Railway Mechanics' Institute, established in 1851. It was originally housed in
Stratford station, and facilities included gymnasium, library, reading room and baths.[94] By 1890 it had a membership of nearly 1,000
(mainly railway workers and their families) of which 170 studied
on courses approved by the Science and Art Department.

A flurry of local initiatives in the 1880s seemed to reflect the
changing national mood towards education, and was spurred by
rapid growth of industry and population. The Thames Iron Works
established sports and social clubs for its workers, and in 1887,
science classes endorsed by the Science and Art Department. The
explicit principle behind these classes was that 'when new jobs
have to be undertaken, and new processes commenced, it is the
man who has educated himself who has the advantage'.[95] Other
institutions linked with industry and providing technical instruction included the Primrose Literary Institute in Silvertown
(founded in 1888 and connected with the Royal Primrose Soap
Works), and the Tate Institute (founded in Silvertown by sugar
manufacturers in 1889). The Carpenters' Company which owned
a large tract of land at Stratford on which it had built an estate,
opened a technical institute close by in 1886: classes included
plumbing, joinery, carpentry, cookery, geometry and mechanical
drawing. A swimming pool and secondary school were added

later. Science and Art Department classes were also held by the local YMCA (founded 1885), the Church Institute (founded 1886) and three West Ham Board schools.[96] University Extension lectures were periodically held in West Ham from 1879.[97] Canning Town Women's Settlement (founded 1892) and Mansfield House University Settlement (founded 1889) also became involved in adult education.[98]

When West Ham established its own technical institute, 1,595 students enrolled in the first year, and much of the educational work of earlier providers was eventually subsumed within the new institution. Early civic pronouncements on the need for the technical institute echoed familiar themes. On laying the foundation stone in 1896, the Mayor suggested that education would allow workers in West Ham to 'better themselves' and raise their wages.[99] Whilst the guest of honour at inauguration, philanthropist John Passmore Edwards argued that 'West Ham was trying to keep up with other countries; and if other large towns in Great Britain had imitated their example Germany would not be so far ahead'.[100]

A productive relationship with commerce and industry was aspired to in principle but not easily achieved. There was some cause for early optimism: the Great Eastern Railway Mechanics' Institute committee was active in the campaign to establish the new technical institute, and the railway's chief engineer was later invited to sit on the governing body. The company endowed scholarships, as did the Thames Iron Works and others. However, in 1906 the technical institute hosted a conference with eleven local manufacturers, the local trades council and Stratford Co-operative Society, with the purpose of tailoring the work of the institute to meet the needs of local employers. The Principal proposed a range of measures, including allowing company employees to attend day courses, placements for students and favourable rates of pay for those who attended approved courses, but the response was disappointing.[101]

HM Inspectors later acknowledged some inherent problems in co-ordinating the institute's work with local industry. First, the nature of local industry was not predisposed towards education: the borough was not dependent upon one major employer, but upon a very diverse range of industries: whilst the requirements of some employers, particularly in the docks, was for unskilled and casual labour. Second, West Ham's proximity to London meant that a considerable proportion of local people worked elsewhere in the metropolis, which broadened the range of employers' needs even further. Nevertheless, the absence of any definite scheme in 1921, was considered 'somewhat anomalous'.[102]

Technical education was not the only educational activity relevant to the London economy. By the end of the nineteenth century, the importance to London of education for commerce became more apparent than it had been hitherto, when the emphasis had been on the training of artisans. But even though the commercial workforce had grown more than six-fold from 1851 to 1901 (Table 2.2), commercial education was as badly neglected as technical. Again, there were expressions of the need for education to assist Britain's economic competitiveness. Although Pollard asserts that British skills in commerce and finance were not seriously questioned before 1914,[103] the Royal Commission on the Depression of Trade and Industry in 1886 recorded: 'In the matter of education we seem to be particularly deficient as compared with some of our foreign competitors, and this remark applies not only to what is usually called technical education, but to the ordinary commercial education which is required in mercantile houses, and especially the knowledge of foreign languages'.[104] In 1893 an American commentator recorded Britain's 'extraordinary backwardness' [105] in this field.

Commercial education was difficult to advance under the Technical Instruction Act. It was not until 1895 that the LCC first made grants towards existing classes run by the London Chamber of Commerce; commercial education was intended to come under the aegis of the London School of Economics, just founded (by the Webbs and others), 'for the higher study of economics and political science and training suitable for those engaged in administration or business'.[106] LSE and other institutions subsequently received further support from the LCC. As with technical education, commercial education to be successful relied on a foundation in earlier education. In London, as elsewhere, this was often lacking, and the LCC could make little progress with commercial education until an effective secondary education system in London was developed.[107] London employers also appeared reluctant. A survey of 42 employers in 1899 only found three – a firm of bankers, a milling engineer and a railway company – in favour of higher commercial education, and only the first of these actually took graduates.[108]

It also became clear that the educational demands of the London economy were not limited to the improvement of workers' skills. A more scientific orientation was necessary. Higher education – at university level – was needed to develop and improve industrial processes. London, it was argued was falling behind other European capitals in the provision of advanced scientific facilities.[109] At this stage, these facilities, insofar as they existed, were mainly within the colleges of the University of London and other 'recognized' institutions. The University, set up in 1836, was, initially, simply an examining body for students from University and King's Colleges, and other approved institutions. Sanderson reports that London University's contribution to industrial science was greater than that of any other British university and he records the particular relevance of its chemistry to London industry.[110] At King's College, Sir Herbert Jackson ran courses on laundry chemistry for the National Laundry Association and through his researches showed how imported products could be made for a third of the price locally. At University College in the 1880s, chemical studies were closely related to industry, in particular to chemical works in Willesden. Brewing science was developed and courses in bread making, soap glass and cement offered for London manufacturers. In 1887, the arrival of Ramsey transformed University College's chemistry 'from that of a technical college to high science', though Sanderson argues that his work nonetheless kept in close touch with developments in chemical manufacture in London. Similar examples can be cited for electrical engineering, such as Sir Ambrose Fleming's contribution as consultant to Ferranti for equipment for London's power supply. In the opening decade of the twentieth century, the University developed further industrial links, particularly in the emerging electrical, telecommunications and wireless industry, and in aeronautics and the motor industry (in which Imperial College was prominent). The Great Eastern Railway Company used the engineering department at East London College for training.

But it was not all good news. London University, in Saint's view showed 'little consciousness of its civic obligations' and even Webb at the LCC 'spent less time in reminding the university of its municipal debt to London and Londoners as a whole than towards making it a centre of national endeavour'.[111] Sanderson, too, records some of the University's failings in its relationship with industry in the years up to 1914. There were 'curious curricular gaps' – in electro-chemistry, in the chemical using trades, such as leather, rubber and clothing (which abounded in London), in gas engineering (although London was a major gas producer) and in nautical fields, although London was a major port.[112]

The University's contribution to the formation of human capital was also modest. Output from the University was low. Sanderson estimates the output of science graduates in 1901 as about 300[113] and some of those came from the polytechnics. The fault did not all lie with the University. Industry was slow in contributing to the University and reluctant to take on graduates. Supply of scientific graduates was widely held to exceed demand from London employers in the 1900s.[114]

The University was, however, significant in the development of higher education in non-university institutions. The 1898 University of London Act enabled non-university colleges in London to have 'recognized' teachers and to offer internal degrees of the University. By 1914, some 30 such colleges had this status. Thus institutions such as the polytechnics and West Ham Technical Institute were able to offer degree courses from their foundation. Moreover, even non-recognized institutions could offer external degrees.

Numbers of internal students of the University of London were nearly 2,700 in 1904–5 and rose to nearly 5,000 in 1912–13 (Table 2.5). The majority of these were in schools and colleges of the University: only just over 800 were in institutions with recognized teachers in 1912–13. It is difficult to offer definitive observations on the relationship of this education to the London economy. It is clear, however, that only a small proportion of these students were studying engineering subjects which might be regarded as most directly relevant to manufacture. In 1904–5 the numbers were 215; and, though by 1912–13 they had more than doubled, they were below 500, suggesting an annual output of fewer than 200.[115] Only a small proportion of these students were in institutions with recognized teachers (36 in 1906–7 and 75 in 1912–13). Numbers in science were, however, higher, reaching nearly 1400 in 1912–13, but this was little more than numbers in arts or medicine. Again,

Table 2.5   *Internal students of London University 1904–5 to 1914–15*

	Institutions with recognized teachers	Incorporated colleges and schools	Total
1904/5	N/A	N/A	2,673
1905/6	N/A	N/A	3,032
1906/7	590	2,886	3,476
1907/8	624	3,115	3,648
1908/9	603	3,483	4,086
1909/10	645	3,740	4,260
1910/11	754	3,786	4,424
1911/12	770	4,016	4,786
1912/13	834	4,036	4,870
1913/14	N/A	N/A	N/A

Source: LCC, *London Statistics*, (annual) vols 15–25

the institutions with recognized teachers provided for the minority of these, but it was a larger one (349 in 1906–7 and 468 in 1912–13). Several institutions with recognized teachers, however, had no students on internal degree courses at all in this period; these included Woolwich Polytechnic in 1906–7 and Finsbury Technical College from 1907–8 to 1912–13.

These modest numbers contrast with those attending the public institutions in London. Table 2.6 summarizes day and evening enrolments in polytechnics, technical institutes and schools of art receiving LCC assistance in 1912–13. Over 55,000 students were enrolled, more than 6,000 of them day students. A further 3,500

Table 2.6   *Enrolments in LCC assisted institutions 1912–13*

	Art	Other courses		Total
	Day and evening	Day	Evening	
Aided institutions				
Polytechnics	1,417	2,987	22,149	
Technical institutes	1,109	253	6,055	
Total	2,526	3,240	28,204	33,970
Maintained institutions	4,309	,512	6,776	11,597

Source: LCC, *London Statistics*, vol. 24

were enrolled in training colleges. These figures are dwarfed by those for evening classes in the polytechnics and technical institutes (despite the criticisms of Llewellyn Smith). The LCC Education Officer compared statistical returns from polytechnics and technical institutes in 1908–9 and the 1901 Census data, although occupational groups were not classified as in the Census. Using these data we have estimated that, overall, up to 6 per cent of men within the LCC area (nearly 93,000 out of just under 1.5 million) attended evening classes. Up to 4 per cent of women (almost 60,000 out of 1.8 million) did so. The Education Officer noted that, whilst the figures do not imply that students were attending classes which had 'a direct bearing on their occupation', it could be assumed that 'in a very large proportion of the cases, that is the fact'.[116] The data show a considerable attendance by men in important London industries – electrical and mechanical engineering, shipbuilding and metal occupations (more than 10,000), the building trades (over 5,300), and from commerce clerks totalled nearly 30,000. Amongst women, there were nearly 10,000 clerks. Some occupational groups were more represented than others. The 1,900 male and 5,300 female teachers each represented about a quarter of those in these occupations in the Census, and about 28 per cent of male clerks attended classes, but only about 2 per cent of male labourers did so and only 1 per cent of female domestic servants.

The University connection was also a mixed blessing. It raised questions about the autonomy of the non-university institutions, and of the relationship of the syllabuses to local industrial needs. It presented issues which later became known as 'academic drift',[117] the tendency of non-university institutions to ape their university counterparts and thus to neglect the purposes for which they were founded. For example, West Ham Technical Institute was taken to task by HMI Dr Ball in 1903 when he told management to 'look to the requirements of the locality. This place is surrounded by chemical works. Could you not induce the employees of labour to send their apprentices here? A deal of work could be done in connection with the trades. This is not being taken into consideration much in the curriculum here'.[118]

The Royal Commission on University Education in London had quite different reservations about the effects of the relationship in 1913, in that 'the London polytechnics, and the institutions which may be grouped with them ... cannot be said to have a common aim in university work in the sense that they have made any attempt to differentiate university from other students, or to arrange even their day courses so as to avoid competition between different institutions'.[119] On the other hand University recognition of individual tutors had a beneficial effect for institutions, 'the benefit of attracting a better type of lecturer', according to Sydney Webb.[120]

By the 1930s the problems posed by these relationships was the subject of internal Board of Education memoranda. The county's senior HMI articulated the Board's view that the primary role of technical colleges was to meet the requirements of industry and commerce, consequently 'in the provinces the main problem is disentangling technical work from that of universities, whilst in London the problem is that of keeping the University out of the Polytechnic.'[121] Thus were the battle lines of the binary debate of the 1960s already drawn up in the early years of higher education in London.

CONCLUSION

This chapter has discussed some of the ways in which higher education and the economy developed in London. Initially, higher education played little part in the development of the London economy. The fact that the industrial revolution in Britain was well under way by the time that anything resembling higher education existed in London raises some questions about the contribution of higher education to economic growth, in London and elsewhere. A main pre-condition for economic and industrial development in the late eighteenth and early nineteenth century was the success of agriculture. The growth of agricultural output from the 1750s sustained population growth over several decades without increases in food prices, and permitted the expansion of manufacture, development of technical invention, scientific advance and of economic institutions which facilitated overseas trading.[122] The industrial revolution was, too, as Bronowski argues,[123] initiated by mainly self-made men (Brindley, the great canal builder, could not spell the word 'navigator').

Nevertheless, as Musgrave argues,[124] education – particularly technical education – was seen by a prescient few as essential for national and metropolitan development and its neglect in London and England, particularly by contrast with other cities and other countries, was lamented. These – the spur of foreign competition, and the key figures arguing for it – were the two 'constant stimuli' to the demand for technical education in the second half of the nineteenth and first half of the twentieth century. Although England had enjoyed an enviable reputation in science since the Elizabethan age, by 1800, 'organised science had made little progress since the days of Newton' a century or so earlier.[125] The absence of an adequate school system was held to be a conspicuous cause of England's failure, and this was contrasted with France and Germany, amongst others. Education was undervalued by industrial leaders because Britain had achieved its economic dominance largely without it. The class system ensured that the esoteric values of the public schools and ancient universities were aped at all levels and helped to ensured that the British 'entered the twentieth century and the age of modern science and technology as a spectacularly ill-educated people'.[126]

Technical education was neglected, although it was eventually recognized as necessary to enable workmen and artisans to understand the principles underlying their trades. But it is significant that the forerunners of technical education, the mechanics' institutes, developed from classes in Glasgow rather than London. In the metropolis industry relied on the craft skills of its workers and the in-house apprenticeship system to maintain its competitiveness, rather than on education and technical innovation. The ship building industry, for example that on the Thames, diminished as technical complexity in the industry increased, making the apprenticeship system inadequate to teach the necessary skills and knowledge and through lack of investment in research.[127]

Shipbuilding and silk weaving are two examples of substantial London-based industries which had collapsed long before technical education had even become an issue. However, the contemplation of the loss of these industries and the threat to others, became, for some, part of the stimulus for education. The social consequences of the loss of these and other industries, the expansion of sweated labour, and widespread deprivation also contributed to the demands.

For much of the century, technical and higher education provision in London was struggling to catch up with this historic neglect. It took numerous Commissions and Enquiries to argue the case.

It was sporadic, usually local and relied on a mixture of individual, municipal, corporate and state initiative. Government responsibility was even split between departments, and divisions of social class affected its development. This was not all bad news. Pollard, whilst criticizing the state for failing to support and direct education, recognizes the flexibility and diversity of the voluntary provision,[128] and he is less critical than some of the failures of British education and science.[129]

It took the dissenters at University College (the 'godless institution in Gower Street') to initiate university education in London and to establish chairs in science and engineering. The University soon took on a national role, and though it made a direct contribution to the London economy, its output of graduates in science and engineering was modest. But it also offered a route for students in the emerging technical colleges to gain higher education. It took the creative burst of state supported municipal enterprise of the 1880s and 1890s to remedy the deficiency in technical education and start to develop a system of technical education to support the development of the London economy. It took even longer to develop education for commerce, despite its central role in the London economy.

It was, if anything, the polytechnics and technical colleges which pioneered education relevant to the economy in London, and many indeed, continue as the 'new universities' to do so today. Their development largely set the pattern for post-school education in London for much of the twentieth century. There were more students in these colleges, albeit far fewer at degree level, than in the University of London. Their growth was fired by their local links, their own ambitions and those of their students. They increasingly made links with local industry and other employers in the opening decade of the twentieth century, and this development continued after the First World War as the National Certificate Scheme (introduced in the 1920s) enabled them to offer national qualifications for courses created locally. New colleges too were built, as at Barking and Walthamstow in metropolitan Essex, to meet the needs of local industry and in West London as industry developed along the Great West Road and the adjacent suburbs of Middlesex. It was this kind of development, at a time when enrolments in the universities were broadly static, that caused concern within the Board of Education about the respective functions of the university and technical college sectors. It was this issue of the relationship of different kinds of higher education institution to the economy which, as much as any other, eventually led to the announcement of a 'binary' policy in higher education in the 1960s, and which were resolved – at least formally – only by the 'unification' of higher education in the 1992 Further and Higher Education Act.

Thus, the relationship between higher education and London's economy is of more than just historical relevance. It was in the nineteenth century that the idea that education is important for national economic success first began to be extensively aired and to receive widespread acknowledgement in Britain. The consequences for London were seen in the voluntary provision, central government policy and local government action that followed. Since then, the political, economic and social geography of London (and the rest of the world) have changed, often dramatically. But the economic imperative has persisted as a driving force in higher education policy. In 1997, the Central London Training and Enterprise Council published a research report which showed that many links existed between London business and higher education, and that higher education was an important part of the London economy, but it also concluded that 'if London businesses are to increase their competitiveness within a global market, relationships between Higher Education Institutions ... and business in London need to be dramatically improved.'[130] The lessons of history may still need to be learned.

NOTE

The authors wish to acknowledge the generous response of local history librarians in many London boroughs who responded to our requests for information, and the helpful staff at the London Metropolitan Archive.

APPENDIX

TECHNICAL AND ART EDUCATION PROVISION IN THE LCC AREA 1896

London Statistics 1895–96 records the following provision of 'institutions where instruction is given in science and technology' and where 'instruction in art is given' within the LCC area in February 1896.

Institutions where instruction is given in science and technology
Fifty-three institutions are listed of which two are outside the LCC area. Thames Ironworks and The Carpenters Company School were both in West Ham borough, but their inclusion presumably reflects their importance, though interestingly the Great Eastern Railway Mechanics Institute which pre-dates both is not included.

The institutions are grouped in four categories, and those which were aided by the LCC Technical Education Board are asterisked.

'Colleges of university rank including technical colleges'
1. City and Guilds Finsbury Technical College
2. Kings College
3. University College*
4. Bedford College*
5. City and Guilds Central College
6. Royal College of Science
7. Kings College (Ladies Department)

'Polytechnics'
8. People's Palace
9. City of London College*
10. Birkbeck Institution*
11. Northampton Institute*
12. Northern Polytechnic*
13. Regent Street Polytechnic*
14. South West London Polytechnic*
15. Battersea Polytechnic*

16. Borough Polytechnic*
17. Goldsmiths' Institute
18. Woolwich Polytechnic*

'Technical Institutes'
19. Carpenters' Company's School Stratford (outside London)
20. Whitechapel Craft School*
21. Leather Trades' School
22. Shoreditch Municipal Technical School*
23. St Bride Foundation Institute*
24. Trades' Training School
25. Westminster Technical Institute*
26. Westbourne Park Institute*
27. Wandsworth Technical Institute*
28. Norwood Technical Institute* } Branches of Borough
29. Herolds' Institute*   } Polytechnic
30. Mechanics' Institution*

'Institutions where evening science classes are held'
31. Thames Iron Works' classes (outside London)
32. Bow and Bromley Institute* (to be incorporated shortly with the People's Palace)
33. North East London Institute
34. Hackney Institute
35. Toynbee Hall
36. City of London YMCA Aldersgate Street
37. St Thomas Charterhouse evening classes
38. Highbury Institute and School of Art
39. Working Men's College*
40. Exeter Hall YMCA
41. Clarendon Square evening classes*
42. Aldenham Institute*
43. William Ellis School evening classes*
44. Queen's Park Institute*
45. Church Institute Upper Tooting
46. Ferndale Road Science and Art classes
47. Brixton Science and art classes
48. Stockwell Orphanage*
49. Morley Memorial College*
50. Camberwell Green (Greencoat School) evening classes*

51. Bermondsey Settlement*
52. Clyde Street science and art classes
53. Addey and Stanhope evening classes

Art schools and classes: institutions where instruction in art is given

'Art schools attached to institutions of university rank including technical colleges'
1. City and Guilds Finsbury Technical College
2. Kings College Art School
3. Slade School of Art, University College
4. National Art Training School, South Kensington
5. City and Guilds South London Technical Art School
6. People's Palace
7. City of London College*   ⎫
8. Birkbeck Institution*   ⎬   City Polytechnic
9. Northampton Institute*   ⎭
10. Northern Polytechnic*
11. Regent Street Polytechnic*
12. South West London Polytechnic*
13. Battersea Polytechnic*
14. Borough Polytechnic*
15. Goldsmiths' Institute
16. Woolwich Polytechnic*

'Technical Art Schools and Institutes'
17. Whitechapel Craft School*
18. Shoreditch Municipal Technical School*
19. North London and Hackney School of Art*
20. Clapton and Stamford Hill School of Art*
21. Camden School of Art*
22. Central Art Department Bolt Court*
23. St Bride Foundation Institute*
24. Royal Female School of Art*
25. St Martin's School of Art*
26. Westminster School of Art*
27. Westminster Technical Institute*
28. Hammersmith School of Art*
29. Putney School of Art*
30. Clapham School of Art*

31.   Lambeth School of Art*
32.   Blackheath Lee and Lewisham School of Art*

'Other Institutions where art teaching is given'
A total of 23, of which 12 were aided by the Board.

CHAPTER THREE

Higher education in the London community

Anne J. Kershen

The Shorter Oxford Dictionary defines community in several ways;
from the general, 'A body of people organised into a political,
municipal or social unity' or 'A body of persons living together
and practising community of goods' to the more specific, 'the little
communities ... [called] Neighbourhoods' – definitions which
originated in the eighteenth century. The late nineteenth century
introduced a new concept, one which acknowledged the increasing
number of alien arrivals and the sectioning of the capital. Thus we
find; 'The Jewish Community' or 'the people of a district'.[1] With
such diversity of definition and content it becomes clear that any
limited study of 'The London Community' in the late nineteenth
and early twentieth centuries has to be specifically directed.
Therefore, for the purposes of this chapter, I intend to concentrate
on a particular section of the capital's population within clearly
defined geographic and chronological boundaries, in this instance
the working class[2] of East London in the years between 1887 and
1931. The period under examination begins with the arrival of the
'university of the poor', the People's Palace, in the East End in
1887 and closes with an embittered debate over the role of that
'university' within the locality 44 years later.[3] It is an exploration of
the response of a community – one defined by geographic location
and economic status – towards the provision of higher education
within its midst and of the conflict of recreation and leisure versus
education. In addition it is a questioning of the attitudes of the
educationalists towards the East London community.

THE SETTING

Nineteenth century London was a city in constant flux. The prizes
of industry and empire brought with them urban development on

a scale never before experienced. During the century's span the population increased sevenfold as the city extended its boundaries in all directions. The elegant environs of the royal parks provided prestigious mansions for the aristocracy; the emerging middle class made their base in the pleasant surroundings of areas such as Barnsbury, Bloomsbury and Bayswater, whilst the lower classes were to be found in locations such as Somers Town, Seven Dials and, of course, the East End. Though few of the poorer members of society enjoyed the benefits of industry and empire all were affected by its impact. Not only did London burst her boundaries, she changed her composition. The city had long been a magnet to incomers, both from home and abroad,[4] but never more than in the nineteenth century when earlier trickles became floods. The native unemployed migrated to London where it was believed, mistakenly, that work was always to be found. Large numbers of immigrants from Ireland and eastern Europe were drawn to London, most particularly to East London, the traditional first point of settlement for immigrants. To a promised land which all too often proved to be a pathway to exploitation and deprivation.

It was Charles Booth, in his revelatory first volume of *Life and Labour of the People of London*,[5] published in 1889, who first revealed the true extent of the plight of the people of East London to the nation and to the world. For the first in what was to be a 17 volumed work, Booth concentrated solely on East London, as he believed it held the worst examples of poverty in the capital. In addition to the text, Booth produced a map of poverty. Streets were to be shaded according to levels of poverty, the poorest and most deprived areas appearing as black, the most affluent glinting gold. The colour which predominated in East London was pink, denoting a predominantly working-class population in regular but poorly paid employment. There were irregular, and frequent, patches of threatening black and impressive lines of red, particularly along the main thoroughfares where lived those aspiring to, or already members of, the middle class. Gold did not feature. East London housed a population composed of the semi-skilled and unskilled mingled with the artisan and shopkeeper. By the third quarter of the nineteenth century industry and empire had bequeathed an industrial structure which was small scale, seasonal and casual, its work forced engaged in the finishing trades, building, ship repair, dock labour and the manufacture of clothing.[6] The density of sub-divisional tailoring work(sweat)shops, many run by immigrants from Eastern Europe, led to East London's becoming an area synonymous with sweated labour, a condition which thrived on economic necessity and man's inhumanity to man. As the traditional first point of settlement for immigrants, East London, and most particularly its East End, had become, by the early 1880s, an overcrowded abyss, which, as well as drawing to it the poor, hopeless and helpless, criminal classes and aliens, attracted those who sought to resolve the sad condition of man by means of moral and spiritual uplift and educational fulfilment. For, as men such as Samuel Barnett and Arnold Toynbee believed, it was through education that man might hope to lift himself out of the depths and enter the world of opportunity.

Any discussion of the availability and uptake of higher education has first to take account of what the higher levels would build upon. Before the passage of the 1870 Education Act, East London offered a selection of primary and secondary educational institutions which varied widely in quality and cost. For those members of the poor who wanted to learn there were ragged, voluntary and Church run schools. Those who could afford a small fee were able to take advantage of the local private and dame schools, which, according to Maclure, ranged from 'appalling ... to good', at a cost of 9d or less a week.[7] At the eastern tip of the Mile End Road the Bancroft Almshouses, administered by the Drapers' Company, in addition to providing accommodation for the elderly, offered schooling to boys between the ages of 7 and 15. From 1870 onwards Board Schools blossomed, some such as Christ Church in Brick lane, having evolved from eighteenth century church schools. The alien, so often criticized for his lack of cleanliness, wage undercutting and rack renting, could not be faulted in the education of his children. In fact, the sons and daughters of the immigrants were frequently congratulated by school inspectors for their regular attendance and for their 'excellent work ... and perseverance'.[8] There were a number of Jewish day schools in the East End, the largest and the best being the Jews' Free School which opened in 1817 with 102 boys enrolled.[9] By 1881 the school held almost 3,000 pupils. The need for specifically Jewish schools reduced following the 1870 Act which ensured free non-denominational education. By the close of the century, Christ Church School, in Brick Lane, was composed of over 95 per cent Jewish children, as a result Jewish religious instruction was made available after hours on school premises.[10] From 1870 onwards some form of elementary education, if not yet free, was available for all. A tidying up Act was passed 6 six years later which required that parents ensure their children attend primary school, even if this meant recourse to the Board of Guardians to cover the cost, but it was not until 1891 that elementary education became available for all without charge.

In traditional working-class families of low incomes and irregular employment all those old enough to earn a wage were expected to do so. The experience of work was something known to children long before school leaving age, the majority working before and after school hours in order to supplement the family budget. Only a minority of parents, those who could afford it or those who took a longer view, sought to advance their children's vocational opportunities by taking advantage of what secondary and higher education was available. Some lower middle-class or artisan families even sent their children to Board school in order to qualify for assisted secondary education, a practice which may well have misled those at the time seeking to establish the attitude of the poorer classes towards secondary education.

Provision for the further education of the London working man began in the early years of the nineteenth century. But it was during the 1870s that provision for the further and higher education of the working man and woman moved on a pace.

It was during this period that the focus on 'technical education' heightened. This resulted from concerns raised over the disappointing standard manifested by British workmen – by comparison to their European peers – at the Paris Exhibition of 1867. Support for improved teaching came from several sources. Sir Sydney Waterlow, the Lord Mayor of London, suggested that 'Evening Lectures be delivered . . . and that a fund be formed for founding a college to develop Technical Education'.[11] He pressured for support from the Livery Companies and for the involvement of the Prince of Wales. At the same time, what proved to be a short-lived guild for the Promotion of Technical and Higher Education among the Working Classes of the United Kingdom was founded, based on the belief that technical education should be 'what working men themselves wanted'.[12] Gladstone took up the issue and called for methods of instruction that would enable the British workman to 'hold his position in the world'. The Drapers' Livery Company pressured for the furtherance of the cause of technical education for the working population through the provision of elementary and advanced teaching. The outcome was the creation of the City and Guilds Institute and the birth of a national scheme of technical education.[13] What followed was the establishment of a number of metropolitan technical schools in which students would be trained to take the Institute's examinations. Amongst these were the City of London College in Moorfields, Quintin Hogg's Polytechnic in Regent Street and the restructured Finsbury Technical College. In 1884 the Central Institute – which in 1911 became Imperial College – was opened in South Kensington to provide would-be teachers and managers with a scientifically biased technical education. The elitist King's College in the Strand acknowledged that working men could not attend its daytime courses and in the 1870s began a series of evening classes. However, the paucity of equipment and fittings discouraged many artisans from attending. Even though the need for an increased provision of technical training for the working class had been recognized, by 1884 there was a general consensus that this had been insufficient and that technical education still required special attention. The City Livery Companies and a government sponsored Royal Commission set about examining the current state of technical education. Their findings revealed the major problems to be shortage of good teachers and the inability of the working man to afford the time or money required to benefit from further and higher education.[14] They recommended that increased provision be made so that the British workman could become better acquainted with the tools of his trade and the principles by which that trade operated. An overt recognition of the need for Britain to remain Great and perhaps a covert indication of the concerns over increasing numbers of immigrants 'taking the jobs of Englishmen'.[15]

It takes little imagination to recognize that the majority of the people of East London fell into the category of those least able to afford the time or money to take advantage of further and higher technical education. None of those institutions referred to above were within easy access, all required travelling time and expense. As was noted in the Deed of the People's Palace Committee, in 1885, the 'technical College at south Kensington and classes at Finsbury are out of the reaches of the East End artisans'.[16]

Therefore, what was available for the late nineteenth century East Londoner who wished to avail himself, or herself, of the benefits of further and higher education closer to home? In essence, prior to 1884, little or nothing, though the seeds were being sown. In 1875 a Balliol graduate, Arnold Toynbee, had his first encounter with the 'city of darkest night',[17] when he took rooms in Commercial Road. His confrontation with poverty and deprivation and his attempts to feed the poorly nourished East Enders with knowledge, left their mark and, following his untimely death at the age of 30, Toynbee's friend, the Reverend Samuel Barnett, Vicar of St. Jude's, Whitechapel, suggested that the most fitting memorial to the young man would be the founding of a university settlement in the East End, where students and graduates from Oxford and Cambridge could spend time to both research conditions of poverty and to bring education and recreation to the local community. In 1884 Toynbee Hall was established as a University Settlement in Spitalfields, just off the Whitechapel Road, in the heartland of the Jewish immigrant quarter. In that same year Oxford House, in Bethnal Green, slightly to the north-east of Toynbee, opened its doors. Toynbee was conceived as a 'club house, of which the condition of membership was interest in the poor, and goodwill towards their needs.... Some had taken classes or reading parties. Others had worked at education.' Whilst the intention was to improve the lot of the poorly educated classes, in reality the studentship was composed of 'schoolmasters, clerks and artisans'.[18] The very poor and exploited, those who worked long and hard for few rewards chose to spend their brief leisure time in the warm and welcoming environment of the public house rather than in the colder realms of learning.

It was an educational establishment, to the east of the university settlements, which was eventually to bring higher education within the grasp of the local community. The Beaumont (Philosophical) Institution, founded by the benevolent Barber Beaumont, was opened in Beaumont Square, E1,[19] in 1840 with the stated intention of providing persons in the neighbourhood 'the means of meeting together for mental and moral improvement'. Beaumont died only a year later and by 1879 the Institute's funds had been depleted to a level which forced its closure. Fortunately, this was not the end, the Institute's function and popularity was such that a debate began immediately as to the form and location of the successor. There was a manifest concern that the lower middle class 'inhabitants of Beaumont Square and surrounding neighbourhood should be afforded intellectual improvement and rational recreation by means of libraries, access to reading of newspapers and journals, lectures and other means for the diffusion of useful and entertaining knowledge.'[20] In this statement we find the essence of future debates and conflicts surrounding what became the People's Palace. Was its main focus to be learning or relaxation and entertainment? How were the needs of the local community to be addressed? There was little doubt in the mind of one of those who attended a meeting in June 1882 at which the structure of the new body was discussed. It should provide 'for the East End the educational advantages of the City of London College and the evening classes at King's College plus library, reading room and recreation and social intercourse',[21] no small order! The trustees of the Beaumont Institute had already fixed their sights on the old Bancroft School and Almshouses as the location of their new project, for which additional funding was vital. The Drapers' Company, which in common with other Livery Companies, had publicly stated its belief that training for the artisan and craftsman was a priority, offered £20,000 towards the cost on condition that a technical school was included in the plans. However, more than the Drapers' money was needed if the People's Palace was to become a reality.

A UNIVERSITY FOR THE POOR

It was a popular novel set in Stepney, written by Walter Besant, that acted as the catalyst for the establishment of an institution which would 'place within the reach of the dense population of the East End of London the means of technical education and rational enjoyment.'[22] Besant's novel, *All Sorts and Conditions of Men*, which appeared in 1882, was an articulation of his belief that for the neglected working class of East London, cultural uplift and guidance was the pathway to a more rewarding and productive life. He considered East Londoners to be a forgotten people, who had 'no part nor share of London'. Angela Messenger, the novel's heroine, dreamt of creating a Palace of Joy in Stepney, one which had classrooms, a dancing room, children's playroom, a library and other rooms, 'where tired people might rest, quiet and talk, the women with tea and work, the men with tobacco'.[23] The book, with its fairy tale perception of, and prescription for, the problem of poverty may have been far from reality but it fired the imagination of those with money to realize Besant's dream even though few had ever ventured east of Aldgate Pump.

Support for a palace of education and culture was also forthcoming from members of the local community, English and alien. In February 1886, the editor of the *Jewish World* published a report of a meeting, held at the family home of the Abrahams and Gluckstein's in Whitechapel, to establish a local committee to promote the erecting of a 'People's Palace' for East London. The Chairman of the committee, Sir Edmund Hay Currie clearly articulated the mutually agreed aim which was to, 'establish a university of higher education in the East End'; the People's Palace would combine 'a university of education and recreation'.[24] It should perhaps be noted that, whilst the fund-raising committee had a strong local and alien flavour, its President being one Lewis Levy – by name identifiable as a Jew,[25] as were at least six other members of the committee – the list of trustees declared class, affluence and respectability, comprising as it did Sir Edmund Hay Currie, Spencer Charrington and the Reverend S. Barnett.[26] The setting up of the committee, which immediately received the Queen's patronage, and the declaration of intent, received a broad spectrum of press coverage. The editor of the *London Evening Standard* considered that the creation of such an institution, a 'university for artisans', would, 'work a social change'. He also understood the nature of the area and its people as he accurately noted that East London was not 'a complete community' but one in which 'the poor dwelt in all their poverty alone and out of view.'[27] Reports of the proposed creation of a People's Palace appeared in *The Times, Leeds Mercury, Grocers' Journal, Bristol Mercury, Christian Chronicle, Cambridge Review* and *East London Leader*, the latter stating that local (would-be) students would now have 'placed within their reach the riches of learning'.[28] The editor of the *Jewish Chronicle*, writing in an atmosphere of increasing anti-alienism, declared that he was 'pleased to see so many Jews had subscribed',[29] and an article in *The Times*, reflecting on the current high levels of unemployment and worker unrest, viewed the project as one which would 'give almost immediate employment to East London'.[30]

Within the year sufficient money had been raised to enable the

Prince of Wales to lay the foundation stone for the recreational and cultural centre. Of the records that do remain there appears no evidence of any large sum raised by the local community, and no record of any substantial individual Jewish bequests, though there were a number of sizeable donations. The estate of Barber Beaumont provided £12,150, Sir Edward Cecil-Guiness £14,000 for the Winter Gardens whilst the Earl of Rosebery funded the swimming pool.[31] In 1887 Queen Victoria opened the Queen's Hall and laid the foundation stone for the technical schools. Even in those early days some members of the local community were convinced that the Palace was not for 'the likes of themselves'; a letter published in the *Echo* revealed the sentiments of one who had watched the Queen's visit, 'I saw a constant stream of carriages rolling along from the West End, but no working men and women pouring into the Hall.'[32] Perhaps his, or her, head was turned the other way when the 3,000 chosen dockers, railway workers and others earning between one pound and thirty shillings a week, entered the reception.

By October 1888 all the basic facilities of the People's Palace – the Queen's Hall, the library, swimming baths, the gymnasium and technical schools – were up and running, the technical schools being the last to open with courses on offer to men and women between the ages of 15 and 25. The Palace's recreational facilities were well used. In its first year the Gymnasium could claim 1,500 members and the swimming bath 69,463 entrants.[33] The *Daily Telegraph* asserted that the swimming bath was in fact the first of its size to 'be placed at the service of working men'.[34] The Charity Commission's report on Lord Roseberry's gift had a less charitable ring, concluding that, 'a few warm baths are badly needed, as sometimes people come from their work so dirty as to be hardly fit to be admitted ... without previous ablutions.'[35] Cleansing and beneficial the baths may have been thought by some, but to one local they were too expensive, the one shilling charge for entry being 'far too large a sum', and one which put the baths out of the reach of many. It was recommended that 'at one penny a time hundreds more would take advantage of the facility'.[36] Others living close to the Palace lost no time in complaining about the noise of the building work and of the 'playing of classical music in the evening'.[37]

The recitals, readings and exhibitions were well attended[38] and provided for a variety of tastes. Entertainments included a 'Lecture on Ceylon' (entry 2d, 1d for students), Grand Concerts (free entry) and a performance of the Messiah (entry 3d). The Poultry and Pigeon Show (entry 2d) held in October 1887 attracted an attendance of 36,000, the Chrysanthemum Show, which opened on November 16 in a dense fog, drew 19,650, whilst the Cats and Rabbits Show was attended by 24,225. In addition to the special events the twice weekly concerts attracted average audiences of 2,500. No evidence exists to determine the composition of the audiences in those early years of the People's Palace; free entry, warmth and entertainment might well have drawn support from the poorer classes for the grand concerts, but would they have paid to hear a lecture on Ceylon or a performance of the Messiah? Whilst the Charity Commission recommended that the 'Queen's Hall be used for lectures, meetings, musical and other events suited for the recreation and instruction of the poorer classes',[39] it would appear that in terms of *recreation*, it was the members of the local community who were well above Booth's poverty line who were was being accommodated.

It was the educational side of the People's Palace that Hay Currie considered his priority. His plan was to create an institution which would provide a complete education for the working man. 'A technical university at which every East End workman who is to stand high as a master of his trade must graduate.'[40] Adopting a proactive approach to student recruitment, Hay Currie suggested that the Palace's technical school should be informed, by elementary headmasters in Tower Hamlets and Hackney, of all boys[41] leaving school after having taken the 'Government Examination' so that they could be asked to attend an interview at the Palace to discuss their future education and work. Those who had achieved seventh grade should be offered scholarships in the Day Technical School for two years, these to be followed by entry into an appropriate place of work with subsequent training in theory and science to be continued at evening classes. For those whom it suited, further teaching should be made available in French and book-keeping. At this point Hay Currie's higher education ambitions tailed off; those who wished to continue their education were recommended to attend either Finsbury Technical College or South Kensington College and take the more advanced examinations there, it was not until the first decade of the next century that those attending what became East

London College, could take their higher education to its graduate conclusion.

Hay Currie was determined that fees be kept low in order that the poor could overcome their mistrust of 'anything new set amongst them and [so] will come in fast-increasing numbers', a suggestion that the breadth of admissions was not all that had been anticipated. In spite of this, Currie sincerely believed that the poorer members of the East London community were availing themselves of what was on offer at the Palace, it was just they were not always identifiable. As he explained:

> I believe that this question often arises in the minds of good friends of the Palace, who visit the institution with the expectation of finding the halls and corridors swarming with ragged men and women with no boots ... the silent struggles which are going on in every direction among the decent poor to keep a respectable appearance even at the expense of misery and semi-starvation, are heart breaking ... the noisy complainer who stands at the out-relief door of the workhouse is often much better off than many of the quiet people in decent well worn clothes who are to be met at every turn in Mile End, Stepney, Limehouse and Poplar. Of course, a certain leaven of a more fortunate class are still found among the audience at a People's Palace concert, although it may often require the eyes of an expert in East End matters to distinguish between the two classes.[42]

Currie's words are further confirmation of the heterogeneous nature of the local community and also of his attempts to convince himself, and others, that the People's Palace was attracting the needy and deprived members of the local population. He appears to have overlooked the fact that it was not only scholarships which the poor needed but compensation for lost earnings. In its first academic year – 1888-9 – more than 3,700 boys/men and girls/women enrolled for the variety of courses on offer. These included evening classes in art and music as well as those of a strict vocational nature. Trade classes covered cabinet making, carpentry and joinery, brickwork and masonry, electrical engineering, plumbing, printing, tailors' cutting,[43] upholsterers' cutting and draping and land surveying and levelling. The latter was advertised as £20 for the course, whilst the others ranged from six shillings per term to ten shillings per session. In addition, there were classes to facilitate entry into the Civil Service. For women the People's Palace provided classes in dressmaking, millinery and cookery at ten shillings and six pence per term as well as in elementary reading, writing and arithmetic.[44] From content and cost it is clear that the vocational classes were organized for would-be artisans and white collar workers and it appears most likely that they came from similar backgrounds as the application records show that requests for prospectuses came from addresses in more affluent – pale pink and red – locations of Bow, Limehouse, Old Ford Road, Bethnal Green, Brixton, Plaistow, Forest Gate and Stoke Newington; there was even one from as far afield as Manchester. There were few requests from the poor and immigrant areas of Spitalfields and St. George's in the East, the areas shaded light blue, dark blue and black on Booth's map.[45]

The appointment of James Hatton as new Director of Evening Classes in 1892, in preference to one Oscar Wilde, who though considered a 'high class university man with some experience of technical institutions' was passed over because of doubts about his organizational ability and rapport with working men,[46] was the precursor to increased and accelerated academic ambition, the culmination being acceptance of the College as a School of the University of London in 1907, and the emergence of a student ambience at the East London Technical College. The student magazine, the *Palace Journal*, first appeared in 1895. It signals the collegiate environment that was evolving with the creation of student societies for engineering (founded 1893), shorthand and typing (founded 1895) and chemistry (founded 1893). Student sports societies were also established, amongst them a cricket club which ran three elevens. The Club president was N. Cohen – one of the few Jewish sounding names to occur in the student lists of the time.[47] It is perhaps relevant at this time to consider the paucity of Jewish students at the College throughout the period under examination. The author's research has shown that it was hardly economically viable for the children of the poorer members of the Jewish community to continue their education after primary level.[48] It was also unusual for the offspring of the more affluent entrepreneurial immigrant to take advantage of higher education. Fathers were eager for their sons to join them 'in the business' as soon as possible, or at least once they completed their secondary education.[49] The further or higher education of the female off-spring of all would not have been on the agenda.

In spite of criticism that the 'People's Palace had not exercized the amount of influence upon the locality which Sir Walter [Besant] was able to place to the credit of the Palace of his story', there was at least one success story from the East End. Albert Smith, a Dr. Barnado's boy being trained as a printer, was reported as having shown great talent in the art classes held at the Palace and having gained a scholarship to art college. Perhaps his institutional background, which did not impose the kinship demands on wage earning at an early age, had facilitated his pursuit of an artistic career.[50]

A SCHOOL OF THE UNIVERSITY OF LONDON

In 1896 Hatton was appointed Director of Studies of East London Technical College. He became the driving force behind the College's programme of higher and further education, catering for entry from the age of 15 – into preparatory class – through to the award of a university degree with honours.[51] In 1906 the Day School was closed and the College renamed East London College in preparation for its recognition as a school of the University of London. The eschewing of the title 'Technical' is indicative of a new status and reflective of a metaphorical move away from East London to a location in the capital as a player in the City's main institution of higher education.

The change was confirmed by the College's newly stated objectives. These were:

> to promote higher education in East London in various branches of a liberal education for world quality students to take degrees of London and other universities of the U.K. and to give instruction in science and technology as would be serviceable to students who intended to pursue a trade or profession in which a knowledge of science is required.[52]

This was a departure from the original objectives of the college, as laid down by the Charity Commission document in February 1892. These had had a stated intention to promote the 'industrial skill, general knowledge, health and well-being of young men and women belonging to the poorer classes'. Fourteen years on the needs of the poorer members of the East London community were eschewed in favour of a broad range of courses and higher charges. The evidence of change is there as early as the 1900–01 session. Evening classes now provided for Matriculation, Intermediate and Final B. Sc. levels, whilst mechanical engineering, physics, electrical engineering were also on offer. The 'Trade' range had been significantly reduced, though still carrying an artisanal profile. For the latter classes cost between ten shillings and seven shillings and six pence per term. The People's Palace Calendars, which advertised the range and cost of classes available throughout the decade of the 1890s, provide the opportunity to identify a positive move towards a more academic profile.[53] By the time of its admission in 1907 as a School of the University of London in Arts, Science and Engineering, the East London College was a 'university of the poor' no longer. The separation between recreation and leisure for the local community and higher education for all (who could afford fees and time) was made formal and public in 1909 when the People's Palace and the College split. The lacuna which had been covert became overt as the people of East London increasingly viewed the College as an educational institution which just happened to be located in the Mile End Road.

It is clear from those records which are available that East London College did not fulfil the dreams of its creators by enrolling large numbers of the impoverished local community. But had any of the visionaries really believed that the deprived and the needy, the poorly educated, the casual worker and the shift worker, would overnight develop such a thirst for knowledge and education that they would, or could, sacrifice all for academe? This is not to suggest that the East End harboured none with academic ability and ambition, it did, but in the days when the welfare state was in its infancy, and free higher education yet another dream, only the fortunate and dedicated few could avail themselves of what East London College had to offer. The Minutes of the College Vestry Committee reveal that by 1907 the College Senate had clearly decided that its role was one which looked beyond the immediate community, beyond the capital and, as is evident from the student records, beyond the nation's shores. As part of London University the College was adopting its character, one that saw itself as a centre for higher education based in London with its courses available for both national and international students, rather than one which was for Londoners alone. In determining the fee structure from 1907 onwards it was recorded that:

> The Senate, while recognising the special conditions of the East End of London, are of the opinion that some attempt should be made to place the fees ... on a more uniform basis ... and it would probably be possible to devise a scheme which would render the classes of the College open to the inhabitants of the East End under approximately the same financial conditions at present, and at the same time to avoid undue competition with other schools or institutions in the University.[54]

In other words, the fees were to be set at a level equal to the other schools of the University of London, such as King's College and University College, though there was a *possibility* that some *concessions* might be made for the local poor. In fact, as has already been illustrated, the number of vocational classes had been reduced in favour of those with an academic bias. Those that remained were very much for the aristocrats of labour.[55]

This chapter is about the people of East London, and by way of conclusion it looks at the student records of East London College in the years between 1908 and 1931 to discover how the local community responded to the university in its midst.

In the academic year 1908–09, the College's three degree faculties were composed of the following student numbers, Arts (29), Engineering (9) and Science.(52) According to McDonnell's research,[56] five out of the 91 had Jewish sounding names – including one Jacob Brodetsky – three appeared to come from Irish middle-class backgrounds whilst the majority were of 'solid English stock'.[57] Less than a quarter of the students had an East London postal address. Evidence shows that most were residents of suburbia, availing themselves of the benefits of road, rail and underground transport which for those who could afford it, linked East London to the rest of the capital and its suburbs as well as places further afield such as Plymouth, Leatherhead and Suffolk. McDonnell's research further reveals that the greater percentage of students came from educated backgrounds with parents who were teachers, doctors, ministers of religion and white collar workers.

The 1912–13 List of Matriculated and Registered Internal

Students ilustrates that the Arts (146 students) and Science (164 students) faculties attracted far more students than Engineering (48 students).[58] Of the total enrolled, less than 1 per cent of the student body for that year is listed with addresses in the immediate vicinity of the East End while no more than 27 per cent is recorded as living within the wider perimeters of East London. Overall the intake from Greater London was just under 50 per cent. The list provides evidence that East London College's reputation had spread to France and Germany. Conformation of the College's broad catchment area is to be found in the Record Book of those killed in the First World War. Of the 40 fatalities recorded, 20 were listed as having addresses in the East London area, three only from the East End, two of which were Jewish sounding names. The remaining 20 addresses illustrate the widening of the College's net, they run from Newcastle to Devon and from Kent to Middlesex. The bias towards science is evident in that more than three-quarters of the men killed had been awarded or were registered as reading for, the degree of Bachelor of Science.[59]

The post First World War student intake shows little change on the previous decade. A faculty of medicine now existed and, of the 589 registered for day and evening university courses in 1922–3, 71 students were registered as reading medicine. Yet again, the local community was poorly represented, only 16 recorded as students living close by. And though 116 came from East London the bulk, 184, were from Greater London. There were also 16 foreign students registered for that session, engineering attracting those from Armenia, Ceylon, Rumania and Greece, science drawing two with address in Palestine, whilst three South Africans showed a preference for medicine.[60] By no stretch of the imagination could the East London College any longer claim to be a college for the local 'poor' community. Though perhaps some of those attending were East Enders who had been part of the post First World War move out north, north-west and north to the suburbs.

The final set of student entry statistics examined here are taken from the academic year 1930–1, the session during which the Queen's Hall was destroyed by fire. The fire, which occurred during the early hours of 25 February 1931, was the catalyst which brought out into the open the bitterness which had been developing between those who saw the People's Palace as a centre for recreation and the governors and academic body of East London College, a college which had become increasingly a part of the University of London and decreasingly a vehicle of economic and intellectual improvement for the poor of the East End.

By the beginning of the fourth decade of the twentieth century East London College, now an established School of the University of London, with a developing degree programme, was awaiting the granting of the Royal Charter, an event which took place in 1934 when the College was renamed Queen Mary College. In spite of an article which appeared in the *Daily Telegraph* in May 1928, which sought to suggest that the College, 'brings within the reach and to the very doors of the poorest in pocket, the 'Neglected Half of London', a chance to satisfy the zest for culture and thirst for learning that take wealthier men to the older universities',[61] the list of students attending day and evening courses during 1930–1 contained only 16 with local addresses and a mere 54 from within the larger radius of East London. Foreign student numbers were on the ascendancy and for that session stood at 36. There was a stronger Jewish presence than in previous years, though the majority of those with Jewish sounding names gave addresses in Palestine rather than the East End. The constant factor was the marked preference for scientific study.[62]

Further evidence of the gulf that now existed between the local community and the College is to be found in the College student magazine which contained few references to the local area and even fewer contributions from members of the local community. What did appear was contemptuous rather than fond. J. Noel Reamsley, in an uncomplimentary article about the Mile End Road presents an unsavoury view:

> Shops with dirty windows behind which it would not be difficult to imagine the enactment of all the darkest deeds in the criminal category ... a chop house with quaint hieroglyphics – meant to be English ... in the Near Far East there is a man of tender years, of an alien persuasion and bearing a wealth of superfluous tissue.'[63]

All the negative values of the East End, its criminality, poverty, illiteracy and alieness portrayed by a less than sympathetic student.

It was the fire that destroyed the Queen's Hall and the debate that followed about its rebuilding and the role of the Palace and the College in relation to the local community which manifestly ended Besant's and Hay Currie's dreams. In place of community spirit was division and distrust, the belief that if the educationalists won then the People's Palace would be lost to the people of the East End. This sentiment was supported by an article which appeared in the *Jewish Guardian* and which referred to, 'The destruction of the large hall of the People's Palace [as] a distinct loss to the social life of the East End in general as well as to the Jewish population.'[64] Recent research has shown that few, if any, of the local Jewish community were engaged in academic or even vocational studies at the College. Their attachment was to the People's Palace as a centre of entertainment; 'We regularly went to tea dances and to concerts and theatrical performances'[65] reminisced one East Ender, another recalled attending a concert given by the Jewish *chazan*[66] Rev. Rosenblatt at which the audience was in excess of 2,000. None of the 60 interviewed[67] had attended classes at the College. The *East London Advertiser* highlighted the lacuna between education and recreation and the separate communities those two activities served, 'It has to be remembered that the students are not drawn in any great numbers from East London ... whilst the People's Palace and all that it stands for, is essentially an East End institution.'[68] As the editor of the *East London Observer* succinctly pointed out in the November of that year, 'The problem really resolves itself into a question of College versus Palace. The point is whether the major object should be University Education or whether it should be Popular Recreation.'[69] A bitter dispute followed, with the outcome a victory for education. The College succeeded in taking over the Queen's Hall site as well as the library and the club rooms to use for academic purposes, local events were to be catered for on a site nearby.[70]

CONCLUSION

What is clear is that, even in the early years of the twentieth century, the People's Palace was perceived purely as a place of entertainment by the poor whose 'university' it was intended it should be. The majority of the local poor, were too tired and worked too long hours to be able to avail themselves of the learning that was on offer. What attracted was a haven from the harsh reality of working life, as Besant had written some 20 years earlier, a place where 'tired people might rest, quiet'. As the above has shown those that did take the opportunity of further and higher education were, in the main, those who had the time and the money.[71] But the local community were not the only ones who spoilt Besant's, Hay Currie's and the *London Evening Standard's* dreams. James Hatton had chosen the route of the University of London and once a part of that body local allegiance became secondary to the ambitions of the capital's primary centre for higher education. All the Schools under the University's umbrella played their role as educators for the nation and the civilized world. Within 20 years of the foundation of the People's Palace, education for the London community, the nation and those who came from overseas had taken precedence over the recreational and educational needs of the East London community.

Note
I should like to express my thanks to Anselm Nye, archivst at Queen Mary and Westfield College and Josh Levy for their help in researching the material for this chapter.

CHAPTER FOUR

Class and gender aspects of higher education in London: the origins of London Polytechnics

Miriam E. David

What education is for is a very topical and controversial question, capable of many different kinds of answer, from the philosophical to the prosaic. I hope to address the question from my own social scientific vantage point, and starting with the origins of South Bank University, about 190 years ago.[1] The buildings at the Elephant and Castle and especially Borough Road, are a vital part of England's educational legacy, having been used for both voluntary and municipal educational provision for a wide range of ages, and both sexes, but largely for the 'poorer classes'. I hope to show the different kinds of arguments advanced in the public arena for the provision of education in the past and the common threads in the current policy debates about education. In particular, I hope to illustrate the dilemmas posed about whether education should only be provided as an end in itself meeting private family or individual needs or as a wider public service, serving the needs of either the economy or the social system, or being used in the service of wider socio-economic changes, such as reducing differences between individuals whether male or female, on the basis of parental socio-economic backgrounds of privilege or poverty.

George Bernard Shaw, the playwright, was one of the early members of the Fabian Society which he joined in the early 1880s, together with Sidney Webb. Webb, with the Fabian society, had an important role in creating the London Polytechnics including what became known in 1892 as Borough Polytechnic Institute. Shaw wrote about some of the dilemmas of creating higher education in his play *Man and Superman*, published in 1903 and first performed in 1905. The play is essentially about the 'life force' and attempts to forge new relationships between men and women. A second issue is the question of reducing class distinctions through education in the interests of social progress. In one dialogue between Tanner, the progressive hero of the play and referred to as a member of the Idle Rich Class and Straker, his chauffeur and car mechanic, Shaw[2] satirises class distinctions through education. He sees 'Enry Straker as New Man, with technical and mechanical skills, not possessed by the middle and upper classes, and a force for the future:

Tanner: But this chap has been educated. What's more, he knows that we havnt. What was that board school of yours, Straker?

Straker: Sherbrooke Road.

Tanner: Sherbrooke Road! Would any of us say Rugby! Harrow! Eton! in that tone of intellectual snobbery? Sherbrooke Road is a place where boys learn something: Eton is a boy farm where we are sent because we are nuisances at home and because in after life, whenever a Duke is mentioned we can claim him as an old school fellow.

Straker: You don't know nothing about it, Mr Tanner. It's not the board school that does it: *it's the Polytechnic.*

Tanner: His university, Octavius. Not Oxford, Cambridge, Durham, Dublin or Glasgow. Not even those non-conformist holes in Wales. No, Tavy. Regent Street! Chelsea! *the Borough!* – I don't know half their confounded names: these are his universities, not mere shops for selling class limitations like ours. You despise Oxford, Enry, don't you?

Straker: No, I don't. Very nice sort of place, Oxford, I should think, for people that like that sort of place. The teach you to be a gentleman there. In the polytechnic they teach you to be an engineer or such like. See?

Arguments about whether educational institutions should serve particular purposes, providing specific knowledge, skills or social privilege or prestige for one class and/or gender have raged since the origins of state involvement in educational provision, nationally and internationally. They are also particularly pertinent today, in the current debates about educational provisions, finances and standards and the extent to which the state should be involved, as compared to private and/or voluntary organizations in providing education. Unlike Governments over the past 150 years, over the last 18 years, Conservative Governments believed that the balance ought to be struck by families having the freedom to choose appropriate education on the basis of their own resources rather than with some kind of state subsidy, effectively seeing education as an entirely private matter, and not ironing out differences in life chances between men and women, rich or poor, black or white. This approach is likely to be modified now, rather than fundamentally altered, by the New Labour Government.

We begin with a case study of the origins of Borough Road both as an elementary school and training institution and as a Polytechnic, reviewing the arguments about education provision on a class and gender basis, and looking at ways in which these arguments developed and were implemented from their early beginnings. I shall discuss how education came to be seen as an essential component in the growth and development of social progress and especially the Welfare State in the aftermath of the Second World War. I shall also briefly look at the critical involvement of social scientists in the processes of both analysing and arguing for educational provision and expansion as a basis for economic growth. Their arguments focused on the necessary relationship between families, especially mothers and the education system, for children's successful educational performance and achievements. I shall conclude by looking at the ways in which these debates were transformed over the past 18 years under Tory administrations from ones about the necessity of education for both economic growth and social progress, back to Victorian values and towards education again being seen more narrowly for private family goals and/or as an end in itself, rather than a question of state investment for the wider public good. The New Labour Government, however, has already proposed to tip the balance back to state provision but for essentially individual goals. The common thread throughout the policy process has been the balance between families and the state with women's role as mothers supporting the family, socially and economically, vital if often invisible.

THE ORIGINS OF BOROUGH ROAD AS AN
EDUCATIONAL INSTITUTION

Although the origins of Borough Polytechnic in themselves offer us a fascinating insight into the history of educational provision in the late nineteenth century, the buildings at Borough Road had an even older educational pedigree. In reviewing the use of the buildings in Borough Road from the early nineteenth century we are afforded what is probably a unique history of educational provision for the poor and English educational history in microcosm. The Polytechnic was established in 1892 in buildings that were bought from the British and Foreign Schools Society. This society had been founded in early 1814 by followers of Joseph Lancaster, a Quaker philanthropist. Given the lack of schooling, except what private arrangements rich families chose to make for their own children, Lancaster had set up a school in Borough Road in 1798 to provide rudimentary religious education as a form of 'moral rescue' for poor children in Southwark from nonconformist families. This led to the setting up of more schools, and a teacher training department in 1808, all using the same method of teaching known as the 'monitorial system', that is, older children teaching groups of younger children. As Tropp[3] noted:

> One of the earliest of Lancaster's projects was the establishment of a department attached to his school at Borough Road for the training of senior monitors, in order that they in turn might take charge of monitorial schools.

The Borough Road Training Department was founded in 1808, became an essential component in the spreading of these educational ideas among Whigs, Unitarians and Evangelicals. A rival organization, known as the National Society for Promoting the Education of the Poor, was founded in 1811 by Bell, an Anglican clergyman, who also used a version of the monitorial system. Together these two organisations became known as the charity schools movement (see Chapter nine).

These initiatives were entirely dependent upon charitable contributions from their religious backers. Given religious disagreements education remained entirely a private, individual parental responsibility. The Established Church had, however, begun to assume some responsibility for elementary education. There were also widespread charitable foundations and endowments together with a network of Grammar Schools from medieval times.[4] In fact, Lancaster fell into financial difficulties and after an argument with the British and Foreign Schools Society left in 1814. In 1818 he went to the USA to establish his monitorial system and it quickly found popularity there too. It has recently been reconsidered as an efficient and effective educational method in the USA.[5]

The British and Foreign Schools Society in England continued to influence the spread of charitable schooling for poor children, such that during the course of the nineteenth century it established over 4,000 schools for boys and girls. Training continued to be provided at Borough Road, usually to young adult men and women since a minimum age of entry was set, well above that of the age of leaving school. The students were usually Sunday School teachers who were often financed by their religious employers. Tropp claims that 'the majority of recruits to such teaching were men who had tried other professions and failed.'[6]

Given the successful spread of charity schools, despite lack of public financial aid, by the 1830s consideration was given to state support for school buildings. In 1833 the first grant of £20,000 was given to aid private subscription of school buildings. The question of teacher supply was also seen as a matter for public resolution. The first Secretary of the Committee of Council on Education 1839–49, Sir James Kay Shuttleworth, was particularly keen to aid the further establishment of such schools and to this end devised a modified form of training known as the pupil-teacher system. Initially, he was not able to gain public support and so he established a private training college in Battersea, which later became part of the rival National Society. By the late 1840s a scheme of public state support in the form of scholarships for training had been created. Women in particular were encouraged to be pupil-teachers so that by the end of the 1860s they consti-tuted almost a half of the teaching workforce. They were drawn from the same poor backgrounds as their own charges and kept on in elementary schools for five years before going on to the training at age 18.[7] This was seen as an effective method of educating poor children, supplemented later by payments from the Science and Art Department. In the 1860s the government grew concerned about excessive public expenditure and devised a scheme which became known as 'payment by results' to ensure that teachers were both efficient and effective, measured against their pupils' examination results: six different standards for ages 7 to 12 were created for the examinations: the early origins perhaps of standardized testing and the National Curriculum?

By the end of the 1860s, the Government had become extensively involved in supporting religious education, through grants to pay for teachers' training and salaries as well as support for school buildings. Provision was usually by religious bodies on a voluntary basis. The recognition that it was in the interest of the state to support schooling for the masses as a way of maintaining social control and order was an essential part of its involvement with charity schools. It led to the setting up, through the first major piece of educational legislation, the Elementary Education Act of 1870 (Forster's Act), of a parallel system. The aim was to ensure national provision and school boards were to provide elementary schools in areas without charity schools. By the 1890s the two systems of state and charity schools were becoming merged, with many of the schools of the British and Foreign Schools Society incorporated into the school board system, which by this stage was providing compulsory education for 5 to 12 year olds. The Borough Road Training College was also merged into the state system of teacher training and no longer only provided for the poor of the locality: hence its move to Isleworth in 1890.

One major influence on these developments was Joshua Fitch who had been a pupil and later the principal at Borough Road and later became an HMI, involved in the Royal Commissions on elementary education. He was also involved in promoting developments in women's education, based on his own experiences, given that there had been female trainees from the beginning. His career resonated with that of the first woman director and later Vice Chancellor of South Bank. She had come to her post from having been senior Chief HMI responsible for schools in the 1980s.[8]

By the late 1880s, not only had arguments that the state should be involved in providing a basic education for all children found acceptance on grounds of both social order and social improvement but consideration was also given to the distinctiveness of particular forms on the basis of class, religion and gender. There was a political consensus on the need for education but not on its form of organization. In particular, there were disagreements over both the extent of state support and involvement in providing more than a basic, and free, elementary education. The system of public and endowed grammar schools for middle- and upper-class boys was codified and regularized into three or four grades in the 1860s, including opening up some opportunities for the provision of such schools for girls. However, the state did not finance the schools but merely allowed for the use of funding on a charitable or endowed basis. Families were still to be free to choose the kinds of education best suited to their financial means. Although separate girls' schools were established in the aftermath of these reforms, there was never any intention of transforming women's role within the Victorian family. Such secondary, further and higher educational opportunities chiefly for middle-class girls would not inevitably lead to positions of economic independence in adult life, but mainly, on marriage, to traditional positions within the family.

Despite all this state involvement in the redesign and development of the education system, streamlining its finances and systematizing it in accordance with a more clearly differentiated social structure, concern was increasingly expressed that the British education system did not match that of Germany in terms of technical education for industrial economy. Matthew Arnold's report, for example, drew unfavourable comparisons between British and German higher education, seeing the latter's technical high schools as infinitely superior.[9] In the 1880s, therefore, attention was given to how to create both the administrative and financial machinery to develop such education. In London, it was decided that funds from the City of London Parochial Charities should be used to provide technical and commercial education for the poorer inhabitants (see Chapter five). County and borough councils were established in the late 1880s and given powers to provide technical instruction. They were also given further powers to use funds from a local customs and excise tax, know as the 'whisky money', to support such developments.[10] By 1890, the stage was set for a massive expansion of educational provision above the elementary level, partially supported by central or local government, in order to improve Britain's industrial competitiveness and to ensure social progress. Tories and Whigs were in agreement on the broad ends for different reasons. The Tories were concerned about social order and improvement whereas the Whigs were more concerned about economic developments and 'national efficiency'. For example, in 1882, Quintin Hogg, a Tory, had reopened Regent Street Polytechnic to provide both technical eduction and facilities for leisure for the poorer classes in central London. It had originally opened in 1838, modelled on the Parisian

Ecole Polytechnique, for the exhibition of objects connected with the industrial arts and providing a laboratory and lecture theatre. The Liberals also pressed for expansion of technical education through the various Royal Commissions on education.

Perhaps one of the most important influences, however, on the form of development was the creation of the Fabian Society in the early 1880s, set up by 'members of the extreme democratic wing of the liberal party'.[11] Shaw and Webb joined with the express purpose of campaigning for social improvements to achieve national efficiency. Sidney Webb together with his wife Beatrice, also began to develop modern methods of social investigation as a basis for attempting to influence government action.[12] Both the Webbs and Fabian Society were very influential in the creation of new educational institutions which promoted new educational forms as a basis for national efficiency. However, they were not concerned about changing the relationships between the family and the state or promoting women's role in public life. Indeed, Beatrice Webb deliberately eschewed such changes.[13] Sidney Webb became the chair of the London County Council's Technical Education Board in 1892, which was influential in creating the London Polytechnic Institutes.[14]

In examining the origins of Borough Polytechnic it is also necessary briefly to detail the origins of the London School of Economics (LSE). It could be described (after Dickens) as a 'tale of two institutions' across the river, instead of across the channel. In 1894, the Webbs were successful in obtaining private and London County Council (LCC) financial support for the establishment of LSE, eventually to become a constituent college of London University.[15] The aims in setting up LSE were to develop commercial education for the workforce of London and 'the application of scientific thinking to politics' and to use 'state intervention in place of an uncaring individualistic ethic'.[16] The LSE slowly developed the social sciences not only on a Fabian socialist basis but particularly, drawing on the Webbs' early examples, as methods for aiding government action for national efficiency. Many of the sources that I have drawn on for this review of the socio-historical development of education were researched by scholars at the LSE. Olive Banks, one of the most significant of these scholars, in reviewing the development of the sociology of education has claimed that the subject:

may really be said to have begun as a regular academic discipline in the research carried out at the London School of Economics in the years after the Second World War. The interest amongst this group of sociologists at this time was largely with problems of social structure and the economy, and they were fascinated, in Jean Floud's own words, 'by the spectacle of educational institutions struggling to the new purposes of an advanced industrial economy' ... the early sociology of education was rooted very firmly in sociology rather than education ... another influence has been its interest in educational policy.[17]

The LSE's origins were similar but the developments were rather different from those of Borough Polytechnic, despite the fact that the Fabians' intentions were that they should both be part of a more extended system of higher education. Webb was particularly keen for Borough Polytechnic also to become affiliated to London University but other members of the Institute did not want it to diverge from its commitment to working-class education. London University was reconstituted in the late 1890s so that teachers at places like Borough could become 'recognized teachers' of the University and courses could become part of internal degrees. There was no question of Borough – or any of the other Polytechnic Institutes – becoming part of the University. But some such as the Peoples' Palace (Queen Mary College) began to move in that direction. In 1904 Webb published a survey entitled London Education which boasted of the achievements of the London Polytechnics. He:

> boasted that even the new provincial Universities, with all their dignity of charters and chancellors, diplomas and degrees often do less work of a University grade than a London polytechnic.[18]

Webb and Hewins pushed LSE towards joining London University but the early intention was clearly to provide 'commercial education'. Borough was more broadly based in terms of subjects. LSE did not set out to cater for women. Part of the reason for the differential development of Borough from LSE was that its origins lay in a different political milieu from that wished for it by the Fabians. In 1889, a South London Polytechnic Council was set up composed of both Liberals and Tories. They were 'convinced of the urgent need in this country of technical and commercial education'.[19] They decided on three Polytechnic Institutes in south

London – one at New Cross (later Goldsmiths'), one at the Elephant and Castle and one at Battersea (later Surrey University). The Council had difficulty finding a site for the Borough but eventually negotiated with the British and Foreign Schools Society to buy their buildings. This was inspired by the Charity Commissioners in their disposal of City of London Parochial Charities funds: an offer to match sums raised on voluntary basis and the influence of Evan Spicer in raising funds. In 1889, Sir Phillip Magnus, a member of the South London Polytechnic Council, the LCC, and later to become a governor of Borough (given his work for the City and Guilds and the fact that he also became an MP), published a clear case for all three Polytechnics, modelled on that of Regent Street. The intention was social improvement not social mobility, maintaining a class and gender based system of education, whilst at the same time expanding the amount of technical education for the working class. Although there was some confusion in his argument over whether the Institutes should be for working men only or also working women, the purposes were clear:

> The new Polytechnic which is to be the centre of the intellectual life of the artisan population of every district in London has two distinct functions to which a third is in the process of being added. It is intended to afford facilities for the technical and commercial eduction of young men and women engaged in different occupations, and to provide, at the same time, healthy recreation in the form of music, lectures, popular readings, physical exercises and social gatherings. It is both a school and a club; and whilst the scope of school is narrowed by a distinct bias toward bread-winning pursuits, the objects of the club are widened so as to include many forms of amusement which are foreign to club life, as understood by the frequenters of Pall Mall and St James's Street.[20]

In elaborating his views of the purposes of such education, he made clear how its focus was on moral and social improvement as well as control, rather than any form of social change:

> The institute ... is essentially a corporation of working men and women bound together by the sympathy of kindred occupations and bent on mutual improvement by all such agencies, other than religious, as are calculated to promote their intellectual physical, moral and material well-being.... To improve the lives and to increase

the happiness of the labouring population are, per se, objects to be aimed at. Those occupied with pleasant pursuits can scarcely realise the monotony of the ordinary workman's existence.... It is no more than charitable to infer that *many of the lapses into immorality and sometimes into other forms of vice, are the result, particularly among women, of sheer dullness,* [*sic.*]*of the absence of all legitimate means of mental excitement* ... what is wanting is some sort of counter attraction.... These wants the new Polytechnic supplies. But it does much more. It draws in the children of the poorer classes, and trains them early, before there has been time for the effects of their elementary education to wear off.'[21]

The Polytechnic Institutes were thus conceived of as chiefly forms of adult or evening education in technical or commercial subjects as was LSE, but with the addition of day trade and technical schools for children above the school leaving age. Given the acquisition of the building through the funding from the City of London Parochial Charities, the Polytechnic opened in 1892. It rapidly began to receive financial support not only from voluntary and charitable contributions but also from the newly established Technical Education Board (TEB) of the London County Council (LCC). In the same year that the Polytechnic opened, Sidney Webb was elected to the LCC as a member for Deptford and almost immediately became chair of the TEB. He was only one of six Fabians elected to the LCC but they were to wield an influence far in excess of their small number, given an LCC of 118 members. Despite Webb's previous lack of experience or apparent interest, he quickly developed it, to quote Brennan:

Sidney's entry into the educational world was not dictated by any particular interest in elementary education nor for that matter in the endowed grammar schools. Parliament had given educational responsibilities to the new authorities. As far as the LCC was concerned these powers had been allowed to go by default. The situation called out to be exploited. It was the subsequent experience of being responsible for the conceiving and execution of policies in the field of technical education that provided the practical frame of reference for the Webbs' instrumental theory of education to germinate and grow.'[22]

Webb's instrumental theory was that education should be more than humanistic and contribute to work, employment and the developments of the labour force. Under Webb's influence and in co-operation with City Parochial Charities' Foundation the TEB began to develop all the London Polytechnics into day as well as evening schools and also to finance the development of the LSE. As a result Webb was able to write, in his preface to the first official history of the Polytechnic, in 1910 that:

> The story of the Borough Polytechnic affords a more than usually interesting example of the happy cooperation of endowment and municipal aid, of voluntary initiative and collective control.[23]

That 'happy cooperation' was for a clear purpose of providing 'supplementary' education for working men and women as laid down in the official aims:

> The object of the institute is the promotion of industrial skill, general knowledge, health, and well-being of young men and women belonging to the poorer classes. . . . The classes and lectures shall not be designed or arranged so as to be in substitution for practical experience of the workshop or place of business, but so as to be supplementary thereto.[24]

During the first 10 years provision of evening technical courses developed rapidly for both men and women largely in the age range 16 to 25, albeit that the provision was largely for the separate sexes. Although the schemes of administration laid down that it 'shall so far as practicable be arranged for and open to the uses of both sexes' certain facilities were to be provided for each sex separately, namely a common room and a refreshment room, and eventually separate gymnasia. A male principal was appointed but a 'Lady Superintendent' was also appointed to take charge of the women's departments.[25]

The range of evening classes was wide: from special trade classes through to arts and crafts to higher commercial and general classes, languages (English, French, German, Italian and Spanish), commercial and local government law, economics, banking and currency, machinery of business, accountancy, etc. – not unlike the spread of subjects today. There were also special technical and domestic economy classes for women, including needlework, embroidery, millinery, dressmaking, cooking, laundry-work, sick nursing, home management and care of children. Five different day schools were also set up including a technical day school for boys, a trade school for girls, domestic economy for girls, music and a national school of bakery (which still exists as part of the University and provides the basis for the staff dining room as a training restaurant) and confectionery. One of the first of these, influenced by the TEB, was the domestic economy school for girls set up on extremely narrow lines to prepare girls for work, the family, well in keeping with the times, as noted by Dyhouse.[26]

> The school was intended to give a thorough training in the various household arts to girls who had passed through elementary schools and were exempt from school attendance. It aimed to prepare them for home life and not to become teachers of domestic economy.[27]

Given the assumed nature and needs of the locality, which according to Booth's surveys of the 1890s was extremely poor, this school was afternoons only.[28] Evening trade classes for women were not very successful, given the limited number of women workers, as both Purvis (1989) and Dyhouse (1989) have recently noted more generally.[29] Single women had quite high participation rates and such classes were popular elsewhere – especially typing and shorthand – but on marriage women were no longer able to do such work. Instead, a day continuation school with preparatory trade training as well as general education and artistic training was started with waistcoat-making selected as the trade for experiment.

Given the TEB's definition of technical education as 'the teaching of every conceivable subject other than ancient Greek and theology'[30] there was a proliferation of day and evening vocational courses in the Polytechnics. To assist the development of higher elementary education the idea of a 'scholarship ladder' was devised by Webb and accepted by the TEB. Initially 500 junior county scholarships were given with a maintenance grant 'to compensate parents to some extent for the loss of their children's earnings'. By 1904 this scheme had been extended with the addition of intermediate scholarships for pupils aged 16 to 19 years old, and for those taking technical or continued instruction and the most, domestic economy scholarships for both girls and women. These schemes greatly influenced the growth of trade schools and higher elementary education in London albeit that these schemes all remained rigidly socially and sexually distinctive.

Changes in the educational and administrative machinery of

government also complemented these local developments. For example, curiously and much to the anger of his former allies, the Liberals, Webb helped the Tories to devise the 1902 and 1903 Education Acts. There had been much friction between the TEB and the London School Board. The two Acts abolished the school boards and put in their place composite local education authorities (LEAs) based on the counties and county boroughs. Each was to provide its own form of secondary education by means of incorporating endowed and voluntary grammar and technical schools, on a fee-paying basis but with the possible award of selective, financial scholarships. It also entailed subsidizing the efforts of religious bodies which was anathema to the Liberals. The LEAs gained responsibility for most state education including technical and secondary education, through the scholarship system, excluding only the Universities and fee-paying public and independent schools.

Within this revised and streamlined system, ostensibly to achieve national efficiency through education, Borough Polytechnic remained committed, in the early 1900s, to providing suitable education for the young men and women of the locality rather than encouraging a more middle-class and professional ethos through extending its University work.[31] Although some evening students were registered for London University degrees, the then principal preferred to concentrate on technical education for workers in contrast with the principal at Battersea Polytechnic.[32] This latter institution eventually became Surrey University in the transformation of Technological Institutes to Universities in the early 1960s by the Tories, whereas Borough Polytechnic remained the prototype for the creation of the binary system of higher education as developed by Anthony Crosland for the Labour Government in the latter part of the 1960s.[33]

The Polytechnic, by 1910, had developed into a rather complex institution, providing, on the one hand, higher elementary education for working-class boys and girls and, on the other, part-time evening education, of a largely technical kind for working men and women, although figures indicate that there was always twice as much provision for men as women, inevitably perhaps given the expectation that married women were primarily to be occupied with their home lives. However, some non-technical education was provided in Morley College then based in the Old

Vic and a part of the Polytechnic. This College's courses were largely for women and more oriented to leisure but there was no record of knowing how popular the courses were. The two Institutes separated in the 1920s, with the famous social scientist, (later Baroness) Barbara Wootton, becoming Morley's first principal before she moved to London University and LSE by the Second World War. The educational provisions at the Polytechnic were provided in a complex mix of government and voluntary support, such that Webb could write, in what now seems almost prophetic language that:

> It is one of the special problems in Democracy which make the twentieth century so interesting to discover how we can most successfully fit the voluntary agency in the governmental framework so as to secure the maximum advantages of both. The problem confronts us in the domain of public health, in that of lunacy, in that of the provision for the aged on the one hand and the able-boded unemployed on the other. But in no branch of public action does it confront us more definitely than that in education and in no place is the problem so momentous as in the vast wilderness of London. In the matter of university education for the metropolis, for instance, the whole future hangs on its solution. It is because I am convinced of the great advantage that the Borough Polytechnic has derived from its independence in administration and freedom to start new experiments that I venture to express the hope that the happy relationship between the polytechnic and the London County Council will not be departed from.[34]

The 'new experiments' have continued albeit on relatively traditional class and gender lines up until the present and in parallel with developments in the other London Polytechnics and London University: points to which I shall return.

EDUCATION REFORM FOR ECONOMIC OPPORTUNITY:
CONTRADICTORY REORGANIZATIONS OF SECONDARY AND HIGHER
EDUCATION

Moving from these early developments in education provision for national efficiency in Victorian times and the early twentieth century I now want to look briefly at how educational reforms were developed and implemented after the First World War and up to the present day, when the term 'educational reform' has become the official terminology for educational policy. During the 1920s and 1930s there was a growing recognition of the need to try to fit education more closely to the needs of an increasingly diverse economic system. These aims were translated into policy proposals and solutions but only implemented after the Second World War. There was a measure of party political agreement in the 1940s on the need for educational and social provision to secure greater economic growth. Such views were advanced by economists, such as Keynes, in the 1930s, as well as politicians and formulated as policy prescriptions by Beveridge in his now famous report *Social Insurance and Allied Services* published in 1942 which set the framework for the development of the Welfare State.[35] The 1944 Education Act was one of several measures to secure such developments. It was passed by a war-time coalition Government and demonstrated some commitment to the principle of equality of educational opportunity by making secondary education free for the children of those parents who chose it. Private education was not, however, abolished and indeed the system of direct grants, introduced in 1926, to extend the scholarship system to civic grammar schools that selected academically able children from LEA schools was extended.[36] Nevertheless, the underlying aim was to select children for suitable education at all levels on the basis of their ages, aptitudes and abilities, rather than on their parents' socio-economic circumstances, whilst accepting that a small minority would continue to avail themselves of independent, private or public school education. Higher education was not considered at this stage except to extend the system of scholarships to widen access to existing opportunities. Of course, the system of higher education remained socially selective.[37]

In the next 20 to 30 years, social scientists were increasingly drawn into the policy process in both an official capacity and as independent social researchers to analyse the effectiveness of particular educational reforms in meeting the goal of equality of educational opportunity and proposing refinements to those measures. As mentioned before, this involvement of social scientists in both the policy process and the analysis of educational and other social reforms was continued and developed in particular at the LSE, drawing on the Fabian tradition. It focused upon the analysis of earlier educational reforms and on policy developments to achieve social and job mobility through education. Olive Banks'

careful and now classic study, published in 1955, of the development of English secondary education between 1900 and 1944
reached important conclusions about the role of education in
society. She argued:

> This attempt to use the secondary schools as a means to 'unite
> instead of divide the nation' raises in an interesting way the whole
> problem of the relationship between the education system and the
> social structure ... much recent educational policy has under-
> estimated the influence of the social and occupational structure on
> the development of the secondary schools ... the popularity which
> the grammar schools have always enjoyed in the eyes of parents is
> derived ultimately from their social role....'[38]

She drew the conclusion that:

> While the precise relationship between the school and society is
> still not understood, it is reasonably clear that the history of English
> secondary education has been profoundly influenced by its role in
> selection for social mobility. As a result, purely educational reforms
> have foundered whenever they have set themselves against the
> selective function of the schools.[39]

Despite these pessimistic conclusions, educational reforms to
reduce the selective function of schools and education more
generally continued to be tried and suggested by social scientists.
American policy-oriented research often provided the model.[40] In
Britain, the policy developments that eventually gave rise to the
breakdown of the party political consensus over commitment to
reducing parental disparities in resources, such as parental privilege or parental poverty, were not that of so-called compensatory
education from the USA but rather the expansion of equal
educational opportunities in secondary and higher education.[41] It
is now a matter of some curiosity that the Labour Governments
of the 1960s aimed to reduce social selection by first attempting to
abolish tri- or bi-partite secondary education (grammar, technical
and secondary modern schools) and create comprehensive schooling and second by attempting to create binary higher education.
Circular 10/65 entitled *The Reorganisation of Secondary Education
on Comprehensive Lines* and issued in 1965 was the Labour
Government's first official policy pronouncement.[42] This was followed, in 1966, by resource constraints on capital building projects

for selective grammar schools to ensure LEAs moved towards comprehensive education. However, in that same year, the Labour Secretary of State for Education announced, in his Woolwich speech, a new binary policy for higher eduction. There would continue to be universities funded through the University Grants Committee (UGC), some of which had been set up as recently as the early 1960s such as the new technological Universities (e.g. Brunel, Bath Surrey, Salford) and the greenfield Universities (e.g. East Anglian, Lancaster, Sussex, York, Warwick)[43] and through the Robbins Report (1963). In parallel there would be Polytechnics funded through LEAs. The plan in 1966 was to create 30 new Polytechnics by 1970, a process which became known as 'academic drift'.[44] In 1970 Borough Polytechnic became known as the Polytechnic of the South Bank.

Initially successive Tory Governments in the 1950s and the early 1960s had accepted informally the policy of comprehensive education but the Labour Government's persistent pursuit of it in the late 1960s, along with the expansion of higher education, from the Robbins Committee's report of 1963[45] began to raise doubts about educational standards in the minds of some of the Right. Initially criticism was confined to a récherché group of pamphleteers – the Black Paperites – who dubbed the policies 'egalitarianism'. No social scientific evidence was collected to demonstrate the effectiveness of these policies in reducing class differentials in educational opportunities either in secondary or higher education. Nevertheless, the rhetoric of the policy, to provide equal educational opportunities and reduce socio-economic differences on the basis of parental socio-economic circumstances, by means especially of providing comprehensive rather than selective secondary education became the butt of New Right critiques of educational policy. So, too, did higher education expansion with the phrase 'more means worse' attitude to University expansion in particular. The Right began to argue that such secondary and higher education lowered educational standards and produced mediocrity. They therefore began to argue for more parental rights to determine the choice of schools as an assertion of traditional Tory values of individualism and parental responsibility. At the same time, evidence was presented of successive economic crises and the mismatch between educational provision and the needs of the economy.[46]

A shifting political consensus began to emerge of the need to redesign the education system to fit it more closely both to the needs of industry and the wishes of parents, seen as relatively synonymous, rather than to achieve equal educational opportunities. For example, with respect to school policy, as a result of the Great Debate in Education, a common core curriculum and the making of education more accountable, especially to parents, was proposed by Prime Minister Callaghan in 1976 to the Labour Government. This was despite the fact that social research evidence failed to demonstrate that the purposes of education, in terms of equality of opportunity, had in any small measure been achieved. Neither official reports nor the academic studies such as the Oxford Mobility studies showed tendencies to reduce class differences for boys in educational opportunities and the growth of the economy.[47] However, the political pressure was increasingly in the direction of making the whole education system from early childhood to higher education better oriented to its consumers, both industry and parents. To the latter end proposals were formulated also to further involve parents in the political rather than purely educational process. Similarly higher education was being streamlined particularly with the introduction in 1972 of the Council for National Academic Awards (CNAA) and the National Advisory Board (NAB) for public sector higher education. The UGC for the Universities began a process of quinquennial planning in an effort to be efficient.

EDUCATIONAL REFORM: A NEW ERA?

After the 1970s changes in the political complexion of government were the occasion for a redefinition of the purposes of social and educational services provided by the state. (This transformation occurred not only in England but in other advanced countries, with New Right governments, particularly the USA. There the commitment to the new pursuit of 'educational excellence' was earlier and more explicit than in Britain.[48] Instead of education being harnessed to economic growth and social progress, it was blamed for the successive economic crises sustained. The Conservatives began to reassert values of individualism and parental responsibility for education. State involvement in educational provision came to be viewed more cautiously, rather than as a necessity for economic growth. Attempts were made to curtail public expenditure on education replacing it with the possibility of private sources of funding and to achieve greater efficiency within given resources. The underlying theme was one best described as the process of privatization, whereby Government reduced its own role as provider of social and educational services and allowed for alternative provision by private and/or voluntary organizations and/or the private family. By the same token, most social scientists as analysts of the public policy process were distanced from this process. Those who continued to be involved tended to be economists and/or businessmen with an appropriate philosophical approach: in Mrs Thatcher's words 'one of us'.

The transformation of education to one based more on private and/or family resources took place through both financial reductions and educational legislation. Three Education Acts in the 1980s, shifted the balance between the state, local government and families in their respective financial responsibilities.[49] The Education Reform Act 1988, marked the culmination of this process, with its chief architect, Kenneth Baker, seeing it as heralding a new *era*: specifically of 'standards, freedom and choice'. The aim was to create a market in education at all levels, from early childhood through to higher education. This was the first piece of educational legislation to cover both schools and higher education making all educational institutions more financially autonomous. Through the market, education provision would become more responsive to the needs of the consumer rather than the providers, seen as the educational establishment, especially the teachers. In the first place, educational institutions, previously reliant on state financial and bureaucratic LEA control, were given more financial responsibilities to manage themselves with greater business criteria. In the case of Universities the UGC was recreated as the Universities Funding Council (UFC) and in the case of Polytechnics, the relationships with local authorities were severed completely and NAB was turned into the Polytechnics and Colleges Funding Council (PCFC). In the case of schools, local management of schools (LMS) entailed local authorities setting only the per capita financial criteria. In all cases the governing bodies were given greater freedom to determine how to allocate funding as between staff and curricula, allowing for the development of institutional performance criteria: a return in some respects to the nineteenth century system of payment by results.

Chances are also opened up to find additional sources of income other than that provided by the state to ensure an adequate provision of teaching resources. In other words, state financial support was no longer deemed to be adequate for the purposes of meeting a full curriculum, except the National Curriculum, and required to be supplemented with private and/or parental support. With respect to compulsory education, a market began to be created with the provision first of financial aid to a few academically able children of 'poor' parents at private schools, through the Assisted Places Scheme, secondly open enrolment in state schools, and the possibility of schools opting out of LEA control to grant-maintained schools (GMS) or city technology college (CTC) status. The consumers were said to be the parents who were to be given both the right to express their voice in the management of schools and the freedom to choose schools in accordance with their wishes, whether state or grant maintained, city technology colleges or purely private schools. The argument was that this process of consumer choice would raise standards and thereby improve the whole education system. Brown (1990) has labelled this era as the 'wave' of the ideology of parentocracy to contrast it with the previous 'wave' of the ideology of meritocracy.[50] This introduced a period of tremendous critical policy analysis and social research especially on whether parental choice does exist and to what extent it may raise standards and improve schools. In fact, most of the evidence that has been collected about parental choice, as it has begun to be defined over the last 10 years, shows that parents' wishes for the schooling of their children are complex and not just focused on standards, as demonstrated by public examination results and league tables. The research evidence seemed to show that, despite various policy changes, education remains tied to social selection on the basis of parental background and socio-economic circumstances.[51] And indeed, despite the rhetoric about choice creating better educational standards, it seems likely that in so far as it exists it reinforces social differentiation.

Another argument has been that such consumer choice will lead to the closure of poor or bad schools. However, the evidence suggested that parental choice did affect children in some schools adversely, whilst not necessarily leading to their closure. Evidence has also shown the difficulty of schools in certain areas being able to meet their statutory requirements in terms of the provision of teaching, such that unqualified teaching help is increasingly being used to supplement teaching staff. Beginnings perhaps of the return to the monitorial system for children in poor, inner city areas, such as Southwark, Tower Hamlets or Hackney? Evidence has also been collected of the extent to which changes in the system produce benefits for the relatively middle class, despite their being presented as ways to assist poor but academically able children to benefit from private schooling. Edwards, Fitz and Whitty[52] demonstrated the extent to which the Assisted Places Scheme (abolished by New Labour in 1997) benefitted the lower middle classes rather than the working class, to the extent that 40 per cent of the children were from lone parent mothers with substantial amounts of education.

Higher education was similarly transformed through this period and made subject to increasingly severe resources constraints, whilst at the same time being expected to meet the needs of consumers, through the expansion of places for students. Moreover, a series of moves to introduce quality assurance has also been made. Throughout the 1980s Polytechnics and Universities were expected to expand in response to either growing demand or increasing levels of unemployment. By the end of the 1980s in the ERA 1988, the system of funding for higher education has also been changed with the establishment of two separate funding bodies PCFC and UFC, modelled on their former bodies, NAB and the UGC respectively. However, they remained relatively distinct, with a system of dual support for the universities in which research featured prominently, whilst the Polytechnics continued only with funding for teaching.

In the 1990s there have been further attempts to systematize higher education such that, under the terms of the Further and Higher Education Act 1992, all polytechnics were afforded the opportunity to apply to become universities. Furthermore, the funding of higher education has been rationalized under one main funding body, the Higher Education Funding Council (HEFC). Dual funding no longer operates in the same way with much of the funding for teaching and research allocated through HEFC's selective mechanisms and criteria. Thus South Bank along with the other original four nineteenth century London polytechnic institutes, has become known as a University. In the summer of

1992 it applied for incorporation as a new University. South Bank, in common with these other London institutions, continues to cater for the same kinds of clientele as it has done now for over 100 years, that is a mix of mainly lower middle-class or working-class students from the local communities of London studying for vocational scientific or engineering qualifications together with the social sciences and some limited humanities. There is now a more even balance of men and women, albeit that many of the women students are mature, and from ethnic minority groups. This mix continues the trends set in place when Borough Polytechnic was first established, but the types of courses pursued now are somewhat more advanced and include, also in common with other institutions of higher education, a sizable proportion of postgraduate studies, including research.

However, the post-war period has also witnessed enormous changes in the nature of the economy and the family structure in part attributable to the massive expansion of education, particularly in the last 30 years. In terms of higher education, both full- and part-time, women have increasingly been drawn in, in the last 20 years. The expansion took place mainly in Polytechnics and Colleges rather than in the previously designated Universities. Women now account for half the students in higher education, many of them mature students. South Bank University, formerly Polytechnic, the successor to Borough Polytechnic, expanded partly along the lines of its initial nineteenth century developments, and partly accommodating more mature women students on both a full- and part-time basis, in keeping with the national trends in the 1980s. What is particularly noticeable is the extent to which these women students tend still to be drawn from the locality. However the locality, and the student clientele has been transformed in terms of the proportion of minority ethnic groups. The original aims of the former Polytechnic have been somewhat modified given the wider changes in the socio-economic and family system. However, Magnus' view that such education would reduce women's lapses into immorality and/or vice is not the reason. It is more to do with economic necessity for such women to become more highly educated both for themselves and their children.

Much of the higher educational expansion has involved women with families, who have either followed the social pattern prescribed for them in traditional educational ideologies: of school followed by marriage and family, followed by part-time employment or higher education. This certainly seems to be the case from the evidence uncovered by one of my former postgraduate researchers, Dr Rosalind Edwards.[53] In participating in higher education either on a full-time or part-time basis they are participating at their own or their families expense rather that with full state support. Either way, these women have increasingly been drawn into education as a prelude to paid employment as evidence grows of a changing labour market, often referred to as the demographic time bomb: the need to find alternate sources of skilled labour as the balance between the dependent population and the labour force shifts. Given the education policy changes towards a market in education provision, these women are increasingly having to gain the skills and knowledge on their own account, without the benefit of state support.

By 1997, there was an increasingly diversified education system in terms of provision for various social groups, on the basis of class, race and gender. Although the system has expanded massively from its origins in the nineteenth century, disparities remain, and indeed are being reinforced between provision for the rich and poor, men and women. There is some evidence to suggest that compulsory education is no longer a fact for some children in poor inner city areas (and especially those from minority ethnic groups) such as Hackney and Tower Hamlets. The Government may no longer see its obligation necessarily to provide for these children, except by means of modest grants to the LEAs and through the specification of the National Curriculum and its associated key stages for testing pupil performance. In essence, there may be a return to the situation that prevailed in the early nineteenth century with a patchwork of voluntary charitable effort rather than statutory and compulsory services.

And similarly at the level of higher education, Government commitment is no longer to the full provision of these services, but as Webb noted earlier, to a mix of voluntary charitable and state and individual support for educational experiments. Webb had hoped to retain the relationship between local government and education, especially the Polytechnics, as a basis for major educational experiments. This relationship also reached its demise in the new era. Emphasis is now on self-help and parental input. The Dearing Committee, set up under the last Conservative administration, to review funding of higher education underlined this by suggesting greater individual and parental input to fund higher education.

CONCLUSIONS

To conclude, I hope that I have shown that the purposes of education and their effects over the last 160 or so years have been in the direction of economic and social progress, spreading the benefits of more education to wider groups and age ranges, as well as more to women. Nevertheless, the expansion of education has remained socially selective and stubbornly resistant, despite a variety of measures in the heyday of educational opportunities and the ever-increasing use of family support, to either social or sexual redistribution. Moreover, few measures have affected the distribution of education and economic opportunities between the sexes, because women have been relied upon to maintain the family. Indeed, women as mothers have been drawn into the education system both to support their own children's educational progress and more recently to develop the skills to support and care for their families economically. In the last two decades the process of privatization, of education among other social services, has increasingly made families more dependent upon their own resources and choices in relation to education. This process has already brought about great diversity of access to different kinds of education amongst families with different backgrounds and structures, including minority ethnic groups and lone parent households. It is likely that family diversity will continue to increase, returning England, albeit at a higher level, to the situation that prevailed 150 years ago where Government grants were provided only to top up the essentially private and voluntary system of education, differentiated along class and gender lines. Education is currently seen as being in individual and private family interests rather than to sustain a more caring society or to sustain the economy. Higher education is increasingly seen as a benefit to the individual rather than as a general social good. As it has become more widely available and diverse Government has become less willing to fund it and state priorities are now located elsewhere in the system. Despite changes of Government this situation is unlikely to be rapidly reversed, giving rise to continuing concerns about resources constraints and public expenditure.

Social scientists were, during the past 18 years of Tory Government distanced from official social analysis of the effects of social and educational policy changes. I argued in my inaugural lecture in Fabian terms that as social analysts we still have a vital and continuing role to point to the effects of education and social policies on different social groups, different types of families and their individual members. This Fabian argument is now being accepted by the New Labour Government. It has appointed over twice as many professional advisors as the previous Tory administration. The Government is itself made up of a higher proportion than ever before of University- and Polytechnic-educated recruits, including almost a quarter of women in the 419 Labour MPs. Moreover, many of them are professional educators, former school teachers and University academics, from across the spectrum of higher education. Perhaps most interesting of all the Minister of Higher Education, Baroness Blackstone, was educated at LSE in the quintessential Fabian subject – social administration – which she then went on to teach at LSE for the first 8 years of her career. Thus Webb's ambitions for higher education have, in some senses, now become true.

CHAPTER FIVE

The City of London and higher education

Sean Glynn

The eponymous City had been synonymous with London for many centuries but urban growth and spread, particularly after the Great Plague of 1665 and the Great Fire of 1666 meant that by the early nineteenth century the famous Square Mile retained only about one-tenth of London's population. By the end of the century the City's (night-time) population, as defined in the Census, formed only a tiny part of the Metropolitan whole and had been in sharp absolute decline for several decades.[1] While London burgeoned in area and population the City remained confined, at least in official and administrative terms, to more or less that area which had been contained by the original Roman walls and defined in a succession of medieval Charters.[2]

While the City is clearly defined in terms of administrative area it is not an easy matter to say exactly what the City was in broader terms. We do need to attempt this in order to consider the role of the City in the development of London's system of higher education. Beyond this we have to examine what the City did in relation to higher education and why it acted as it did. What clearly emerges from the story is that the City played an important and unique role through a variety of institutions and initiatives. In the final quarter of the nineteenth century City-related institutions were playing a leading role in the establishment of higher education and City funds were highly important both in aggregate and strategic ways. Ironically perhaps, this was against a background of broad indifference to higher education in terms of City opinion.

THE ROLE OF THE CITY CORPORATION

The City was represented and governed by the Corporation of London on the basis of over 100 Royal Charters awarded over seven centuries.[3] These had been threatened in the late seventeenth century under the Stuarts but were restored and firmly maintained from 1688 onwards. William III, in return for City support, re-established the old Charters and repealed the new ones of 1684. From this time the City was not inconvenienced by outside interference or investigation until the 1830s.[4] The City continued to be defined as the ancient 600 acres extending from Temple to the Tower with adjacent Liberties, such as the Artilliary in Spitalfields. Also, the City had purchased the Shrievalty of Middlesex and various rights in Southwark. It had monopoly rights over markets within seven miles and collected coal duties within 12 miles as well as governing 80 miles of river from Staines to the Medway. In the words of Sheppard, it was 'replete with privilege' and adopted a 'posture of strict defence of its established rights'.

The Corporation was headed by the Lord Mayor and two Sheriffs and had four Principal Courts. These were the Court of Aldermen, which, in the early nineteenth century, had 26 members elected for life; the Court of Common Council, which included the Aldermen and 200 common citizens elected annually by the freemen ratepayers; the Court of Common Hall, which included the Mayor and Aldermen together with the 12,000 or more liverymen of the City Livery Companies; finally there was the Court of Wardmote which provided the essential foundation of the whole structure. This was held separately in each of 26 wards and ratepayers (freemen or otherwise) were entitled to attend the Wardmotes. It was these Wardmotes which elected the Ward Officers (beadles, clerks, constables) as well as Common Councillors and Aldermen. The Lord Mayor and Sheriffs were chosen from the 26 Aldermen and elected on an annual basis by the Court of Common Hall. The City also elected four Members of Parliament, usually chosen from the Aldermen. The Court of Aldermen, which met weekly, had traditionally run the City but after 1815 its influence waned and was challenged by Common Council. By the second half of the nineteenth century Common Council was dominating City government, often in conflict with the Aldermen and Common Hall. According to the Webbs, by the 1830s Common Council had become 'the supreme organ of administration, itself wielding the whole power of government, and reducing the Lord Mayor and Aldermen to a mere magistracy'.[5] The livery franchise remained and was resented by Common Council. Common Hall selected the Lord Mayor and other officials as well as the City Members of Parliament. But it was a large and unwieldy body which could be manipulated and out-manoeuvred. In the early nineteenth century the City MPs were invariably Whig or Liberal and sometimes radical. Later the City changed its allegience to Conservative and became, to some extent, a Liberal target. This was to have important implications, indirectly, for education.[6]

It will be clear that the Livery Companies were an integral part of City government and that their members had an important political role. Company organization was complex and varied and, in Lang's words, 'it is so difficult to lay down hard and fast definitions of exactly what they are'.[7] There are problems in making generalizations but certain features in common can be distinguished. All the Companies were at least nominally linked with a particular trade, craft or 'mistery' and historically they had fulfilled some of the functions of modern trade associations and trade unions.[8] They had commenced as mutual benefit associations, at first on a voluntary basis, then governed by Wardens and bye-laws under the City Corporation, and eventually coming under the protection and control of Royal Charters.[9] Partly for tax avoidance reasons, money had often been left in trust to the Companies by their wealthier members who wished to avoid *mortmain* on their estates.[10] Most Companies were presided over by a Master and one or two Wardens, elected annually, from a Court of about 20 Assistants. Members of the Court were elected from the Liverymen of the Company when a vacancy arose. The Liverymen were recruited from the ranks of the Freemen, usually on payment of a fee. At the bottom of the hierarchy were the Journeymen of the Company.[11]

With the rise of City property values after the mid eighteenth century some of the Companies became very wealthy and 12 leading Companies gradually emerged.[12] But most of the others appear to have languished and some ceased to exist. By the early nineteenth century most of the 89 Companies existing had lost control over their particular trades and were unable to impose 'closed shops' or to regulate trading or apprenticeship.[13] Membership declined sharply in the early half of the century and the middle years marked what has been called 'the nadir of company fortunes'.[14] Most members had no connection whatsoever with the relevant trade or 'mistery' and joined companies only for political, social and personal reasons. Individuals paid 'fees and fines' for these reasons and the amounts paid varied with the prestige and influence of individual companies, the main tangible benefit being a vote in Common Hall. These highly unusual, archaic and often obscure bodies came under sustained attack from the 1830s onwards and came to fear abolition. Largely as a result, they were to play a remarkable and important role in the establishment of higher education in London and beyond. In the longer run this played a significant part in the revival and rehabilitation of many companies.

After being seriously threatened in the later seventeenth century the City had secured its constitution and autonomy after the 'Silent Revolution' of 1688 and resolved to defend it. The basic strategy, which had been in place since the sixteenth century, was to deny any external jurisdiction over the Square Mile while, at the same time, refusing to accept much in the way of responsibilities beyond it. The legal basis and rationale for this rested in the Royal Charters which had been obtained over centuries and defended through the City's considerable influence at national level.

When 'municipal reform' reared its head in the 1830s Commissioners were appointed and Sir Francis Palgrave and others conducted a massive and painstaking investigation during 1833–5.[15] In the end, the Corporation was held to be a reasonably efficient and 'open' municipal authority with a relatively wide franchise.[16] The City was more or less a ratepayer democracy and demands for reform were not much in evidence. As a result, the City was excluded, as was London as a whole, from the Municipal Reform Act of 1835. However, the City did not escape criticism: 'The corruption of the City's body politic was laid bare: the freedom was anachronistic, the Livery franchise absurd, the Court of Aldermen oligarchic, and the ward system inequitable.' The companies were 'mere charitable trusts', at best, and 'self-regarding clubs' in most cases.[17] Attention was also drawn to failures in City administration including the lack of sewers and failure to control nuisances and pollution arising, for example, from slaughterhouses, markets and prisons. The City had failed to extend the Port until the late eighteenth century, it had neglected the river, failed to deal with crime and refused to establish or allow new markets.[18]

From the 1830s onwards the City became a target, albeit intermittantly, for radicals and reformers ranging from Lord Brougham to W.E. Gladstone. The *Times* identified the City as a favourite target and the assault was to continue in various forms until the 1890s through the press, Parliament and several public enquiries.[19] In the event, the City proved to be remarkably well able to defend itself through a variety of means, although some of these also were, in turn, subjected to criticism and public scrutiny.[20] Through this lengthy process of being attacked and seeking to defend and preserve itself the City became centrally involved in some greater and national issues. In particular, the public health controversy of the 1840s, the campaign for a London-wide government, and the education question. It has been said that the City was 'institutionally and spiritually ... at variance with the new Victorian zeitgeist'.[21] In 1854 a Royal Commission examined the City Corporation once again.[22] The City again defended itself successfully and, although criticisms were made and reforms recommended, there was no fundamental change.[23] Reforms were made in the franchise and 'freedom' ceased to be pressed on retailers in the City. Also, the *metage* (levy charges for measurement of imports by sea) was commuted to a fixed charge in 1873 (for 30 years) with the proceeds dedicated to 'open spaces' for London. In 1861 the Coal Duties, levied over a radius of 20 miles, were dedicated, in part, to the Thames Embankment with the remainder to go to the Corporation.[24] In various ways, therefore, the Corporation sought to deflect and counter criticism.

In 1829 London gained its first general authority in the Metropolitan Police but the City was specifically excluded, creating its own up-dated policing arrangements. This seems to have established a precedent which has been maintained to the present time.[25] The City also had its own Commission for Sewers, which was one of eight in the Metropolis. When public health became an issue in the 1840s the City Commission appointed John Simon (later Sir John) as Health Officer and this proved to be an inspired choice. After various battles against City institutions and personalities ('the defenders of the filth') Simon was largely instrumental in ensuring that the City emerged triumphant over Edwin Chadwick in the so-called battle for public health.[26] While the City had representation on the Metropolitan Board of Works, established in the early 1850s, it devoted a good deal of energy to opposing its activities, most particularly where the Square Mile was directly affected.[27] The MBW was seen as an interfering rival and a threat by the Corporation, even where its activities were clearly beneficial. In the long struggle over a government for London (see Chapter one) the City allied itself with the Vestries, which, in differing forms, provided local government for the remainder of the capital. In the words of W.A. Robson, 'The record of the City Corporation in delaying, obstructing or defeating legislation aimed at the reform of London government between 1835 and 1880 was one of unbroken success'.[28]

ECONOMIC AND SOCIAL CHANGE IN THE CITY OF LONDON
Traditionally the City's demands for higher education had been a reflection of economic, social and religious development.[29] The City elite, over many centuries, had usually aspired to become rural gentry where success in commerce, manufacturing, retailing and professional activity made that possible.[30] Insofar as higher education was called upon, the usual recourse was to Oxford and Cambridge which remained England's only universities until the second quarter of the nineteenth century. Gresham College was established in 1579 on the basis of a legacy of Sir Thomas Gresham, founder of the Royal Exchange. The bequest included Gresham's house in Bishopsgate (after his wife's death) and rents from the Royal Exchange which were left under the joint control of the City Corporation and the Mercer's Company. Seven Professorships in a range of subjects were to be appointed with the duty of offering occasional lectures. The College operated at Bishopsgate during 1579–1768 and then at the old Royal Exchange until 1843. However, the College failed to develop successfully as a centre for teaching and learning despite several attempts to extend its activities. Although Oxbridge satisfied higher social aspirations and religious needs for Anglican communicants, it failed to cater for the middle classes and non-Anglicans. Their needs were met by a long succession of lesser establishments culminating in the University of London which commenced in the 1820s.[31] The Dissenting Academies, which flourished in the seventeenth and eighteenth centuries, were important forerunners.[32]

The economic life of the City also produced important demands for higher education. As a major centre of specialization the City required high degrees of skill and expertise in a wide range of activities including law, medicine, navigation, languages, book-keeping and mathematics. High levels of skill relating to service and manufacturing activity and the marketing, transhipment and processing of a variety of products including grain, sugar, furs, tea, coffee, precious metals and timber.[33] A variety of efforts were made to meet these various and diverse needs. City interests had established and endowed grammar schools and scholarships from which a minority of the most able pupils moved on to Oxford and Cambridge colleges.[34] These, in turn, were generously supported by City funds. It has been estimated that between 1480 and 1660 London donors gave Oxford and Cambridge £92,000 for fellow-ships and scholarships and this represented nearly five per cent of total City charitable donations.[35] Over time the City had also become the main national centre for training and learning in the higher professions. There were important medical foundations within and near the City, including St. Bartholomew's and St. Thomas's as well as the Royal College of Physicians. Also, the main national centres for the study and practice of Law were based in adjacent situations at Temple, Lincoln's and Gray's Inns. The Law Society first established entrance examinations in 1836 and the Inns of Court followed in 1852, albeit on a voluntary basis.[36] Several other, less exalted professional groups had their own City Companies and these included the Surgeons, Apothecaries and Attorneys. By virtue of its important economic activities, therefore, the City had traditionally been heavily involved in vocational training at all levels and this included areas which are now an important part of higher education. Also, the Guild Companies had, traditionally, assumed a responsibility for the supervision of training and entry into the trades and professions.

The City itself changed dramatically over time in terms of function and physical and human structure. The teeming life and mixed economy of the medieval City gave way to the modern centre of international finance and commerce, populated by an army of clerical workers by day and depopulated by night.[37] The most dramatic phase of this transition occurred during the second half of the nineteenth century.[38] The Census (i.e. officially resi-dent) population of the City peaked in 1851at 130,000 and fell to 114,000 by 1861. In the 1860s population fell by one-third to 76,000 in 1871 and there was a similar reduction in the 1870s. By 1901 the City had a Census population of only 27,000.[39] Enquiries in the 1850s revealed that none of the Aldermen and less than a quarter of the Common Councilmen actually lived in the City and that the institutions of the City were dominated by shopkeepers and small tradesmen ratepayers. Leading figures in commerce and finance were notably absent from City governing bodies and played little or no part in running the City.[40]

The City was substantially rebuilt during the Victorian era and changed dramatically in appearance.[41] The building of the new Royal Exchange, opened in 1844, marks the commencement of particularly rapid change in physical layout, upward projection and appearance.[42] Retail shops, workshops and domestic dwellings were replaced with larger, new buildings for use as offices and warehouses. Streets were widened and new thoroughfares (such as Queen Victoria Street and Holborn Viaduct) constructed. There were new markets at Leadenhall, Smithfield, Billingsgate and Spitalfields and railways eventually penetrated the Square Mile, facilitating the growing population of commuters.[43] The main economic changes involved the eastward shift of the Port and dockside activities to locatities beyond the City; the decline, disappearance and re-location of manufacturing activities; the decline of retailing: and the emergence of new financial and commodity markets.[44] These developments were closely linked with Britain's imperial, financial and trading role in the rapidly growing international economy. The City became an international centre with functions and connections which extended throughout the world.[45] These developments translated into rapidly rising site rental and freehold values and falling resident population. The poor, in particular, were forced out of the City by rising rents and this had implications for the disposition of charitable funds.

THE CITY AND GUILDS OF LONDON INSTITUTION

We now turn specifically to the development of higher education and to an examination of the City's involvement. During the 1870s a series of initiatives and complex lobbying and negotiations eventually gave rise to the City and Guilds of London Institution. City and Guilds became, and remains, a household name throughout and beyond Britain. This important development was to lead to a national system of technical and vocational education and examination as well as giving rise to a number of new educational establishments. These included the City and Guilds of London Central Institution, which has been described as Britain's first 'Industrial University', the City and Guilds of London Technical College at Finsbury, which became a model for technical institutions throughout the country, and the City and Guilds Art School in Kennington Park Road.[46]

Several London Livery Companies acted alone in supporting educational activities and initiatives connected with their trades. One such was the Clothworkers' Company which, from 1870, supported the Leeds Textile Industries' School which was to form a nucleus for Leeds University.[47] On 24 November 1871, Thomas Hughes MP wrote to the Lord Mayor of London suggesting that the City should lead an initiative in 'education for industry'.[48] Hughes is usually remembered for his authorship of *Tom Brown's Schooldays* and rather less for his long involvement in the promotion of popular education. He had been one of the founders of the Working Men's College and was its Principal during 1872–83.[49] On the 20 December 1871, the Lord Mayor sent a circular to all Masters, Prime Wardens and Upper Bailiffs of Livery Companies convening a meeting at the Mansion House on 10 January 1872, 'with the ultimate object of initiating a movement for the encouragement of Art, Manufacture, and Technical Education in connection with the City of London'. This meeting established a Committee to represent the Corporation and the Companies with a nominal membership of 88 consisting of representatives from the 76 Companies together with 11 members from the Corporation and the Lord Mayor.[50]

During the following five years a series of meetings and negotiations took place alongside intensive informal activities and public pronouncements in Parliament and elsewhere. The essential point of these activities involved a small group of influential individuals attempting to pressurise, provoke and persuade the reluctant Livery Companies to make a commitment of resources.[51] Among these the most important appears to have been Sir Sydney Waterlow who was part of a sucessful family partnership in printing and stationary and a member of the Clothworkers' Company.[52] Waterlow became Lord Mayor in February 1873, and lost no time in proposing evening lectures in Livery Halls and the establishment of a fund 'for founding a college and to develop

Technical Education'.[53] Information was gathered by the Corporation on schools in the Metropolitan area and the activities of the Livery Companies in promoting education. Twenty-five of the 76 Companies failed to produce any response to the survey. The majority of Companies had no educational activities at all and only 19 were able to indicate any actual activities or intentions.

It became clear that important pressures would have to be applied. A conference was held at Marlborough House, on 21 July 1873, convened by Prince Albert in his capacity as President of the Commissioners of the 1851 Exhibition, 'with the view of discussing how technical instruction might be promoted by the City Companies acting in concert with the International Exhibitions'.[54] By the end of 1873 the campaign appeared to have failed. Waterlow's term as Lord Mayor had ended and the majority of companies had indicated lack of interest. There was a renewed initiative two years later following Gladstone's speech at Greenwich in November, 1875, in which he stressed the need to 'give instruction in science' and to 'improve the knowledge of the British artist and workman'. Gladstone attacked the Companies for their misuse of funds, spending on lavish dinners while doling out small sums to charity, and suggested that they should 'fulfill the purpose for which they were founded'.[55] This attack was followed in December 1875, by Thomas Huxley, in his Presidential Address to the Society of Arts. Huxley informed the Society that funding for technical education was indeed available:

> There are in the City of London ... the possessors of enormous wealth who are the inheritors of the property and traditions of the old Guilds of London, which were meant for this very purpose, and if the people of this country do not insist on this wealth being applied to its proper purpose, they deserve to be taxed down to their shoes.[56]

Huxley drew a rather unflattering analogy between the reluctant Companies and a donkey: 'the animal is moving and by a judicious exhibition of carrots in the front and kicks behind we shall get him to a fine trot presently'.[57]

There was a further meeting of the Companies and the Corporation at the Mansion House on 3 July 1876 and a Provisional Committee was established under Lord Selbourne, a Liberal Lord Chancellor and Master of the Mercers' Company. It was resolved:

That it is desirable that the attention of the Livery Companies be directed towards the promotion of education, not only in the metropolis, but throughout the country, and especially to technical education, with the view of educating young artisans and others in the scientific and artistic branches of their trades'.[58]

Against a background of reluctance and resistance from most Companies and the City Corporation some of the leading Companies began to take independent action. In December 1876, Waterlow submitted a motion to the Court of the Clothworkers' Company which proposed to 'initiate a movement for establishing in London a City and Guilds Industrial Institute or University, with affiliated branches for ... the provinces'. This was to substitute for the 'superceded system of apprenticeship' and the Company was to devote £2,000 per annum towards the project in co-operation with other Companies and Gresham College.[59] The Clothworkers began to make common cause in this venture with the Drapers and then the Mercers.[60] In February 1877, nine Companies met in the Drapers' Hall and passed resolutions calling for the foundation of an Institute and in June, 1877, a General Committee and Executive was established by a meeting of Company representatives at the Mercers' Hall. The Executive Committee, again under Lord Selbourne, called for reports from six eminent figures. These were Sir William Armstrong, industrialist; George Bartley, philanthropist; Sir John Donnelly, educationalist; Captain Douglas Galton, scientist; Professor Thomas Huxley, scientist; and Henry Truman Wood of the Society of Arts.[61] In 1878 the Executive Committee issued its own report entitled *Technical Education*. This contained detailed plans for a Central Institution and local trade schools, with the former designed to promote research and to supply teachers and what were referred to as 'superior workmen'. The overall aim was to improve general knowledge of scientific principles rather than to institute formal craft training.[62]

The decision to establish a City and Guilds of London Institute for the Advancement of Technical Education was formally taken by a meeting at the Mercers' Hall on 11 December 1878.[63] From the beginning there were close links with the Society of Arts and in 1879–80 a transfer of technical education from the Society to the Institute was arranged with the help of the Drapers' and

Goldsmiths' Companies which had been approached previously by the Society.[64] The first examinations under the Institute were held on 22 May 1879, in 23 centres, with 16 subjects being offered and seven actually sat. This represented a transfer of Society of Arts examinations which had been organized since 1873.

The Institute, from headquarters at Gresham College, set out to offer examination facilities wherever there was an appropriate class with sufficient candidates. Local committees were established to conduct examinations and to supervise syllabuses. Teaching was carried out in schools, colleges and evening institutions under the Science and Arts Department's system of payment by results, as well as under local School Boards and other relevant bodies. Teachers were recognized initially under Science and Arts Department qualifications. In 1880 the Institute became registered as a company and appointed Phillip Magnus, later Sir Phillip, a Reformed Jewish Rabbi and scholar, as full-time Director and Secretary. This proved to be an inspired choice and Magnus became an active and influential figure in higher education over many years.[65]

In 1879 the Institute established evening classes in applied sciences in the Middle Class School in Cowper Street, Finsbury. This was the origin of Finsbury Technical College which was established in a new building in 1883. Day and evening classes were organized and Finsbury became a model for Technical Institutes nationally. Lambeth Art School, which had been established in 1854, had developed an extension for 'industrial arts' in Kennington Park Road. After being threatened with closure in 1878 this was taken over by the Institute and extended into two houses which were purchased at 122 and 124 Kennington Park Road, initially on a personal basis by Sir Sydney Waterlow.[66] This became the City and Guilds of London Art School.

In the early years there was a good deal of disagreement over the site for a Central Institution. The Corporation and some Companies favoured a City location near the City of London School even after a site in South Kensington had been offered by the Commissioners of the Great Exhibition of 1851. There had been problems regarding cost and availability in the City but the offer of a free location did not resolve the issue. The City had to be pressed and persuaded but this was achieved and the Central Institution opened in Exhibition Road, South Kensington in

1884.[67] Conflict between the City and South Kensington and between Magnus and the Executive Committee continued over many years. One result of these problems seems to have been that the Drapers' Company turned its main attention to the People's Palace.[68] Also, the Goldsmiths' Company decided to fund a new Technical Institute at New Cross which eventually became Goldsmiths' College. In 1893 the Central Institution became the Central Technical College and in 1911 it was renamed the City and Guilds of London College. In 1907 a Departmental Committee appointed by the Board of Trade proposed the establishment in South Kensington of a grouping of science and technology colleges. The Royal College of Science, the Royal School of Mines and the Central Technical College became Imperial College in 1907 and, in the following year, this became a School of the University of London.[69]

In 1889 the Leather Trades' School in Bethnal Green was taken over by City and Guilds Institution with financial support from the Leathersellers' and Cordwainers' Companies and the Boot and Shoe Manufacturers' Association. In 1913 this became the Cordwainers' Technical College with the Cordwainers' Company assuming sole responsibility.

In its early years the City and Guilds Institute achieved a great deal in spite of many serious difficulties. The support of a few major Companies and the energies and dedication of a few individuals was crucial. Support from the Corporation and the majority of Companies was not wholehearted and there were, in particular, financial difficulties.[70] These made it necessary to rely as far as possible on existing institutions and to turn to other support where this became available. There were also many organizational difficulties including the shortage of teachers, high examination failure rates in the early years and difficulties in striking a balance between academic and commercial considerations. What endured was the subject organization and validation side of activities while teaching and research went elsewhere. The Central Institution became part of London University and Finsbury Technical College was closed in 1926 after losing its original role to rival institutions and falling into financial difficulties.[71]

In the 1870s the City and Guilds venture had been an important pioneering development in technical and vocational education at a time when government was unwilling to act. By the early 1890s, however, public sector involvement began to crowd out and threaten City and Guilds activity in virtually all areas. Enhanced public activity in educational provision was the result of several developments. The Technical Instruction Act of 1889 made local rates available for technical education. Further funds came in the form of the 'whisky money' (see Chapter one). Also, in London, the City Parochial Charities Foundation emerged as a major provider for higher education and this is discussed below.

By the late 1890s the funding of technical education had passed largely to public and quasi-public bodies and both the Corporation and the Companies reduced their contributions to City and Guilds. The result was a financial crisis and the need to organize an appeal.[72] In December 1904, a meeting at the Saddlers' Hall passed a motion of regret which seems to have resulted in contributions being restored to former levels. Nevertheless, by the time of the First World War the future looked 'ominous' for City and Guilds.[73] After the Second World War a new role in the supervision of vocational education was created and the Institution gained a new lease of life in quite different circumstances.

THE CITY OF LONDON PAROCHIAL CHARITIES

The foundation of the City and Guilds Institution in 1878 did not bring to an end the criticism of and attacks on the Corporation and the Livery Companies. On the contrary, in the 1880s both were seriously threatened with abolition. There had been demands for a Royal Commission for many years and these were pressed by J.F.B. Firth, James Beal, William Gilbert, J.R. Phillips, W.H. James and many others in the Press and Parliament. Demands were made that the Companies be reformed or abolished and their funds re-appropriated for public use.[74] In 1880, when the Liberals were returned to power under Gladstone, Sir William Harcourt, Home Secretary, lost little time before setting up a Royal Commission to enquire into the Livery Companies.[75] In seeking to defend themselves the Companies found that the City and Guilds Institute was one of their few strongs suits. While the Royal Commission was sitting the City Corporation was also facing a threat of extinction under Harcourt's Bill of 1884 which sought to establish a municipal authority for the whole of London.[76] In the event, Harcourt's Bill failed, but in seeking to defend itself the City had resorted to dubious tactics and some deplorable, if not criminal methods, which were later laid bare by a Select Committee of Inquiry.[77] From this inquiry, 'A nauseous story emerged: reform meetings had been disrupted by paid bully boys; forged tickets to meetings of the Reform League had been printed and circulated in order to pack its meetings with opponents; and a bogus antireform body, the Metropolitan Rate-payer's Protection Association, had been created and generously subsidised . . .'.[78]

In seeking to defend the Companies before the Royal Commission Lord Selbourne argued that they had *private*, as distinct from *trust* property, and that most Guild funds fell into the former category.[79] The evidence taken revealed that there was indeed great wealth involved. Property worth £15 million and an annual income in excess of £750,000, and rising rapidly. Out of this income only about £200,000 was directly committed to charity and the remainder, nearly £600,000, was devoted to Company purposes. About £100,000 was spent on 'entertainments' and £170,000 on 'maintenance', including attendance fees for members (£40,000) and 'salaries' for officers (£60,000). Since many Companies had refused to supply information and others had been 'economical' with the evidence, it is clear that this was merely an approximation and probably an understatement of Company wealth and appropriation.

The majority report urged and justified state intervention to ensure that Company funds were largely devoted to public purposes on the grounds that the Guilds were both public and municipal bodies. There were dissenting reports from four members of the Commission including Firth who demanded that the Companies be dissolved.

A standing Commission was proposed to reappraise Company expediture and it was suggested that funds should be applied to useful causes regardless of the intentions of the original benefactors. Significantly, several educational bodies had made direct representations to the Commission for financial support from Company funds and there were deputations from five. These were University College, London, King's College, London, the London Society for the extension of University Teaching, the School Board for London and Magee College, Northern Ireland. The Royal Commission, in the event, was not followed by legislation, although this was widely anticipated. Gladstone's Government was much concerned with other issues, Irish Home Rule, in particular, and a private Bill introduced by Sir Charles Dilke failed. While agitation against the City continued it was able to survive until the Salisbury Government (1885–92) came into power. The City had, by the 1880s, come to regard the Conservative Party as its saviour. The Salisbury Government also resolved the London government issue through legislation which made the establishment of the London County Council possible, while leaving the City intact and autonomous. This provided a London-wide authority (excepting the Square Mile) with very limited powers and resources. From the City viewpoint, this was perhaps the ideal solution to a problem which had refused to go away since the 1830s. There was one area where the LCC was soon able to develop and assume remarkably wide powers and that was education. Again, this suited the City because it provided alternative resources to City funds.

The City of London Parochial Charities Act of 1883 was perhaps the most successful City reform during the nineteenth century. It followed a long history of investigation of City charities by the Charity Commissioners. These investigations had occurred, intermittently, since the early years of the century, but were in earnest from the 1860s when City charities became a matter for frequent public comment. By this time the population of the City was in sharp absolute decline and poor and destitute people were not evident in large numbers in the Square Mile. But they were elsewhere and it was increasingly argued that areas outside the City should benefit from City charitable bequests.

The parishes of the City had been established largely in the early medieval period (twelfth and thirteenth centuries) in small neighbourhoods around a network of churches. Few churches survived the Great Fire but the parishes remained as originally defined. By the nineteenth century parishes were, in most cases, ludicrously small and the bounderies archaic. One example, which became classic and much quoted, was the parish of St. Mildred, Bread Street (near St. Paul's). In the mid-1860s this had an income of £800 per annum, but only 5 per cent of this went to the poor with the rest going mainly to 'administrative expenses'. There were only two inhabited houses remaining in the parish which consisted mainly of offices and warehouses.[80] In these circumstances it is hardly surprising that parish funds became an issue.

In many cases also the original purposes of trusts had become outmoded. Funds to be devoted to 'the burning of heathens' were unlikely to be called upon and even worthy benefactions to 'the poor of the parish' had limited relevance in the depopulated City.[81]

In the 1860s many members of the clergy began to give their support to reform of parochial charities and the Rev. William Rogers of St. Botolf's, Bishopsgate became a leading figure in pressing for the use of parochial funds to support education. In 1865 Rogers established the Corporation for Middle Class Education and he was supported by the Bishop of London (Tait) who called in the House of Lords for City parochial funds to be devoted to middle-class education throughout the metropolis.[82] These views were supported by *The Times* and taken up by Firth and other critics of the City institutions. However, proposals for change were resisted by the City vestries, churchwardens and trusts which clashed repeatedly with reforming clergy. This resistance was eventually organized and led by Edward Freshfield, a City solicitor, who put the case for local control of City funds.[83]

In August, 1878, Disraeli established a Royal Commission and this reported in 1880, providing 'irrefutable evidence of maladministration stretching over decades'.[84] Legislation eventually followed in 1883 when James Bryce, MP for Tower Hamlets, successfully introduced the City of London Parochial Charities Act.[85] However, this was preceded by a struggle involving a campaign of resistance by elements in the City. Two Bills were introduced in 1882 and a Select Committe was appointed to consider both.[86]

The task of implementing the Act of 1883 was given to the Charity Commissioners and action was several years in gestation. The Charity Commissioners had operated on a permanent basis since 1853 and from time to time they had given attention to City Charities. Nineteenth century Britain had inherited a complex array of charitable trusts and endowments, many of which were archaic and badly administered. Even before the Charitable Trusts Act of 1853 the Commissioners had shown a preference for devoting the proceeds of charitable endowments to educational purposes rather than to the direct relief of poverty. Post-elementary and middle-class education, rather than education for the poor and destitute, was often the beneficiary of their activities and it has been suggested that 'the Charity Commission was increasingly regarded as a body which wanted to see virtually all charity funds put to educational ends'.[87]

However, in dealing with the City Charities the Commissioners had a complex problem on their hands and there were a number of competing claimants. The City vestries were often active and well organized in seeking to retain control and many had influential members. Also, it was increasingly clear that opportunities for dispensing charitable funds within the Square Mile were limited while there were pressing needs beyond. Indeed, the East End which became notorious for poverty and deprivation in the 1880s was on the edge of the City.[88] In all, a total of 112 parishes were surveyed and 107 of these came directly under the first part of the Scheme. The remaining five, larger parishes, came under a Scheme whereby their funds were devoted largely to local needs. It was accepted that a large part of the funds would be devoted to the Established Church and to religious purposes. Also, in the 1860s 'open spaces' agitation had led to the establishment of Victoria Park and the City had also purchased and taken control of Epping Forest during the period 1871–82.[89] Efforts to preserve and devote parkland areas to public access were popular as was the provision of public amenities such as baths, libraries, hospitals and other facilities. Legislation in 1886 empowered monies to be provided from the City Parochial Charity (CPC) Fund for the provision of 'open spaces' and the Commissioners began to be concerned that the funds were being 'hijacked' for causes which were more popular than education.[90] The Commissioners themselves also came under attack for being secretive, bureaucratic and elitist: in the words of Lord Shaftesbury, 'a body of men who are devoted to high-class education'.[91] In these circumstances, it was the movement for technical education which provided an answer to their problems.

The Royal Commission on Technical Instruction which had reported in 1884 had suggested that endowments might be devoted to secondary and technical education.[92] This coincided with concerns about 'national efficiency', public order and social cohesion which intensified during the 1880s.[93] From these complex circumstances a situation arose where a very large part of the CPC funds were dedicated to 'promote the education of the poorer inhabitants of the Metropolis' and this took the form of a long-term commitment to establish Polytechnics throughout the London metropolitan area.[94] The essential agent in this appears to have been Henry Cunynghame, soldier, barrister, artist, scientist and Civil Servant.[95] Cunynghame was one of three Commissioners appointed in 1884 to deal with London charities. In 1886 he was sent to France to study technical education for the artisan classes and he reported in January 1887.[96] He was then requested to identify and examine similar kinds of instruction available in London and, as a result, he visited the Regent Street Polytechnic.[97] Cunynghame's Report subsequently suggested that Regent Street could be taken as a model and recommended several similiar establishments to serve different areas of London.[98]

Regent Street Polytechnic had commenced in 1838 as a 'Gallery of Arts and Science' organized by Sir George Cayley at 5 Cavendish Square. It aimed at 'the advancement of practical science in connection with agriculture, art and trade'.[99] This became the Royal Polytechnic Institution in 1839 and was devoted to popular science and display.[100] In 1848 the Rev. William Mackenzie had comenced the 'Metropolitan Evening Classes for Young Men' and these were organized throughout London. The Polytechnic Institute became a venue for evening classes and there were 400 students enrolled per term in the 1860s.[101] Trade classes were also organized along with popular lectures in science and classes for specialist workers. In 1861 Mackenzie's evening classes became the City of London College and Quintin Hogg was one of many who worked with this initiative in organising evening classes.

Hogg was an educationalist and wealthy Christian philanthropist with City connections. His earliest ventures in education involved Ragged Schools for destitute boys but evening instruction at higher levels developed from this. In 1878 Hogg established premises in Long Acre, Covent Garden, and evening instruction was commenced there. This included Science and Art Department classes and instruction in Building. By 1880 Hogg was seeking larger premises for his Institute for Young Men and this led to the purchase of the Polytechnic Institute establishment which had been offered for sale in 1882. This was the origin of what became known as the Regent Street Polytechnic. Within 12 months of purchase there were nearly 100 classes with 5,000 enrolments.[102]

While Regent Street seems to have been the main model adopted by the Commissioners, attention was also given to the

'People's Palace' which was in the process of being established in East London in the 1880s.[103] This had developed out of the Bancroft Hospital and the Beaumont Institute. Francis Bancroft, a City Alderman, had left money in trust with the Draper's Company to fund almshouses, a school and the Bancroft Hospital which opened in 1737. Under a separate foundation the Beaumont Institute had been established in 1841 but closed in 1879. The catalyst for a new foundation appears to have come from a popular novel by Walter Besant, *All Sorts and Conditions of Men* (1882), which promoted the idea of a 'People's Palace' devoted to popular entertainment, leisure and enlightenment. The failure of the Beaumont Institute and the shift to another location of the Bancroft Hospital provided both funds and a potential site. In 1882 a meeting at the Mansion House sought to promote the idea of a new Institute devoted to popular culture, entertainment and education: 'It was intended that the institution should not only provide for the East-end the educational advantages of the City of London College and the evening classes at King's College, but would also provide a Library reading rooms and other facilities'.[104]

The first public appeal was launched in 1885 and in June 1886, the Prince of Wales laid the first stone. Use was made of the Bancroft Hospital site, which involved the Drapers, and the Beaumont Trustees were also primarily involved. Queen Victoria opened the Queen's Hall in 1887 and a range of facilities followed including a wide range of evening classes which commenced in 1889–90. As a result of financial difficulties the Drapers' Company became increasingly involved in a leading way and this gave rise to a growing emphasis on the educational side and technical education in particular.

During the later 1880s the aims of the Charity Commissioners with regard to CPC funds were gradually made known. According to *The Times* these were to found 'working men's and women's institutes' to meet 'intellectual and recreative needs' on the 'model of Regent Street Polytechnic'.[105] As a result of informal prompting by the Commissioners, committees were formed in various parts of London with the intention of organizing district colleges.[106] Voluntary efforts were steered and it was indicated that the Commissioners would match monies raised from the general public through voluntary donations.[107] These efforts acquired

Royal patronage and aristocratic support. Earl Cardogan offered a site in Chelsea and the Marquis of Northampton and Earl Compton made an offer in Clerkenwell, later supplemented by grants from the Skinners' and Sadlers' Companies. By 1891, when the Governing Body of the CPC Foundation first met, there were active schemes covering virtually all parts of the metropolis.

The Charity Commissioners also had to decide on the disposition of charitable funds within the City from the five larger City parishes which remained outside the main scheme. It was decided to found institutions with library, reading and meeting facilities.[108] As a result, institutes were established in Bishopsgate and Cripplegate. The Fleet Street Institute for printers was also subsidized by the Foundation. In the parish of St. Botolph, Aldgate, which was just outside the City boundary, serious friction had arisen between the Rev. R.H. Haddon and the local Vestry which had responsibilities, *inter alia*, for the Sir John Cass Trust.[109] Cass had been a City Alderman for the Portsoken ward and also a City MP. His bequest of 1718 had left funds for a school for poor children of the Parish and the endowment included land in Hackney and elsewhere.[110] By the 1880s the value and revenues from these were substantially in excess of the original requirements and strong criticisms were being made about the administration of the trust. The Charity Commissioners intervened and sided with Haddon. This eventually led to the creation, in 1898, of the Sir John Cass Institute in Jewry Street on the basis of trust funds.[111]

Under the Act of 1883 a Central Governing Body for the CPC Foundation was to be established. By the time this actually met in 1891 the Commissioners had made the main decisions and funds were committed far into the future to specific purposes. The basis intention was to found, fund and sustain the London polytechnics and institutes.[112] Both the Corporation and the Livery Companies were critical of and unhappy about these arrangements.[113] The City was allowed four representatives on the Central Governing Body of 21, but there was no Livery Company representation as such. In fact, the Charity commissioners were able to ensure that representation included all possible interests and technical education, in particular, was well represented. Joseph Savory, Lord Mayor of London, became Chairman and remained so for many years. City and Guilds were give direct representation and this included Philip Magnus. Hogg, Webb, Haddon and Freshfield also became members.

The CPC Foundation began its formal existance in 1891 with funds of £410,000 plus various properties. However, £340,000 of this was already committed to the polytechnics and to 'open spaces'.[114] Between 1891 and 1939 the Foundation spent £2.7 million on grants and over 75 per cent of this was devoted to the polytechnics and institutes.[115] This had been more or less mandated by the Charity Commissioners at the outset. In 1891 a sum of £5,350 per annum was mandated for the City Polytechnic, which was a nominal grouping of Birkbeck, City of London and Northampton Colleges, £3,500 to Regent Street, £2,500 to the People's Palace, £2,500 to Borough, £1,500 to Battersea, £1,000 to the South West Polytechnic (Chelsea), £1,500 to the Royal Victoria Hall (Old Vic), and £1,000 to Morley College. Smaller grants were allocated to the Working Men's College, the College for Men and Women, and to the City Institutes, Whitechapel Art Gallery and Chelsea Physic Garden.[116] Some of the above were hardly established in 1891 and there were also plans for Northern and North Western Polytechnics. The latter were slow in gestation but did eventually materialize. The Charity Commissioners had initially been disinclined to give support to Birkbeck and City of London Colleges on the grounds that their students were not, in general, from the 'poorer classes' and they had little in terms of recreational facilities. Neither college fitted the new stereotype of a 'Polytechnic Institute' in terms of size or character. The decision by the Goldsmiths' Company to establish and fund an Institute at New Cross (Goldsmiths' College) released funds previously dedicated and made the City Polytechnic scheme possible whereby Birkbeck, City of London and Northampton Colleges were nominally combined. The sums mentioned seem small in modern terms but should be multiplied by up to 200 to arrive at modern equivalents. An annual endowment of £1,500 was considered equivalent to a capital grant of £50,000 in the 1890s. In modern terms this might represent approximately £10,000,000.

Within a few years of launching its efforts for higher education in London the CPC Foundation found itself with an important public sector partner and rival in the form of the London County Council. Under the Technical Instruction Act of 1889 local authorities were empowered to levy a penny rate for technical education and, in 1890, the 'whisky money' also became available (see Chapter one). The Technical Education Board of the LCC was established in 1893 under the chairmanship of Sidney Webb.[117] Two representatives of the CPCF were appointed to the TEB which had a total membership of 35. In December, 1893, a Conference on the London Polytechnics was held at Temple Gardens by delegates from the LCC, the CPCF and City and Guilds. This resulted in the decision to establish the London Polytechnic Council which first met in 1894.[118] The Council was made up of members of the TEB who were also members of the CPCF Governing Body, or the Council of City and Guilds; the Chairman of the TEB and two members from each of the three constituent bodies. In 1896 members were co-opted to represent Goldsmiths' and the People's Palace. Sir Owen Roberts of the Clothworkers' and City and Guilds was elected Chairman with Webb as Deputy. Hogg and Magnus were also members and it should be clear that the system was under the supervision of a small group of men who moved between different institutions and committees. This arrangement lasted until 1904 when the LCC became the education authority for London and both the TEB and the London Polytechnic Council were superceded. Under the Education Act of 1902 and the Education Act (London) of 1903 the LCC took over public education throughout the metropolitan area and the influence of the City and City institutions declined rapidly. However, City funds continued to be called for and to be devoted to particular institutions and this gave rise to frequent disagreement between the CPCF and the LCC.

In its early years the LCC was dominated by 'Progressive' elements which were hostile towards the City and the arch-enemy Firth was, for a time, deputy Chairman. General legislation for London inevitably came up against the 'anomalous' constitutional status of the Square Mile and, of course, there were regular accusations that the City was not paying its way in terms of London-wide amenities and administration.[119] When the Rosebury Government in the early 1890s began to be influenced by demands for a 'united' London a Royal Commission was established to consider amalgamation.[120] When it became clear that the Royal Commission favoured 'absorption' of the City rather than some loose form of amalgamation the City Corporation withdrew from the Inquiry. Legislation, which would have effectively meant the end of the City of London, was drafted by Webb and others but the Salisbury Conservative Government came into office in 1895 and effectively prevented this. Also, by creating 28 London Boroughs the Salisbury Administration effectively completed the salvation of the City Corporation with the Local Government Act of 1899. In the early twentieth century the Progressive dominance of the LCC began to crumble and from 1907 there were Conservative majorities which lasted until the 1930s.[121] The closing years of the Victorian era saw the commencement of a revival in City institutions. New Liveries were created and the Corporation became more active and effectively organized.

As suggested earlier, the City's demands for higher education were a direct reflection of its social and economic structure. City society at the elite end had always been more flexiblble and open than at national and regional levels, reflecting the economic focus of activity. In the nineteenth century, as Kynaston has argued, 'For all its preponderance of family firms, for all its increasingly hermetic institutional characteristics, the City overall was still a remarkably "open society", capable of attracting talented outsiders and renewing itself'.[122] Notable additions to the City elite included a long line of foreigners, but Rothschilds, Kleinworts and Barings were far from being isolated exceptions, and the Dick Whittington legend of rags to riches still had some relevance. Thomas Holloway, who came from humble and obscure origins in Devon, developed an (eventually) successful trade in ointment and pills in the City of London during the early 1860s.[123] Prior to his decision to found a college for women, which became Royal Holloway College (1886), Holloway proposed to leave his estate to the Lord Mayor and Common Council for the foundation of a hospital.[124]

COMMERCIAL EDUCATION AND THE CITY

Even among the City elite in the mid nineteenth century a university education 'was a rarity'.[125] The Directors of the Bank of England, for example, were 'solid, socially unpretentious members of the London and Home Counties *haute bourgeoisie*'.[126] By the 1880s, successful bankers were marrying into the aristocracy and an integration of old land and new finance was taking place. Gradually, it could be said, the City became more gentlemanly than capitalist and the leaders of finance aspired to the public school and Oxbridge education which was becoming a *sine qua non* amongst the national elite. For these people the very idea of alternative educational establishments was both counterproductive and unthinkable.

At lower social levels there were different needs and considerations. These were, essentially, moral, social and economic. Entry to employment was invariably determined on the basis of social and personal, rather than educational criteria other than what was provided by good elementary and grammar schools. Training was largely *ad hoc*, in service, and job and firm specific with little importance being attached to formal qualifications. However, as the century progressed and the City burgeoned as an employment centre, there were growing concerns about the moral and cultural welfare of the army of clerks and demands and opportunities for training and the acquisition of knowledge and skills outside the firm grew. This was enhanced by the increasing sophistication and systematization of office work and commercial activity and the rise of professionalism.[127] Because of the demands of employment, instruction aimed at meeting these needs usually had to take place in the evenings after the normal working day had ended.

In 1816 an adult school for the poor was established in the form of the City of London Society for the Instruction of Adults. This was supported by the Lord Mayor and Aldermen with a grant of £127.[128] Subsequent educational ventures, while often aimed at the poor or manual workers, were usually taken over by clerical and commercial employees. This happened, for example, to Birkbeck, Regent Street and to the Metropolitan Evening Classes which became City of London College. By 1857 acording to Hudson, the Mechanics' Institute which became Birkbeck College and which was located in the City, had ceased to be an establishment for engineers and manual workers: 'The Institution has been for some years little more than an association of shopkeepers and their apprentices, law copyists and attorney's clerks'.[129] As a result of these demands a series and range of educational establishments were obliged, often as a means of survival, to make drastic changes in their aims and operations. Manual and scientific instruction often gave way to languages, book-keeping and, at a later stage, shorthand and typing. In other examples, where the educational intentions had been more erudite and traditional, the classics and

Hebrew also had to retreat in the face of a growing demand for commercial instruction.

Commercial education encountered serious supply side problems for two reasons. First, the perception of needs, in many cases, only occurred after the commencement of employment and learning could only occur on a part-time and usually evening basis. Traditional educational establishments tended to view these needs as being too varied and specialized, *ad hoc* and ephemeral to deserve attention in the normal curriculum (similar problems have arisen in more recent years with information technology). Also, commercial education was frowned upon by most educationalists. According to James Bryce, writing in 1899, commercial education, 'was understood, in England at least, to mean something 'cheap and nasty', an illiberal education, an education below the level of the conventional gentleman'.[130] As a result of this situation, commercial education, as such, was almost entirely absent from most schools and universities. For these reasons, and because of London's special needs, it was to have an important place in the new arrangements which London developed during the late nineteenth century.

During the last 20 years of the nineteenth century commercial education began to be given the kind of attention which had earlier been devoted to technical and scientific education. These concerns reflected apprehensions in relation to foreign competion and an awareness of the growing importance of employment in service industries and activities. The *Royal Commission on the Depression of Trade and Industry* (1886) had drawn attention to deficiencies in commercial education compared with overseas competitors. This was reinforced in 1887 when *The Times* published a review of over 100 British Consular reports which were strongly critical of overseas commercial representation, stressing, in particular, poor marketing as a result of lack of languages and knowledge of foreign methods and cultures.[131] Few British commercial travellers could quote the foreign customer in his language, weights and measures and currency and business was being lost as a result. At home a good deal of attention was given to the employment of 'foreign clerks', in particular Germans, who were said to be superior by virtue of better Continental provisions in commercial education.

In his *London Education* (1904) Webb pointed out that in

London offices involved in commercial, administrative and government employment there were over 200,000 employees: 'Commercial education in London means, therefore, the education of at least one-fifth of the whole population'.[132] The issue of commercial education was taken up by the LCC and by the London Chamber of Commerce, which was not, primarily, a City institution.

The London Chamber of Commerce was established in 1881 and was one of a number of similar bodies established throughout Britain in the late nineteenth century on the basis of European example.[133] The London Chamber became a leading advocate for, and organizer of, commercial education in London and throughout the country. The Society of Arts had conducted examinations in book-keeping, accounts and political economy since the 1850s and had added shorthand in 1876 and typewriting in 1891. The Oxford and Cambridge Schools Examination Board also held examinations in commercial subjedcts from 1887 and the College of Preceptors established a Mercantile Certificate in 1888. In 1886–7 University College Liverpool launched a two-year curriculum in business studies and this early attempt at management education was followed by King's College, London. Professional and trade bodies also began to establish specialist currricula and to require preparation for examinations. Examinations were established by the Institute of Bankers, the Institute of Actuaries, the Institute of Chartered Accountants and several other associations as well as the Civil Service, the LCC, the Post Office and Railway Companies. In co-operation with the LCC, City of London College and other bodies the London Chamber of Commerce attempted to establish a new national system of commercial education, at all levels, on the basis of existing institutions. In 1887 a Commercial Education Committee was established by the Chamber and a system of examinations in commercial subjects commenced in 1890. With help from the Mitchell Trustees, a City charity, the City of London College set out to develop a system of 'higher commercial education'.[134] In 1898 the London Polytechnic Council gave the College a grant to found a 'higher commercial education' course for day students. When the London School of Economics was established in 1895, on the basis of the Hutchinson bequest, Webb's appreciation of the importance of commercial education and employment was made clear from the outset.[135] The LSE had as its initial aim the teaching of vocational and applied subjects, in particular, to meet the needs of banking, foreign trade, shipping, railway administration, insurance and the Civil Service. It also set out to offer evening instruction to workers in full-time employment. At the outset these intentions were paramount and it is only in retrospect that the emphasis on higher economic and political theory has materialized as an important initial intention of the LSE. Two early steps pointed the School away from its original vocational aims. One was the appointment of Hewins as first Director and the other was the early integration into London University.

In 1897 the TEB established a Sub-Committee on Commercial Education and a series of Conferences to promote the teaching of commercial subjects was organized in the 1890s. In general these activities met with a limited and largely indifferent response and the City was certainly no exception to this. A TEB inquiry reported that views differed widely but that, in general, there was a 'disbelief in commercial education' on the part of empoyers.[136] Evidence supplied to the Inquiry revealed strong business scepticism and a feeling that little more than a sound elementary education combined with good discipline was required. Evidence from educational establishments giving attention to commercial subjects such as City of London College, Goldsmiths' and the LSE indicated that variable and inadequate demand was a serious problem with commercial courses: 'commercial classes are not, as a rule, self-supporting on a scale sufficient to remunerate the teachers'.[137]

The main contribution of the City of London to the development of higher education in London, in both strategic and financial terms, had come most importantly during the last quarter of the nineteenth century. By virtue of timing, City funds, initiatives and institutions had played an important and formative role in the early establishment of the system. However, this had been largely fortuitous, owing much to a small number of individuals and a few important institutions. The vulnerability of the City's position in relation to Victorian public opinion had played an important part in the process and some advantage of this had been taken by those concerned to promote education. Much of what was done was against City opposition and most particularly where it involved a re-deployment of resources. Meanwhile, the City's own concerns about higher education were not much in evidence and seldon articulated. That so much had been done in the name of the City was indeed remarkable.

CHAPTER SIX

The London County Council and higher education

Brenda Weeden

The first London County Council met in 1889 amidst considerable excitement and high expectations of reform. The Local Government Act of 1888 had conferred new powers on existing county councils, but in the case of London the administrative county did not exist and had to be newly defined. London was the national and imperial capital, the world's greatest commercial centre: 'right from the start [the Council] became a vortex of political interest, an arena in which political parties, allied to national political groupings, debated their aims and policies'.[1] Some two-thirds of the members of the first Council belonged to a loose alliance known as the 'Progressives' which was sympathetic to the aims of the London Municipal Reform League. They felt that the opportunity to take control of the London's affairs was long overdue.

The Council had been created to tackle the problems of urbanization. Initially its powers were limited in the face of the continued existence of the single-purpose and often overlapping authorities so disliked by the reformers. Sidney Webb called them 'congeries of local boards, the 5000 members of which, though nominally elected, are practically unknown, unchecked, unsupervised and unaudited'.[2] When the first triennial Council met, administrative reform, control of the utilities and increased powers in areas such as housing were on the agenda; education was not. Elementary education had been the business of the London School Board since Foster's Education Act of 1870. The School Board was directly elected and its work generally respected and admired. In fact the first Council was provided with the means and the money to support technical education, but rejected the opportunity, which was not realized until 1892. That opportunity had been created by the sustained campaigning of the influential supporters of technical education.

The movement for technical education had been gaining support since the work of Lyon Playfair and Henry Cole in the 1850s. The series of trade and industry exhibitions which began in London in 1851 and continued in Paris in 1855, London in 1862 and Paris again in 1867 and 1878, were cited as providing graphic evidence of Britain's industrial decline in the face of growing continental competition. Contemporary concern was exacerbated by perceptions of economic depression in the last quarter of the century. It was argued that technical training for the workforce and an increase in scientific research were needed to modernize and revitalize British industry.

The lobby played a major role in campaigning for and manning the Royal Commission on Technical Education which reported in 1884. Roy McLeod has commented that 'a self-confessed "lobby" acquired the status of a traditionally "neutral" Royal Commission'.[3] Supporters such as Arthur Acland and Henry Roscoe pressed for legislation to support the recommendations in Parliament. Both were founder members of the National Association for the Promotion of Technical Education, established in 1887 to spread the word by means of publications and the work of local committees. Success came in the form of the Technical Instruction Act (1889) which authorized the new counties and county boroughs to create committees to promote technical instruction and to raise a penny rate to support their activities. Supporters of the school boards argued vigorously during the debate that the established education authorities should be given the rating power; the case was made most strongly in relation to London. These protests were overridden by Lord Goschen, 'a convinced centralist who looked to Germany for his model'.[4] In the event, the supporters of the London School Board were right to see trouble ahead.

An additional financial incentive was created when 'whisky money', the revenue resulting from the Local Taxation (Customs and Excise Act) 1890, was allocated to the same local authorities to spend on technical education or relief from the rates. The suggestion was originally made and vigorously pursued by Acland. Although initially rejected, it was subsequently adopted by the

Government as providing a more generally acceptable use for the money than compensating publicans deprived of revenue.

The question of what, if any, proportion of the revenues from the beer and spirit duties should be applied to technical education, was first raised in the London County Council on 7 October 1890 when the Finance Committee presented its revised estimates for the half year ending 31 March 1891. It was decided to place the first allocation of £140,000 for the year 1890–91 to the credit of the general county account for relief of the rates, but a further £23,000 was anticipated for the same year and £163,000 for 1891–92. The Council accepted the recommendation of the Finance Committee that a Special Committee be appointed to decide how that money should be spent. The Committee was appointed on 21 October 1890; it was subsequently authorized to examine witnesses and take evidence. The Special Committee met eight times under the chairmanship of Dr. G.B. Longstaff, and its Report circulated. The debate began on 10 February 1891. It is evident from its minutes that the Council had begun to receive requests for help under the terms of the Technical Instruction Act- for example from Camden School of Art on 20 January 1891.[5] The National Association for the Promotion of Technical Education (NAPTE) was monitoring which councils had decided to devote funds to technical education and, through the work of its local committees, was attempting to advise and cooperate whenever it had an opportunity. It organized a conference in London in December 1890 for local authority representatives to consider how best to utilize the funds for technical instruction, but the LCC declined to participate.

The *Report of the Special Committee on Beer and Spirit Duties* was comparatively short. The Committee had not attempted to prove or even enquire into the general case for technical education, but accepted that it was necessary. The introduction states:

> that wise and patriotic statesmanship should endeavour to encourage or facilitate the technical education of our workmen so as to enable England to maintain that manufacturing supremacy which has been in the past her main source of wealth and power. London, as the greatest commercial, and probably the greatest manufacturing centre in the world, is perhaps more interested in this matter than any other city of the Empire.[6]

The Committee had taken evidence from 22 expert witnesses, all of whom had emphasized the poor and unco-ordinated nature of current provision for technical instruction in London. All had emphasized the needs of existing institutions for funds and the need of artisans for scholarships, though only two, Miss S. Hadland, a retired headmistress, and Sir Henry Roscoe, secretary of NAPTE, had recommended the establishment of the Council's own schools. The others had been against this. The Report commended the organizations which had already made progress in this field, though in the case of the City Companies 'it is earnestly hoped that having regard to the large funds at their disposal they will do a great deal more'.[7] Nevertheless, the Committee made it clear, that if the Council did not act,

> there is no prospect in the immediate future of technical education being developed in London in a sufficiently complete manner and to an adequate extent to prove whether it is capable of producing the results which its advocates claim for it.[8]

The Council, therefore, had to decide whether it would accept the responsibilty for technical education, and, if it did so, how to pay for it. The options were to levy a rate, to utilize the funds from the beer and spirit duties, or to do both. The Committee recommended that the responsibility be accepted, and that technical education be financed from beer and spirit duties only. Its proposed programme, should the first recommendations be accepted, was cautious and not worked out in much detail. It suggested that a Standing Committee be appointed to distribute funds, but that initially it should limit itself to capital grants, introducing maintenance grants dependent upon inspection at a later date.

The first recommendation was immediately countered by an amendment that all the beer and spirit revenues be place in the general account:

> in view of the schemes which the Council now has or may hereafter take in hand for the housing of the working classes, the acquisition of open spaces, and similar efforts for the improvement of the condition of the London poor.[9]

and this amendment, moved by John Benn, was carried by 50 votes to 45. The debate was not concluded until 10 March 1891.

During the intervening adjournments, a further blocking amendment had been added, and the ferocity of its tone appears to indicate that this is where the heart of the opposition lay, in the municipal reformers' emnity towards the City. It amounted to a refusal to devote any Council resources to technical education while the existing funds continue to be diverted by unrepresentative bodies, and went on to call for the disestablishment and disendowment of the City Companies. (*See* Chapter five.) The Special Committee's first recommendation was finally defeated by 40 votes to 46 and the Chairman acknowledged defeat and withdrew the remaining recommendations.

The second Council, returned in 1892, contained a larger Progressive majority. Among them were six members of the Fabian Society, including Sidney Webb. *The London Programme*, written by Webb and first published in 1891 for the election campaign, combined a highly developed case for municipalization with what the author described as his 'life-long acquaintance with London and a very real and deep affection for his native city'.[10] The 1888 Act had made London a county. 'It remains now to make the capital of the Empire also a municipality.'[11] Beatrice Webb wrote in her diary:

> The Progressive leaders of 1892 would have been mightily surprised if they had been told that the LCC of the twentieth century would be far less concerned with material things such as gas and water, docks and markets, tramways and tunnels, than with the education and recreation, medical treatment and adequate maintenance of the five millions of inhabitants within the metropolitan area. And yet the main task accomplished by the Other One during his eighteen years' service on the LCC was its development as the greatest educational authority in the world.[12]

There is little in *The London Programme* to show that Webb had begun (as Beatrice claimed) to develop his thinking on education by 1891. There are passing references to the need for increased educational opportunity as part of a programme of social reform, and Webb apparently accepted that the London School Board was the appropriate authority to implement this. In an attempt to illustrate the true costs of municipalization, Webb devotes one chapter to an imaginary speech supposedly by London's Finance Minister, presenting a model budget. A sum of

£1,350,000 was to be allocated to education, and it was to be given to the London School Board.

> The School Board propose, with the consent of the Education Department, gradually to extend the scope of education given in the schools under their care, taking in manual training and industrial education, so as to provide (with the help of an organized system of continuation classes) for the complete training of every citizen.[13]

NAPTE had campaigned to keep the issue of technical education live during the election, in the hope of reversing the decision of the first Council, producing and circulating a leaflet called *The London County Council and Technical Education: An Appeal to the Electors.*

The presentation of the Annual Estimates by the Finance Committee to the Council on 12 April 1892 provided an opportunity to return to the question of funding for technical education. The amendment was moved by Quintin Hogg, well known as a philanthropist and as the founder of what had become known as the Regent Street Polytechnic. He proposed that £30,000 of the income from the beer and spirit duties to be received during the coming year be placed into a suspense account, and that a Special Committee be appointed to consider what action the Council should take under the Technical Education Acts 'with the power to draw up a scheme or schemes for the consideration of the Council'.[14] The question of assuming responsibility for technical education, which had aroused such opposition only a year before, had been settled without challenge, and in fact the focus of attention had been shifted to the means by which that responsibility should be implemented. On 3 May a motion appointing the 20 members of the Special Committee was 'moved by Mr. Sidney Webb in the absence of Mr. Hogg'.[15] Beatrice Webb wrote that this was his first motion on the Council:

> S.W. has often explained how, in his anxiety to put on the ablest members from the various sections, he found he had not provided for a chairman, as practically all his nominees proved to be already chairmen of other committees. He was, therefore, virtually driven to preside himself.[16]

Webb's reputation as a skillful manipulator and manager of affairs has become legendary. He directed the Committee and later the Technical Education Board with speed and confidence.

On 9 May Webb asked the Council for the power to spend £500 on enquiries into current provision for technical education. Since, he claimed, no person from the Council staff could be spared to assist the Committee, it was necessary to look for advice from elsewhere. It was characteristic of Webb to seek out an expert, and his subsequent temporary appointment of Hubert Llewellyn Smith as inquirer and secretary to the Committee was to prove a master-stroke. Llewellyn Smith had studied mathematics at Oxford and had previous experience of social investigation as an assistant to Charles Booth in his survey of *London Life and Labour*. He had been secretary of NAPTE since 1888, and while in that post had produced, together with Arthur Acland, a report entitled *Technical Education in England and Wales* which was published in 1889. That report included a survey of current provision under three categories: organizations, grades (elementary, secondary and higher instruction) and localities (in which the authors defined the educational needs of particular districts and how far they were met by existing provision). The aim was to show the general reader how much needed to be done, by filling gaps, reorganizing and improving existing agencies and above all in tackling

> the *waste of force* consequent on the overlapping and want of coordination of educational institutions and authorities. . . . Surely something could be done to coordinate the working of all these agencies without destroying the local flexibility of method, which is of as much importance as the harmony of organisation.[17]

The invitation from Sidney Webb to produce a survey and scheme of action for the LCC provided NAPTE with an opportunity to move from propaganda to policy within London, which represented the largest gap in the growing national coverage of technical instruction.

The report which had been scheduled for September 1892 in fact was not completed until just before Christmas. Webb told the Council this was due to the thoroughness of the investigations and the difficulty of working during the summer while classes were closed. Webb was so confident of the authoritative nature of the final report that he suggested that as well as being printed for members of the Council 1,000 copies should be printed for public sale. His confidence was justified when a reprint was ordered a few months later.

Llewellyn Smith's *Report to the Special Committee on Technical Education* was in every way a more substantial document than that produced by the earlier Committee. It was more than twice as long (almost 200 pages) and the text was substantiated by a wealth of newly collected statistical information presented in the form of tables and of maps. The *Report* contained far more than a detailed statistical picture of current provision. It encompassed a comprehensive range of topics, examining how the Council might best act, within the framework of its powers, to improve that provision and suggesting a programme of costed recommendations. The subsequent work of the Technical Education Board has been widely and justifiably admired, but it is difficult to identify an area of policy which did not originate from the *Report*.

The powers which the existing framework of legislation gave to the Council were identified as wide-ranging. Italics have been added to the following passage to emphasize this point:

> The expression 'technical instruction' shall mean instruction in the principles of science and art applicable to industries, and in the application of special branches of science and art to specific industries or employments [this included the educational-classroom and industrial workshop side]. *The County Council is therefore legally entitled to treat technical education as including the whole field of general education minus literature and ancient languages.*[18]

The Council was not allowed to fund the elementary schools which were maintained by the London School Board, but otherwise there was no limit on the age, subject, standard of teaching or social class of the students. The Council could use those funds to supply technical education (by founding its own schools, establishing classes and engaging teachers) or to aid the supply (by providing grants under certain conditions). It was also empowered to increase demand by awarding scholarships and exhibitions to individual students to enable them to attend schools or classes. Except in the case of institutions maintained by the School Board, the Council had to appoint a representative onto the governing body of all institutions which received grants. That representative did not have to be a member of the Council.

The *Report* contains a list of all the institutions currently supplying technical education, classified according to their governing bodies, identifying which were and which were not eligible for Council aid. Llewellyn Smith singled out one particular category in a characteristic suggestion as to how the Council might use its powers to improve quality. He was concerned about a practice called 'farming', where a teacher 'pays all expenses and takes all receipts, thus conducting a private profit school under the wing of a responsible committee'.[19]

> Cases in which the Science and Art Committee is the real governing body of a school, but has an arrangement to farm out the classes to the teacher or teachers, are on a different footing. Such classes may be legally aided by the County Council, but I strongly recommend the Council to insist on the reconstitution of these schools as a condition of aid.[20]

The problem of finding teachers with appropriate skills to combine classroom and workshop teaching is a recurrent theme in the *Report,* and Llewellyn Smith recommended the Council to examine both the quality of teacher training and the level of pay. He did not anticipate serious conflict of interest with other funding authorities, but acknowledged that this was most likely in the case of the School Board in relation to the higher standard work being done by some ex-elementary students.

> Nine tenths however of the work of the County Council will be entirely outside the sphere or influence of the School Board, and the remaining tenth can easily be dealt with by a joint committee, or may be left entirely to the School Board, to which the County Council has a special power to make a grant without representation.[21]

In view of the wide ranging powers which he was recommending for the Council, this failure to anticipate the future conflict with the School Board looks somewhat disingenuous.

Following the same methodology suggested in the earlier NAPTE *Report,* Llewellyn Smith included a chapter which mapped the local distribution of London industries by workers' residence, in order to illustrate where provision of instruction in particular trades should be established or increased. Classes were to be local to make attendance easier, but linked if possible to a centre to ensure quality. For example, there was a need for classes in building and engineering south of the Thames, and he suggested that classes should be established in whatever building was appropriate – for example within the Board Schools – and that the new polytechnic institute at Borough Road should co-ordinate local activity. This was his practical solution to the problem of combining local flexibility with central coordination, and provides one example of the importance of the emerging polytechnics to the policy of the LCC. Once the work of the Technical Education Board was underway, it was the need to fill particular gaps in neglected localities or to meet the need of specialist trades that caused it to move from its preferred policy of aiding supply to direct provision in the form of founding its own institutions.

The *Report* examined the teaching of art, science and technology, manual instruction, commercial subjects and household economy. The chapters follow the same structure, beginning with a consideration of general principles followed by an examination of current provision and a set of costed recommendations. To take the section on art as an example of both the method and the tone, Llewellyn Smith began by dismissing any facile distinction between 'pure' and 'applied' art in the context of technical instruction. 'The working out of design in its appropriate material must spring out of, and not replace, the ordinary teaching of the art school.'[22] He examined the existing schools of art and listed the elements which must be part of the course before the institution could be recognized as a 'Technical Art School' by the County Council. The art classes held by the School Board (both day and evening) were all examined, and an appropriate level of support suggested for each case. The training of art teachers was (predictably) found to be unsatisfactory. Llewellyn Smith suggested that the Council appoint a 'Normal Art Master' who should be allowed to inform himself of developments in the teaching of art by travelling in the provinces and abroad in order to improve the quality of training. 'It is therefore absolutely essential that he should not be clogged with too much detailed routine work.'[23] The technical art schools would act as centres and co-ordinate local activity in the short term, but the Council may in the long term decide to establish its own great municipal art school. The whole programme, including support for schools and classes, training and scholarships, was reckoned to cost in the region of £2,000 for the first year.

Llewellyn Smith saw the support for demand, in the form of scholarships and other awards to students, as possibly an even more important role for the Council than the support for supply of technical education. He proposed that a large number of 'minor scholarships' should be provided for boys and girls leaving the elementary schools (usually at 12 years of age) to allow them to have a year or two of technical education before starting work. He had observed that many of them spent a year or two doing odd jobs after leaving school and before entering the workplace. The instruction should be at a higher grade elementary school, preferably provided without charge. He thought there was a need for a smaller number of awards to enable children to stay at school until 16 or 17, but recommended that the amount be generous and include a maintenance allowance. Unless parents could be compensated for loss of earnings the students would not be allowed to complete a sufficient amount of training. The *Report* suggests ways of co-ordinating the organization of awards across London but makes no recommendation about numbers; the Council would arrive at an appropriate number in the light of experience. Finally, Llewellyn Smith forsaw that a future need might arise for providing scholarships for a few to go from secondary school to university, especially if the hoped-for teaching university was to be established in London.

The supporters of technical education were keenly aware that the development of higher technical education in London was bound up with the vexed question of a teaching university. 'If the low level of the present teaching of science in our intermediate teaching is to be raised, teachers must be trained in connection with higher institutions, where they can see research going on, and engage in it themselves.'[24] This was an area where the continental, particularly the German, example, was much admired. Llewellyn Smith recommended the Council to support whichever model emerged in the highest interests of education, and that £10,000 a year be given to provide for the equipment and maintenance of laboratories, the endowment of professorships and lectureships in chemistry, physics, engineering, commercial law and practice and architecture and for the provision of a certain number of free places for county scholars.

Having provided the Council with a complete programme of action for supporting and developing technical education, Llewellyn Smith allowed himself a 'few observations' on the machinery necessary to ensure the success of that programme. He suggested that the Committee which would be appointed to oversee the work include outside members nominated by bodies such as the School Board and the London Trades Council, to ensure access to as much advice as possible and to avoid competition. Small advisory trade committees could undertake the inspection of purely technological classes, and part-time expert inspectors could deal with the higher level work. The cost of central administration he reckoned would add another £5,000 to his estimated total of £80,000 for the first year's work, and the *Report* ends on that practical note. A passage from an earlier chapter, however, serves to illustrate the comprehensive nature of the role of the London County Council in relation to technical education which the author and the Committee were recommending:

> Private bodies and isolated institutions may, as far as their funds go, do much to supply schools and classes, but the functions of providing facilities of access to the benefits of those classes, whether by spreading far and wide information of their existence, by interesting the great organisations of workmen and employers in them, by linking them together so as to form a connected series, and inducing them to work harmoniously without overlapping, or by selecting scholars specially fitted to take advantage of them, and assisting them pecuniarily while they pursue their studies; all this is essentially the view of a public authority acting over a wide area, and able to take a comprehensive view of the needs of the whole of London, not possible to the representatives of specialised local institutions or sectional interests.[25]

The *Report* was discussed in Council on 7 and 14 February 1893. Seven resolutions were put, covering the acceptance of the *Report* and the administrative and financial arrangements for establishing the Technical Education Board. There was no serious opposition, though John Benn did manage to add an amendment proposing that the City Livery Companies be invited to add a 'fair proportion of their corporate income' to the revenue allocated by the Council. They were subsequently approached, but with little success. The Council allocated £57,000, about a third of the revenue available from beer and spirit duties, to the Board for its first year's work. Together with the £29,000 remaining from the previous year, this met the £85,000 estimated by Llewellyn Smith, and in fact the Board through its 11 years of life operated without becoming a charge on the rates, though it came to take up an increasing proportion of beer and spirit revenues. The Council heartily endorsed the policies and programme outlined in the *Report*. The italics in the following resolution indicate a phrase added during the debate, which served to reinforce rather than detract from the Committee's proposals:

> the Council considers that every district of London ought to be adequately provided with technical education of every grade, rising from the school to the workshop and university, and appropriate to the chief occupations of the inhabitants; that existing institutions of each grade should be systematically coordinated to avoid overlapping, and to provide for continuous education; and that early provision should be made in whatever manner may be found expedient for supplying the gaps at present existing; *that the most pressing want is further inducements and facilities for the poorest parents to keep their children at some secondary or continuation school after leaving the elementary school; that the Council therefore instructs the Technical Education Board to provide as its first duty considerable further facilities for practical and technical education in the poorer and manufacturing districts of London, provided that no scholarship be of less value than £10 per annum;* and that the Council, recognising the value of the most comprehensive report prepared by Mr. Llewellyn Smith, refers it for the general guidance of the Technical Education Board.[26]

Webb's first action was to appoint the members of the Technical Education Board (TEB) along the lines suggested in the *Report*. Twenty members were elected from the Council (Quintin Hogg securing the most votes) and the following organisations were invited to nominate members: three each from the London School Board, the City and Guilds of London Institute and the London Trades Council, two from the Charities Parochial Foundation and one each from the Head Masters Association and the National

Union of Teachers. In addition there were two co-opted members 'one at least of whom should be a woman', and two of the members were to be substantial employers of skilled labour. The total membership was 35, and the formula for creating the Board created an influential precedent: 'It is significant that the device of a mixed delegated committee was later written into the Education Act of 1902 as the pattern for the proposed Education Committees of the new L.E.A.s.'.[27]The Board reported to the Council quarterly but enjoyed considerable independence.

Hubert Llewellyn Smith resigned as Secretary to the Committee in February 1893, at the same time resigning from NAPTE. He was appointed as commissioner for labour at the Board of Trade, beginning a civil service career which culminated in the post of Chief Economic Adviser. He was still under 30 when he wrote his *Report*, so maybe would not have been considered a suitable candidate for the post of Secretary to the TEB. The successful candidate, appointed in June 1893, was William Garnett, Principal of the Durham College of Science in Newcastle, where his success in expanding the fortunes of that College had earned him the nickname 'William the builder'. The staff was to be a small one for the scale of the work in hand. Miss Ella Pybus was appointed as 'lady organizer' of the domestic economy classes. As well as being an experienced teacher of cookery, her career had included working with Miss Beatrice Potter (later Beatrice Webb) as manager of the first block of buildings erected by the East End Dwellings Company in Cartwright Street, Aldgate. Bernard Allen was appointed as assistant secretary in 1897, having previously been an inspector for secondary schools, and it is his *Memoir* of Garnett which provides many anecdotes about this powerful and unconventional personality. A staff of inspectors was gradually appointed: C.W. Kimmins, chief inspector for science, G.J. Frampton, special art examiner, W.R. Lethaby, art adviser, and G.W. Irons, assistant for schools. Initially there was a clerical staff of two, which was gradually expanded to six, as an infrastructure of sub-committees was established to support the work of the TEB. The first offices were at 13 Spring Gardens, adjacent to County Hall, but the need for more space prompted a move to St. Martin's Lane in 1897.

Work on the scholarship scheme started straight away. It took two years to be fully organized and for the famous phrase 'scholarship ladder' to appear in the *Annual Report*. The scheme provided 600 junior scholarships for pupils from public elementary schools, usually aged 13, allowing them a further two more years of approved technical education, either in a higher grade board school or a secondary school. The scholars were given maintenance allowances of £8 for the first year and £12 for the second. The next stage was the intermediate. There were 50 awards to provide further secondary technical education and to allow pupils to remain at school until 16 or 17. The awards were worth £20 a year to the under-15s and £25 to older pupils. Finally there were five county awards available to provide able students with places at university. The awards were allocated by a system of competitive examinations. The TEB took the opportunity to bring together all existing schemes for the award of scholarships for children leaving London elementary schools and combine them into a single examination, administered with the assistance of the Head Masters' Association, 'so as to prevent the unnecessary duplication of examinations, to secure a certain uniformity of standard, and to advertise those scholarships which are little known'.[28]

In due time the TEB was able to report the success of its scheme, as increasing numbers of children came forward to take the scholarship examinations, and some of the more able did progress up the ladder. In its final report, the TEB claimed that of the current 28 senior scholars, 21 had held intermediate scholarships and 14 of those had held junior county awards. A handful of men and fewer women studied at universities at home and abroad. The scheme was administered with some flexibility, and special awards were made in particular cases. The scholarship scheme did not just aim to allow children to stay longer in school, but also to provide opportunities for those in work to attend evening classes in order to increase their skills and improve their prospects. A range of scholarships and exhibitions in domestic economy, art, science and technology was also established. About 2,000 people held awards at any one time, and the cost accounted for just under a third of theTEB's expenditure.

The TEB also began to support existing institutions by awarding grants. This programme was in part driven by the need to find places for the TEB's scholars of a standard appropriate to their needs. It was by means of the conditions which it attached to its grants, and the combination of inspection and advice that it offered to recipients, that the TEB at the end of its life was able to claim a considerable success in improving facilities and raising standards across the range of secondary schools, technical insti- tutes and polytechnics with which its work brought it into contact.

Many of the junior county scholars entered secondary schools. London's endowed secondary schools were of such diverse types and qualitites that the systematizing Llewellyn Smith had not been able to draw up any rules for their treatment, but suggested that each would have to be considered on its merits. About half of London's 90 endowed secondary schools applied for and received help from the Board. The majority of these schools were in a fairly depressed state ('languishing' is Beatrice Webb's word for them) and the new intake of clever scholarship children, plus the additional resources from the TEB, brought about a considerable revival. Grants were made for maintenance, which could include salaries for full-time science teachers, and for equipment, to bring laboratories and workshops up to the appropriate standard. The curriculum had to include those subjects which most interested the TEB, such as drawing, science teaching, manual instruction in subjects such as woodwork for the boys, and household economy, including dressmaking and cooking for the girls. The TEB gath- ered information from its representatives on the governing body, the annual reports submitted by those governing bodies and from the annual inspections. The working relationship with the second- ary schools was evidently a close one, advantageous to both sides.

The TEB was intitially very critical of the facilities available for evening classes, provided by the Science and Art Department classes, the technical institutes and the polytechnics, and embarked upon a liberal grant programme conditional on carrying out its suggested improvements to raise standards. These conditions stated that only students who were qualified by their previous training, or, in the case of trade classes, were already members of the respective trades, be enrolled in classes. Equipment in labora- tories and workshops should be of the required standard, even if that meant using the facilities of a neighbouring institution. Practical classes were to be limited to 20 students under one teacher, workshop classes to 15. To avoid the practice of farming out classes, it was a condition of aid that the committee of management ensured that its teachers were paid an adequate fixed stipend. Teachers of technical subjects were required to have a practical acquaintance with the appropriate industry. The following are the last in a numbered list of points which show how carefully the TEB framed its conditions in the attempt to ensure an improvement in the quality of teaching:

> 6. In several branches of art the individual teaching is to be associated with brief lectures, illustrated on the blackboard or otherwise, and the teaching of design in its application to some branch of industry is essential to securing the highest grade of grants offered by the Board.
> 7. Workshop instruction is always to be associated with class teaching in drawing and in the *principles* of the subjects dealt with in the workshops.
> 8. The classes are to be open at all times to the inspection of the officers duly appointed by the Board.[29]

Subject to these conditions being fulfilled, and satisfactory reports being received from the inspectors, the Board promised attendance, equipment and material grants, plus substantial additional aid for the equipment of lecture rooms, laboratories, art studios and workshops.

It soon became evident that the Board was much happier with provision within the polytechnics than with the smaller local classes and institutes:

> there are too many classes in which the work is not of the standard required by the Board and rather point to the desirability of the establishment of evening schools of technology and science which should affiliate to themselves and reorganise the existing inefficient classes while they should themselves be intimately associated with the nearest polytechnic as the local education centre.[30]

The polytechnics became increasingly important to the work of the Board, which made correspondingly substantial grants to them, amounting to £600,000 during its lifetime. The Board delegated much of the work of inspection, co-ordination and gathering statistics to the London Polytechnic Council, formed following a conference held between the Board, the governing body of the London Parochial Charities and the City and Guilds Institute and representatives from the polytechnics. These diverse institutions provided art teaching, an increasing range and number of technical and trade classes, commercial classes and classes in domestic economy. Several of them had day-time secondary schools, which were also aided by the Board. Polytechnics were characterized not just by the range of subjects taught but also by the different levels of training and education represented in them, and the Board came increasingly to recognize that the highest level deserved the recognition of university status.

The Board had taken every opportunity to influence the ongoing debate about reconstituting the University of London as a teaching university, instead of being simply an examining body. Webb himself had been an active campaigner throughout, anxious that his newly created London School of Economics (founded in 1895 as a result of a bequest to the Fabian Society) should be included within the University, and that its facilities for higher technical education should be more widely available throughout London. The Bill which finally settled the question was piloted through the Commons by R.B. Haldane in 1897, and Beatrice has left an account of Sidney's work behind the scenes. In her diary she wrote 'He thinks he has got all he wants as regards the Technical Education Board and the London School of Economics.'[31] The Act was passed in 1898 and the new statutes came into force in 1900. The TEB had been making capital and maintenance grants to some individual schools of the University in return for access to facilities since 1894. After 1900 the London County Council was given two seats on the newly created Senate, one of which was occupied by Webb, in recognition of the considerable grants it made to the University. In 1902 these amounted to one quarter of its income. The new Statutes included a provision for 'recognized teachers' in other institutions who could involve themselves in the business of boards of studies and faculties, and prepare students who had passed matriculation for internal degrees. This arrangement was a source of great pride to Webb, who wrote that in November 1903 50 polytechnic teachers had been recognized and in six polytechnics '500 duly matriculated undergraduates are to be found working steadily through the various degree courses under the University teachers in these popular institutions'.[32]

Although its stated and preferred policy had always been to work through and support existing institutions, the TEB did sometimes found new ones, to meet a particular case of lack of provision or to take over an institution in difficulties. The first of these was the Central School of Arts and Crafts, established in Regent Street opposite the Polytechnic in 1896. The object of this School was to encourage the industrial application of decorative design. It was intended for advanced students, already working in a trade, many of whom were awarded TEB scholarships. It did not conflict in any way with the Polytechnic's own flourishing School of Art. The School of Arts and Crafts in Camberwell was founded in 1898, and in the same year the Board took over Bolt Court Technical School to found a school of photo engraving for the lithographic industry, and established a school of carriage building within the Regent Street Polytechnic. Similar specialist institutes ('monotechnics') were established for typography and printing, leather dying and tanning, and the furniture trades. Webb's membership of the Board and of the Senate placed him in an ideal position to work for the establishment of a new teacher training college. The London Day Training College was founded with the support of the Board in 1902. It became a school of the University in 1910, and in 1932 its status was changed to a University institute, reflected in the new name of the Institute of Education.

As the scope of the Board's work increased, a series of subcommittees was established to undertake more detailed work in particular areas and widen the Board's range of contacts. At different times particular subjects would be studied in depth – such as trade classes or commercial education – reports commissioned and special provisions made. Conferences were a favourite mechanism for consultation with employers and employed. During its first year the Board arranged four, inviting delegates from the trade unions and representatives of employers from the following groups of trades: building and furniture, engineering and allied trades, paper, printing, lithography and other processes for illustration and chemical industries and miscellaneous handicrafts. The Board also supported the work of the London Society for the Extension of University Teaching, sponsoring a series of Pioneer Lectures 'intended mainly to interest persons of adult age in experimental science, and create among them a demand for more systematic teaching'.[33] From October 1895 it began to publish details of all its activities in the monthly *London Technical Education Gazette*, which came to have a circulation about 4,500.

The later years of the TEB were coloured by its relationship with the London School Board. The work of the two overlapped in the provision of evening classes and of higher grade schools. Short-term solutions for parallel working and cooperation were achieved in practice but in the context of the growing political debate about the future administration of education, conflict was inevitable. Supporters of each body felt that its record of achievement justified its claims to be given wider powers. Political victory went to the LCC, based to a large extent on the success of the Technical Education Board and the vigorous campaigning of Garnett and Webb, but many of the new ideas and schemes being pioneered by the School Board were adopted and developed by the new authority.

The 1870 Act which defined the School Board's powers was sufficiently vague to enable it to widen the scope of its activities beyond the provision of day-time elementary classes. Early attempts to establish evening classes, partly to provide elementary education for those who still needed it, and partly also to provide more advanced work, foundered. Evening schools were opened again from 1882 onwards, initially teaching elementary work under the same conditions as the day schools. In 1885 the Recreative Evening Schools Association was formed, and its members encouraged and supported the introduction of subjects such as physical training, music and singing alongside the vocational subjects which earned Science and Art Department grants. Under this pressure the rules of the Education Department Code were relaxed, enabling the School Board to develop its liberal policy towards evening classes. The 'evening continuation schools', as they became known, began to provide for the social and recreational, as well as the vocational needs of school leavers, and their popularity rose rapidly during the 1890s. By 1902 it has been suggested that well over 60 per cent of school leavers were joining evening classes.[34]

The School Board had also been expanding its day-time work beyond the basic elementary standards into what was in effect secondary education. The advanced teaching was concentrated in particular schools, known as higher grade or central schools. Those which met the Technical Education Board's standards of providing suitable facilities and separate teaching were eligible for grants.

Some junior county scholars took up places in higher grade schools, and pupils from them did well in the intermediate scholarship examinations. The head teachers of the endowed secondary schools began to see the School Board schools as competitors at a time when the issue of co-ordinating the management of secondary schools was high on the political agenda.

A Bill was drafted in 1896 which proposed that the responsibility for secondary education be placed upon the counties and county boroughs. It failed in committee, partly because of the opposition from the school boards and partly because of the deep-rooted objections of the non-conformists to supporting voluntary schools from the rates. In the following year, however, the same issue was raised in a different form. The Science and Art *Directory* introduced Clause VII, which in effect was an invitation to local authorities to take over the responsibility for science and art instruction. Of course the School Board felt that its claim to be recognized as the appropriate authority was superior to that of the TEB. The situation was made more difficult because the School Board had members on the TEB and many supporters among the Progressives in the Council.

The Council's decision to apply for recognition provoked a request from the School Board for a formal hearing at the Science and Art Department, which took place on 1st February 1899. Before that hearing Robert Morant, whom Beatrice Webb described as the principal person in the Education Department, had been in touch with Garnett and discussed how the TEB might best prepare its case, putting forward his own opinion that the School Board's activity in relation to higher grade schools and evening continuation schools was illegal. Garnett next set out to test the School Board position further by persuading representatives of Camden School of Art to make a complaint to the District Auditor concerning the misappropriation of rates. The case was heard by T. Barclay Cockerton, and the label of the 'Cockerton judgement' has become attached to this peculiar incident. Cockerton found against the School Board, and his judgement was upheld in the High Court and the Court of Appeal. An enabling Act had to be passed quickly to enable the Board to continue its work in the short term. All the political cards were stacked against the School Board. Bernard Allen quotes a later comment of Garnett:

The ball which had thus been set rolling by the Technical Education Board in the autumn of 1898 did not stop until the Education Acts of 1902 and 1903 had revolutionised the administration of education throughout the country.[35]

Sidney Webb's influence in shaping and campaigning for the acceptance of those Acts was crucial. He explained his aims in a letter to Graham Wallas:

What I want is (a) the best possible primary schools available to all. (b) the largest possible scholarship system. (c) the best possible evening instruction. (d) the most efficient secondary schools and University colleges. (e) the most thorough provision for post-graduate study and research.[36]

Webb increasingly felt that the most urgent need was to raise standards in all primary schools to a uniform level, and that the most efficient way to do that would be by bringing them all under a single local authority, giving them financial support in return for supervision of individual schools, and providing a means of overall policy control. The county and borough councils were the appropriate authorities to undertake this work. The administrative experience gained on the Technical Education Board had clearly helped to form that view. The pragmatic Webb was prepared to compromise to reach this goal, for example in allowing the heads of voluntary denominational schools a degree of freedom in appointing their staff and in their teaching of religion. Robert Morant was in agreement with his views, and together they worked out their plans for the Bill, but there was a great deal of opposition to be overcome, especially in the case of London. Conservatives were concerned about increasing the powers of the LCC, but in fact many of the Progressives objected to the Bill, combining a reluctance to support denominational schools from the rates with a defence of the democratic virtues of the directly elected school boards. Anglican and Catholic clergy alike were alarmed at the prospect of council control of their schools. The Education Act of 1902 excluded London. The Webbs used every means they could think of to 'get a good authority for London', from private dinner parties for the influential to the columns of the popular press. Success came with the passing of the London Act in 1903, but it had been a bruising and exhausting experience, bringing them sometimes to hope for a Moderate victory in the 1904 Council elections, in case the Progressives should behave vindictively. Their fears were unfounded. A convincing win for the Progressives was followed by an invitation to Sidney to chair the newly established Education Committee. He declined, and instead agreed to head the Scholarships and Higher Education Committee.

The task which faced the LCC on the appointed day, 1 May 1904, was a daunting one. It became responsible for 521 school board schools, with around 485,000 pupils, together with the 438 voluntary schools with a further 175,000 pupils. Inspection revealed that the latter, as anticipated, did not match the standards of the school board schools, either in acommodation or in teaching, and about 20 per cent were subsequently closed down. In addition the authority took over the higher grade schools and evening continuation classes as well as all the institutions maintained and supported by the Technical Education Board. The transition appears to have been remarkably smooth. Some of the former TEB staff continued to work for the Council, Bernard Allen being appointed in charge of higher education and C.W. Kimmins as Chief Inspector. Garnett was not offered an executive post, but sidelined into a position as educational adviser. His behaviour during the conflict with the School Board, during which a confidential memorandum he had written about the LCC plans had been leaked and published in *The Times*, had been considered to be lacking in judgement.

As Webb had foreseen, the initial task was to create administrative unity out of the muddle of overlapping and diverse elements. Outside the sphere of elementary education, this included clarifying the function of higher grade schools and rationalizing the provision of evening classes. There were no dramatic changes of policy, and changes of power on the Council affected the degree of control over spending rather than strategy. The Council, like the Technical Education Board, was concerned to equip young people for the workplace by continuing their training in ways which matched the needs of London's employers. It inherited the scholarship scheme created by the TEB as well as that of the School Board. Webb's first significant contribution in his new position was to press for the number of junior county scholarships to be increased to 1,000, which in turn had to be reflected in a growth in secondary school places. The Council continued to exercise its permissive powers in the field of higher education, continuing to give substantial grants to the polytechnics and the University of London. It was not constrained by any limited definition of education, and could use its powers in imaginative ways. The complete overhaul of evening school provision did not come until 1913, but the resulting scheme included both vocational and non-vocational courses, and pointed the way to the development of an adult education service.

1939 was the LCC's Jubilee Year, and *London Education Service*[37] reviewed the range of educational institutions aided or maintained by the Council. Some were new since 1904. The 'central schools' had been developed as successors to the ill-fated higher grade schools of the London School Board. These schools had the limited objective of enabling the more able elementary school children to be equipped for work. They provided a continuation of elementary education with the addition of a foreign language, and later of practical and science subjects. Nine central schools were opened in 1911; there were 87 by 1939. The age of entry was reduced from 12 to 11, and the initial three year course was extended to four. The day continuation schools were also new, and came about in reponse to the 1918 Fisher Education Act, which established the minimum school leaving age at 14, and recommended compulsory continuation. The LCC responded rapidly and opened its first schools in 1921, declaring eight hours a week compulsory attendance for 14–16 year olds, with the hope of later extending the age to 18. Faced with economic depression, the Government decided to withdraw the element of compulsion, and the LCC reluctantly substituted a more limited voluntary scheme, providing training for commercial or industrial employment.

The LCC continued to support the polytechnics, technical institutions, schools of art and evening institutes, and the description of the process of reorganization aimed at avoiding overlaps and developing a scheme for the whole of London contains echoes of Webb and the TEB:

> definite roles were assigned to the various places of technical education, assistance being given to the voluntary institutions to improve their buildings, equipment and teaching. The evening continuation schools were, in the main, carried on but with slight

modifications until 1913, when a radical reorganisation was effected. The new scheme brought in keener students, better distribution of staff and curriculum and a closer coordination with the work of technical institutions.[38]

The Council continued to pay maintenance and capital grants to the University of London, and 'to pay direct to the colleges concerned the fees of its scholars and for such services as the provision of teachers for evening studies and university extension courses in evening institutes'.[39]

In 1945 the LCC was faced with both the problems of reconstruction and resumption of services, and the implementation of the wider responsibilities placed upon it by the 1944 Education Act, which finally established the right to 'secondary education for all'. The London School Plan for primary and secondary education was produced and approved by 1947 and the London Scheme of Further Education by 1949.

In further education the post-war period was characterized by an explosive growth in numbers, and a change of emphasis from evening to day courses. More and more employers released their employees to take part-time courses at day colleges (formerly called day continuation schools) and technical colleges. Day release, 'block release' and sandwich courses were developed to meet this need. The LCC's existing infrastructure meant that it was well placed to meet the demand for expansion. 'Progress in the previous forty years had in some ways been as remarkable as the more publicized progress of the twenty years that followed.'[40] The demand for full-time advanced level courses also increased, and there was a growing debate about how best to meet the need for higher level work. Following the White Paper on technical education in 1956, 10 colleges nationally were designated as colleges of advanced technology (CATs). Three of these were London polytechnics- Chelsea, Northampton and Battersea. From 1 April 1962 these colleges were directly funded by the Ministry of Education.

The CATs concentrated on the development of full-time and sandwich courses, post-graduate work and research. Part-time and lower level courses took place within the other polytechnics, technical colleges, colleges of commerce and day colleges. These were reorganized into a hierarchy of regional colleges (which offered some advanced work, including post-graduate and research work in specialised fields), area and local colleges. Regional and area colleges were largely for students over 18, and younger students went to local colleges.

The LCC reviewed its progress with regard to the London Scheme of Further Education in a report published in 1961.[41] This review considered the arrangements for implementing the hierarchy of colleges, and also the provision of courses. The Scheme was London-wide, providing a comprehensive range of subjects, many available in specialist centres as part of an integrated system. This was the approach which had justified the existence of a single authority since the time of the TEB, but it was coming under criticism as opposition to the scope and powers of the LCC grew. This opposition was partly political (the triennial Councils elected from 1946–61 were all Labour controlled) but also represented both reaction against its monolithic structure and concerns for the needs of the wider region.

A Royal Commission on Local Government in Greater London was established in 1957. When it reported in 1960, it praised many of the LCC's achievements, noting especially the high reputation of the education service both at home and abroad. Nevertheless, it favoured the adminstration of education by smaller units, which it felt would be more accountable locally. There was a widespread reaction in favour of an integrated system from many sections of public opinion. The London Government Act of 1963 brought about the abolition of the LCC in 1965. Many services were devolved to newly constituted metropolitan borough councils, which were represented on the Greater London Council (GLC). Education was the exception and the Inner London Education Authority (ILEA) was established to administer the service in the former County of London.

The debate was by no means over, and ILEA's existence until its final abolition in 1990 (four years after the demise of the GLC) was a turbulent one. All London education authorities have been high-spending, and ILEA's budget was 'capped' annually from 1985 by the Conservative Government in an increasingly political battle. In his discussion of this troubled period, Stuart Maclure quotes from a report written by Sir Frank Marshall in 1978, following an invitation from the then Conservative-controlled GLC to investigate a series of proposals, including the replacement of ILEA by a statutory joint committee of the inner London boroughs. Marshall reported in favour of retaining a single authority:

> Provision of high-quality specialist facilities (further and higher education, special schools, adult education, youth and careers services) has been built up and managed on the basis of economies of scale in inner London which smaller authorities could not achieve.[42]

In spite of such endorsements, it became increasingly difficult for ILEA to maintain control of higher education in the face of mounting political opposition. Following the Education Reform Act of 1988, higher education colleges, including the polytechnics, were removed from the management of local authorities. Before the abolition of ILEA finally took place, the breakdown of London's integrated system had already begun.

CHAPTER SEVEN

The funding of higher education in London

Arthur R. Chandler

Once it had been accepted that Higher Education was needed it became obvious that special buildings would be required in order to house a large number of adults in their new learning environment. The financial backing of higher education establishments varied considerably. Part of the capital required sometimes came from sales of work and family working days in parks and open spaces, part came from the generosity of wealthy patrons and part came from charities either founded specifically for the purpose or from charities of more ancient origin whose money was transferred to a special trust for this new purpose. These methods of money raising went a very great way to meet the capital needs but everyday expenses and general regular income had to be found from government or civic sources and student fees

EMINENT EDUCATIONAL PHILANTHROPISTS
The Polytechnic movement would not have started, let alone succeeded, had it not been for the philanthropic aspirations of certain wealthy people of the period. It is therefore necessary to see how these philanthropists dedicated their lives.

Quintin Hogg, probably the greatest of the 'Institute Philanthropists', was born in London in 1845. He was educated at Eton and when he left there in 1863 he did not follow the family tradition of going to Oxford but, at the age of 18, entered a firm of tea merchants where he was extremely successful. He later transferred to a sugar merchants' company where he became senior partner. Here his business acumen brought its financial rewards which enabled him to concentrate on what he considered to be his 'main purpose' in life. Because of his Christian beliefs he felt the need to benefit others less fortunate than himself and dedicated most of his life to the provision of education in various forms. This dedication was aimed at helping the working classes.[1]

It is to Quintin Hogg's patient personal work among working boys, and his munificence, that London owes the first model of a Polytechnic institute. In an interesting article published in 1896, Hogg described the beginning of his work among working lads – a reading lesson to two crossing-sweepers in the Adelphi arches near the Strand. This developed successively into a ragged school in 1864 which met within the confines of a small a room in Of Alley (now York Place); into a boys' home in 1868 in Drury Lane; and then in 1871 to separate evening classes in Hanover Street. Seven years later these developed into an evening institute in Long Acre which finally, from 1881 onwards, became the extensive organization at the Regent Street Polytechnic. Here Quintin Hogg proved that, if only the opportunity for innocent recreation and useful instruction were provided, without offensive patronage or irritating restrictions, thousands of working class young men would gladly avail themselves of it. He organized cheap holiday tours for his polytechnic members to many parts of the world – at that time unbelievable to the students concerned. He also helped many students obtain employment by creating a special bureau for that purpose.[2]

South London led the way in the provision of Polytechnic institutes because the movement south of the Thames was directed by Evan Spicer a leading Congregationalist and wholesale stationery and raw paper supplier.[3]

The South London Polytechnic Institutes' Committee organized a very well attended dinner at the Mansion House on 8 June 1888 at which the Prime Minister, the Marquis of Salisbury, was present to support the resolution 'that this meeting, being convinced of the urgent need in this country of technical and commercial education, approves of the scheme for the establishment in South London of Polytechnic Institutes'.[4]

In order to obtain initial support for this venture Evan Spicer records in his papers that he invited 'a few men of worth' to discuss the means by which money could be raised to provide higher education in the South London area. He wrote his original letters concerning this from his offices in Mincing Lane in the City of London. It was from these offices that he controlled his very prosperous paper business, still in existence today.[5]

It does seem however that some of the original meetings were of a more confidential or private nature and, therefore, were held at his home, Belair Mansion, in Dulwich, well away from his business house in the City. He was a man of Christian principles with activities ranging from a Chapel in the grounds of Belair Mansion in which all his family and servants attended prayers every morning, to the more practical application of his wealth in provision for the poor and by offering himself for public service. Evan Spicer was not only a founding trustee of the City Parochial Foundation but also its longest serving as he held office for 46 years from its creation in 1891 until 1937. He was its Chairman for 13 years from 1920–1933. In addition to these duties he was a governor of the Estate and College of God's Gift at Dulwich, where he lived. He was elected the local member of the London County Council and became its Chairman in 1906. His philanthropic services were rewarded with a knighthood from Edward VII.[6]

A local philanthropist in the Woolwich area was T.A. Denny, a bacon merchant, who was instrumental in the creation of Woolwich Polytechnic. The original idea for this establishment came directly from Hogg's influence for Hogg had already established a ragged school in Castle Street, Woolwich, which had great support and was very successful. To this school he first added an institute but eventually split it back into the two separate units, a school and an institute. To this institute came a young man called Frank Didden who decided that it needed a new location and an existence completely on its own. Didden asked Quintin Hogg for advice and, having been told the minimum space needed, he started to look for possible sites. Because the War Office was the main employer and also a comparatively large landowner in the area, it had to agree to the site chosen for the institute. His next task was to find methods of raising money for this new enterprise. In July 1888 a sports meeting was held at Charlton Park which event was described as having taken place in fine weather with a very large attendance. There were gymnastic displays by the London Polytechnic and the Royal Arsenal Gymnastic Society as Didden's work was supported by the Royal Arsenal Munitions Factory. Support also came from the Royal Arsenal Co-operative Society, one of the strongest co-operative societies in the country. Like other such social gatherings the day raised a great deal of money and gained a great deal of support and enthusiasm from the local community.[7]

However, even with all this support and the profit from the various social events, not enough money was raised to purchase a new building. In January 1890, Denny, already mentioned, came to the rescue by personally paying most of the cost of £1,000 for the building that was to house the Polytechnic. He became one of the founding governors of Woolwich Polytechnic and was Chairman of its Board from 1891–4.[8]

Philanthropy was not a male preserve for by the turn of the century Westminster Technical Institute was running under the direct patronage of Baroness Burdett-Coutts. In 1890 she fitted up an old stable near Vincent Square, Westminster, as a workshop for plumbers and metal plate workers. Within this building which became known as St. Stephen's Institute she started a series of technical classes. Three years later a two-storey building, designated the Westminster Technical Institute, was erected on the present site at a cost of about £5,000 to replace the St. Stephens Institute. Facilities for technical and commercial education for the district were made available with the aid of a grant from the Technical Education Board of the London County Council. In 1900 Baroness Burdett-Coutts presented the Institute to the Council and classes were formed for civil engineering, architecture and the building trade. In 1903 the Westminster School of Art was transferred from the Royal Architectural Museum and became part of the Institute. Five years later the Institute was enlarged and re-organized, the building trade classes were transferred and, in co-operation with the Gas Light and Coke Company, instruction in gas supply and the training of gas fitter apprentices was inaugurated. In 1910 a day technical school in cookery was established to provide boys with a three year course of training for the employment of chefs in hotels and restaurants. A school for waiters was added in 1912.[9]

She was a very unusual woman for her times. At the age of 23 Angela Burdett suddenly became possessor of enormous wealth having been left her grandfather's fortune which had been accumulated through Coutts banking house. She immediately had an income of £18,000 per year, a vast sum at that time, and took the surname Burdett-Coutts by Royal Licence. Her father was Sir Francis Burdett who was a public spirited but erratic radical politician always having sympathy for the underdog. Her maternal grandfather was Thomas Coutts, the banker who always employed a great deal of financial caution in all matters. Through her careful benevolence she felt she was following the traditions and aspirations of both father and grandfather.[10]

In memory of her father, she gave over £90,000 to build St. Stephen's Church, its vicarage and schools in the Westminster constituency which he had represented in Parliament for 30 years. She put £15,000 at the disposal of Bishop Blomfield for church building in the diocese of London. Her benefactions were not restricted to London, however, as other communities in Great Britain were to be thankful for her aid as were parts of the Empire including Abeoukuta in Southern Nigeria, Cape Town in South Africa and Adelaide in Australia.[11]

She took a direct interest in all her philanthropic activities. Not only did she read every letter sent to her, sometimes 300 or 400 a day, but she also worked continuously in supervizing the fulfilment of her ideas. Angela Burdett-Coutts was created a Baroness in her own right in 1871. She was heavily involved in the founding, in 1884, of the London Society for the Prevention of Cruelty to Children. Before she started St. Stephen's Institute, she was already building schools to be run in connection with the Church and had donated the cost of the public library and the swimming bath in Great Smith Street, Westminster.[12] She was a legend in her own lifetime being known throughout the City of London and Westminster for her work on behalf of education. She was made a Freeman of the City of London and was also presented with the Freedom of four City Companies. When she died, at the age of 91, 30,000 Londoners reverently filed past her coffin as it lay in state at her house, No. 1 Stratton Street, off Piccadilly.[13]

Thomas Holloway was born in 1800 in Cornwall which county he left at the age of 28 in order to make the proverbial fortune in London. When he reached the capital he met an Italian pill maker called Albinolo and together they set up a patent medicine business. After the death of his business partner, Holloway and his wife put all their energies into making his life's dream of a fortune into a reality.[14]

Holloway's desire to work and make profit was the main purpose of his life – his success was due not just to the long working hours (sometimes 16 hours per day) but to highly calculated advertising. 'Holloway's Pills' were advertised world wide. In 1882 he spent £45,000 on advertisements which created the market for his remedies. The directions for their use were printed in 20 languages including Turkish, Armenian, Arabic, Japanese and Chinese. The profits reached £50,000 per year when the business was at its height. However, he had no children and had no idea what to do with his wealth.[15]

In 1864 Lord Shaftesbury interested Holloway in the plight of the mentally unstable so that when the time came for him to select carefully the projects which he would support, he became fully committed to building a new sanatorium to be used as a caring and curing institution, definitely not as another asylum in which the mentally ill could be locked away and forgotten. Holloway's sanatorium was built at Virginia Water at a cost, including endowment, of £350,000. He then turned his attention to making provision for the higher education of women and threw all his energies into the planning of a new college which would be named after him. In 1874 he purchased an estate at Egham in Surrey in order to establish his college there. He decided that his new building should be an exact replica of Chateau Chambord which he had admired when travelling through France. In addition to an endowment of £200,000, Holloway gave the full cost of £600,000 to recreate the Chateau at Egham in Surrey. A pure gift, no strings attached to other funding, made this an exceptional building in the late Victorian educational world.[16]

THE CITY PAROCHIAL CHARITIES

Whereas the Polytechnics could not have started in the late nineteenth century without the philanthropists of the time, their contribution was not the only provision of funds for the new venture into Higher Education. To understand the financial background to the Polytechnic movement it is necessary to comprehend the provisions of the City of London Parochial Charities Act of 1883.

Within the parishes of the City of London, philanthropy had encouraged the creation of hundreds of charities since the middle ages. By the mid-nineteenth century some of the parishes had disappeared and some of the funds of the charities could not be used, either because the money was no longer needed or because the terms of many of the bequests could not be carried out. One such bequest required that six shillings and eight pence be spent annually on burning heretics, not quite the occupation of Londoners in the 1880s!

The City Charities were usually funded by income from properties, the value of which had greatly increased through the years. In 1883 the parishes had about £1,000 at their disposal and, in order to release this vast sum and make its distribution efficient and helpful to the community in general, the City of London Parochial Charities Act was passed. The Act empowered the Charity Commissioners to appropriate the funds of these ancient and obsolete City Charities and apply them to specific objects within the Metropolitan area. The main object was that of 'Promoting the education of the poorer inhabitants of the Metropolis by technical instruction, secondary education, art education, evening lectures, or other-wise' and 'generally to improve their physical, social and moral condition'.

THE LONDON POLYTECHNICS

In order to carry out these provisions, the Commissioners proposed the establishment of Polytechnic institutes throughout the metropolitan area and offered large sums for endowment on the condition that funds to help in the erection of new buildings were raised by voluntary efforts. A Body of Trustees was appointed by the Charity Commissioners and given the name 'The City Parochial Foundation'. The first Board of Trustees was appointed in 1891 with its offices in Temple Gardens.[17]

Money from the Charity Commissioners went to the Polytechnics and kindred institutions. The term 'kindred institutions' was used by the Foundation to cover a handful of organizations which were generally classed with the Polytechnics for accounting purposes. These were such places as the Old Vic, the Chelsea Physic Garden and the Whitechapel Art Gallery.[18]

The scheme of compulsory annual grants was set out in the central scheme documents and was amended slightly from time to time. The grants actually specified in 1891 consisted of £5,350 to a City Polytechnic which was to be formed by an amalgamation of the existing Birkbeck Institution, the City of London College and the Northampton Institute which was yet to be established (in the proportion of £3,350 to Northampton and £1,000 each to the Birkbeck and the City of London College).

Regent's Street Polytechnic	£ 3,500
People's Palace	£ 3,500
Borough Polytechnic	£ 2,500
Battersea	£ 2,500
South-Western	£ 1,500
Royal Victoria Hall	£ 1,000
Morley College	£ 400
Joint Committee of Working Men's College and College for Men and Women	£ 150 each
The Bow and Bromley and Aldenham Institutes	£150
and an unspecified sum for Bishopsgate Institute.	

In addition the Commissioners could direct that an annual sum not exceeding £5,000 should be paid to any future institution of like nature and under this ruling it was soon found that £3,000 was very quickly required to be paid as obligatory grants to the proposed Northern and North-Western Polytechnics in the proportion £1,500 each.[19]

At the dinner organized by Evan Spicer at the Mansion House on 8 June 1888, the Earl of Rosebery, Liberal Leader, showed his support by sitting next to the Conservative Prime Minister, the Marquis of Salisbury, as he made a public appeal for funds for the South London Polytechnics Committee. Having spoken about Quintin Hogg's work in Regent Street, he went on to talk about 'his friend' Mr Bartley and the work he was doing for the cause in Islington. He congratulated the Trustees of the Victorian Theatre who had offered to sell their building and to give the proceeds to be part of the £150,000 which had to be met for the endowment by the Charity Commissioners for the new Polytechnic system. He pointed out that day students cost two pence per day and evening polytechnic students cost four pence per day but for those whose subjects were within the sphere of the workshop teaching of the various arts and trades the expense increased considerably to as much as one shilling and eight pence per day. Within a few months the appeal had raised £22,000, a huge amount for that time.[20]

By 1889 one year after the dinner the target of £150,000 had been reached and the Commissioners placed on record their perception of the sense of energy and ability by which the South London movement had, under the chairmanship of Evan Spicer, been characterized. Plans were well advanced for the establishment of Polytechnics either by building new premises or adapting existing ones at New Cross already supported by the Goldsmiths' Company, Borough Road, Battersea, Chelsea and Clerkenwell where the Marquis of Northampton had offered to provide a site. At the same time, alongside these plans before the Commissioners was a request for assistance from the Royal Victoria Hall, the Old Vic.[21]

South-west London had been given the promise of a site in Chelsea from the Earl of Cadogan but North London suffered with divided objectives and failed to get anywhere near the local support that existed south of the Thames.[22]

Most embryo Polytechnics had their own fundraising committee. The South London Polytechnics Committee originally raised money, not for one, but three institutes: Battersea, Borough and Goldsmiths'. Evan Spicer became Chairman of this Executive Committee and controlled it from his new offices at 50 Upper Thames Street. The Treasurer was a Walter Wigram with his offices at 343 Walbrook.[23]

Examples of donations given to the Fundraising Committee for the South London Polytechnics included:

Anon (now known to be a Mr Guesdon)	£20,000
Anon (now known to be Mr Edwin Tate)	£10,000
Barclay and Perkins (Brewery)	£1,000
Ecclesiastical Commissioners	£1,000
Worshipful Company of Fishmongers	£ 525
Lord Bishop of Rochester	£ 150
Archbishop of Canterbury	£ 100
Collected from the Clergy of Bermondsey	£ 10 .11s.0d
Collected by J. Theodore Caesar (friend of Spicer)	£ 7.18s.6d

The total sum raised from the first appeal was over £62,000.[24]

It must be appreciated that the Archbishop of Canterbury had to make similar donations to other Polytechnic appeals not only in London but also to establishments being founded elsewhere in his Province. The Bishop of Rochester had only to support those appeals in his own Diocese which, at that time, included the metropolitan area south of the Thames..

Finance for higher education came from three sources, primarily donations from private funds, then grants from the Government in one form or another, and finally from fees paid by students. By the last quarter of the nineteenth century most civic universities and polytechnics were handicapped by lack of funds. Private donations were coming to an end and in 1889 the House of Commons voted the sum of £15,000 per year to be distributed among the universities and colleges. A condition was attached to this money that each establishment should conduct 'an appreciable amount of advanced university work'. This meant that they had to undertake postgraduate research work as well as courses for undergraduates. In July 1919 a body known as the University Grants Committee was established and through its successor body its work continues today.

When founded each Polytechnic institute was an independent organization and, within the limits of its own Trust Deed or foundation rules, was able to determine its own direction. Generally they were based upon schemes of the Charity Commission and this led, to some extent, to ultimate control by the Commissioners as substantial sums of money emanated from the City Parochial Charities. As time went by they were supported in various forms by the London County Council. The majority of the Polytechnics eventually relied upon heavy subsidies from them.[25]

This was a time of change from the Metropolitan Board of Works to the London County Council which was created in 1888 in order to organize and control the many aspects of life within the newly created County of London. Education was to the fore in this planning and included a joint advisory committee with representatives from the City Parochial Charities, the London County Council and the City and Guilds of London Institute. This committee advised on the general supervision of all polytechnics and their funding.

THE PEOPLE'S PALACE CONCEPT

Meanwhile impetus was given to a change in public opinion from another direction. In 1882 Sir Walter Besant described in his novel, *All Sorts and Conditions of Men*, the lack of provision for social intercourse and healthful recreation among the million inhabitants of the East End of London, and sketched out the plan of a 'Palace of Delight' which should supply this need. The idea stimulated public imagination which was then being heavily influenced by the knowledge of conditions in the sweatshops of the garment and other industries. This led to funds being supplied by a private trust and various other donors for the foundation of such a social institute as the social historian/novelist had described. Out of this root has grown, though with many changes on the way, what was originally called the 'People's Palace' and later became the 'East London Technical College'.[26]

As the People's Palace, originally called the Beaumont Institute, was situated in the East End the Commissioners believed it was tailor-made for spreading the Polytechnic education experiment further afield. This Institute had its origins in an earlier idea of founding a philosophical institute in Mile End. This project was heading for failure but was rescued by a combination of peculiar circumstances in the early 1880s. After the publication of *All Sorts and Conditions of Men* in 1882, the Charity Commissioners appointed new Trustees and issued a scheme for new premises on land which belonged to the Drapers' Company. The Company became heavily involved in providing funds for a Technical School and an annual endowment. A new building, the Queen's Hall, was opened there by Queen Victoria in 1887 and the People's Palace prospered.[27]

From the beginning there had been tension between the social activities of the People's Palace with their emphasis on popular entertainment and the increasingly academic work being done at the East London Technical College. In 1907 the College, which by then catered almost entirely for full-time students, was given temporary status as a School of the University of London. The Charity Commissioners therefore decided to separate the two bodies and while the Drapers' Company continued to support the College, the Foundation's grant was allocated to the Palace. East London College, now Queen Mary Westfield College was con-firmed as a School of the University in 1915. The Trustees seemed little inclined to give any additional support to the Palace beyond the obligatory scheme grant refusing in 1922 to cover a deficit of £600 on a series of experimental concerts. The destruction by fire of the Queen's Hall at the centre of the Palace in 1931 created a crisis which resulted in the Drapers' Company favouring adapta-tion of the whole complex for educational use but the Trustees were adamant that there should not be a transfer to the East London College which catered for university students.[28]

Regent Street Polytechnic had led the Polytechnic movement by providing social advantages which came to form the primary object of the People's Palace. One main feature of these institutes was to be the provision of technical instruction for the manual working class. The Drapers' Company took over the People's Palace and set aside a large income for its maintenance.[29]

At New Cross the Goldsmiths' Company undertook the entire charge of funding and maintaining a Polytechnic in the old Royal Naval School which had ceased to be used for its original purpose. This was opened as Goldsmiths' Institute by the Prince of Wales in 1892.

The Clothworkers' Company gave direct donations totalling nearly £20,000 to the Northern Polytechnic at Holloway, and other City Companies helped in their own way. Largely through the energy of Evan Spicer and the special generosity of Sir Henry Tate and Edwin Tate, considerable sums were raised in Southwark and Battersea for setting up Polytechnics in those districts. In Clerkenwell and in South-west London similar schemes were also under way. But except in the cases in which the City Companies had undertaken the entire charge, the available funds were everywhere found to be quite insufficient for the maintenance, and in some cases even for the completion, of the institutions which had been started.[30]

Enthusiasm by local residents for the proposed Battersea Polytechnic was such that in October 1889 Wandsworth Common was the venue for a colourful and exciting event called a 'Polytechnic Bazaar and Fancy Fair'. This had been organized by the Bolingbroke Tradesmen and Rate Payers Club in order to raise £60,000 for the establishment of a 'People's Palace' in the Battersea area. Thousands of people flocked to the Common not only from Battersea, Clapham and Wandsworth, whose inhabitants were to be the beneficiaries, but from all parts of South and North London. Such events were very popular and raised substantial amounts of money for the local Polytechnic Committees.[31]

Plans for the building of Northampton Institute were heavily supported for it had received a capital sum of over £15,000 and its scheme grant of £3,350 from the City Parochial Foundation was second only to those of Regent's Street and People's Palace. In addition the Skinners' Company took a keen interest and was liberal with its support. The site of one and a quarter acres between St. John's Street in Northampton Square on the Northampton Estate in Finsbury was given by the Marquis of Northampton and a competition was held in 1892 to find an architect for the new building. The winning design was submitted by

Edward W. Mountford who was also the architect of Battersea Polytechnic and, incidentally, of the Central Criminal Court in the Old Bailey. Northampton Polytechnic was completed in 1897 and was opened with full civic ceremony by the Lord Mayor in the following year. The Charity Commissioners provided it with a supplementary grant of £1,000 from 1897 and special grants from time to time thereafter.[32]

The original concept of the 'City Polytechnic' died a natural death. A Common Council was set up composed of representatives of the three institutions of the Foundation, the Birkbeck Institution, the City of London College and the Northampton Institute. There had been little co-operation and the joint Polytechnics formally dissolved the association in 1907. The City of London College was subsequently one of the constituent colleges which amalgamated to form the City of London Polytechnic in 1970. That institution, however, has no relationship to that proposed by the Charity Commissioners in 1891. Yet another complication of names is that the Northampton Institute has become the City University.

From its origins, the Northern Polytechnic in Holloway Road, Islington, was supported by the Clothworkers' Company which held a large estate in the surrounding area. Their money was followed by donations from other local interests and a compulsory grant of £1,500 which enabled the Polytechnic to open in 1896. The Trustees of the City Parochial Foundation agreed to frequent special grants including a loan of £10,000 which was later repaid by the Clothworkers whose support throughout had been important in the establishment of this Polytechnic.[33]

The proposed North-Western Polytechnic was also awarded an annual grant of £1,500 but did not progress at all quickly. A site was obtained in Kentish Town Road and the Prince of Wales Road but because of leases it could not be bought out. In 1894, when no progress with the building seemed possible, the Trustees suggested that funds intended for this Polytechnic should be diverted to support the plans for the Polytechnic proposed for Woolwich but this proposal was not approved by the Charity Commissioners. Four years later, with no real progress having been made, the scheme grant was reduced to £500 which sum formed the basis of a building fund until such time as construction could go forward.[34]

THE 'WHISKY MONEY'

In 1890 the Government passed legislation reducing the number of public houses but felt that the dispossessed publicans should be compensated. In order that money could be raised to pay for this compensation, an additional duty was placed on all wines and spirits. The Local Taxation (Custom and Excise) Act of 1890 imposing this duty having been passed, the Government found itself in the unique position of having a considerable financial surplus and not knowing what to do with it. Because many Members of Parliament were against any such scheme for compensating the publicans, Arthur Acland suggested that the money should be given to the County Councils either for assisting technical education or for reducing the rates. After debate some of the original provisions were set aside and surplus money made available in accordance with Acland's amendments.[35]

The majority used this unexpected income for the former purpose and were able to finance technical instruction without the necessity of levying the rate authorized by the Technical Instruction Act. The experience thus acquired by the councils stood them in good stead when in 1902 they were required to take over the administration of education in their areas in place of the School Boards. Such a curious source of revenue, however, brought about one unfortunate result; the funds available for technical education increased whenever drinking increased and diminished with a spread of temperance, so that, if the total abstainers could have persuaded the whole country 'to go dry', there would have been no funds left. Throughout the country a large proportion of the money gathered in was spent on the education of pupils in secondary schools in order to raise the standard of the teaching of science rather than on the provision of technical instruction for older persons. The allocation of the money was different in London where the major part of the 'Whisky money' was used for higher education only.[36]

At this stage the London County Council entered the educational field and in 1892 began to devote its windfall to the promotion of technical education. The Polytechnic institutes, then in various stages of completion, naturally claimed a large share of this new source of educational endowment. These claims were usually accepted and paid in full but only upon the condition that the educational side of each institute was systematically organized on a sound footing, made thoroughly efficient, and greatly extended. Under this influence the Polytechnics, whilst retaining their functions of promoting social intercourse and healthful recreation, became educational institutions of the first importance.

By the early years of the twentieth century a number of Polytechnic institutes and their branches were offering education to students throughout London.

North of the Thames there were:

The East London Technical College, Mile End Road, East, including:

　The Bow and Bromley Institute.

The Northern Polytechnic, Holloway

The Regent Street Polytechnic, Regent Street

The South-West London Polytechnic, Manresa Road, Chelsea

The Sir John Cass Institute, Jewry Street

The City Polytechnic, including:

　The Northampton Institute, Clerkenwell

　Birkbeck College, Bream's Buildings, Chancery Lane

　The City of London College, White Street, Moorfields

South of the Thames there were:

Battersea Polytechnic, Battersea Park Road

Borough Polytechnic, Borough Road, including:

　The Herold's Institute, Bermondsey

　The Norwood Institute, Knight's Hill

　The Goldsmiths' Institute, Lewisham High Road, New Cross

　Woolwich Polytechnic, William Street, Woolwich

The Herolds' Institute is particularly interesting as it was founded specifically to further knowledge of leather and the leather industry which was second only to the docks as an employer within Bermondsey.[37]

Polytechnics working during the session 1903–04 cost just over £1,000,000 of capital outlay. The combined expenditure over the year was £200,000. There were 40,000 registered student members and the receipts from their fees together with other miscellaneous sources was roughly £60,000. This left a deficit of £140,000 to be met by other funds. Private subscriptions were just under £15,000, and contributions from City Liveried Companies accounted for £25,000. The remaining money came from official public bodies – the Board of Education granted £25,000, the City Parochial Charities Fund granted £30,000 and the London County Council gave £50,000 providing it was definitely allocated to the part of the work falling within the statutory definition of technical instruction.[38]

THE ROYAL COMMISSION ON TECHNICAL INSTRUCTION

A Royal Commission on Technical Instruction was appointed in 1884 to review the facilities for technical education in this country and to contrast them with those available on the Continent and in the United States of America. The Commission not only investigated the training given in technical institutions but science teaching from the elementary school upwards. The provision of an adequate number of secondary schools of a 'modern type' was urged. The report made the authorities realize the need not only for first-class technical institutions, but also for an adequate supply of secondary schools in which instruction given would lay the foundation for later technical training. The result of this Commission was the Technical Instruction Act of 1889. The Act was permissive and gave power to the new local authorities, in both counties and county boroughs, to levy a penny rate in order to supply technical instruction by setting up schools and appointing teachers, to aid the supply of technical education by making grants to institutes supplying such education, and to promote technical education by the establishment of exhibitions and scholarships.[39]

This Royal Commission, which had met under the Chairmanship of Sir Bernhard Samuelson, issued its final report in its first year. Its members toured the country addressing audiences, and some of them were involved in setting up a National Association for the Promotion of Technical and Secondary Education in 1886. Under pressures of this kind the first Technical Instruction Act was passed in 1889, enabling the new county and county borough councils to support technical education out of the rates. From then on technical education provided a significant part of the courses offered by the Polytechnic institutes.

The Technical Education Board had its official headquarters in Spring Gardens but, in fact, most of its papers were issued from its office at 116 St Martin's Lane. The Board's report of 1893–4 proved that special treatment was then being shown to all Polytechnics. The Board stated the desirability of appointing an educational principal to direct the teaching work of each Polytechnic. Whereas this appointment would be optional for the Polytechnics already in existence, a condition of recognition of any new Polytechnic would be that a principal would be appointed. The Board made an offer to contribute three-quarters of the cost of the principal's salary providing this sum did not exceed £500 per annum and that the Board approved of the name submitted for appointment.

A further offer was made of £500 per year to each Polytechnic plus a variable grant made up of three parts: i) 10 per cent of all salaries paid to technical teachers, ii) 15 per cent on all voluntary contributions received by the institution, and iii) one penny per hour on all students attending classes in certain subjects coming within the definition of technical instruction. In no case should the Board's contribution exceed £2,500 in any one year.(40)

Consideration was also given for specific grants to cover the cost of new equipment for lecture rooms, laboratories and workshops – each case to be resolved on its merits. Additional grants were made to those Polytechnics that included a domestic economy school on their premises. In the case of the Borough Polytechnic a special grant was given for the establishment of a class in bread making.

Private responses to the situation had begun earlier. The ancient Guilds of the City of London were induced, in 1876, to consider supporting technical education from their unused resources, 'with the view of educating young artisans and others in the scientific and artistic branches of their trades'. The City and Guilds of London Institute had been created to encourage the teaching of practical subjects by conducting examinations but in 1883 it also opened Finsbury Technical College which was to become a model for future technical education. Within its new laboratories there developed a new and dynamic view of science teaching that was soon to be followed by other institutes.[41]

FUNDING THE LONDON POLYTECHNICS
In 1896 working Polytechnics had about 30,000 students between them. These buildings represented a capital outlay of £500,000 and cost £120,000 to maintain. They were:
    Birkbeck Institute
    City of London College, Moorfields
    Woolwich Polytechnic
    Borough Polytechnic

Battersea College
Chelsea
Northern (Holloway) Polytechnic
Northampton Institute, Clerkenwell

At the same time the Sir John Cass Institute found itself with very strong support in Aldgate and therefore soon became a Polytechnic. It provided a treble service to the community as its building included classrooms for a day school and its staff undertook pastoral concern for the Eastern half of the City plus Whitechapel and Spitalfields.[42]

The Polytechnic idea was looked upon by the Charity Commissioners as a two- fold exercise, both giving and receiving. It 'gave' by supporting the 'education and cultural panacea' for urban needs and it aimed to 'receive' by attracting considerable further funds from City companies and other civic circles. The Charity Commissioners made it very clear that all grants would be made conditional on local support. Evening classes were given a great fillip in the mid 1890s by the recognition, for grant purposes, of students over 21 years of age. These classes had really moved from 'the next stage' of education to something adult and really acceptable – 'higher' education.

The boards of governors of individual Polytechnics were reorganized to represent the partnership between the fund providing bodies and the educational establishment. The governors of Battersea for example included three representatives of the City Parochial Foundation, two each from the London County Council and the London School Board, and three from the Technical Education Board. The financing of the Polytechnics was equally complex. In 1895–6 Battersea received £2,500 from endowment, £3,166 in grants for equipment from the Technical Education Board, £1,000 special grant from the Central Governing Body, £2,254 from students' fees, and £653 and £1024 in grants from the Science and Art Department and the City and Guilds Institute respectively. The Technical Education Board provided the highest proportion of continuing revenue, and this remained firm for all the institutions throughout the London Polytechnic Council's life. Heavy demands for equipment grants increased rapidly, clearly brought about by pressure caused by success after success. The same demands applied to the need for costly building extensions.[43]

Once the Polytechnics were being used to capacity, the time

came for application to be made to the City Parochial Foundation for grants for building extensions. Battersea applied for a loan of £2,590 to build additional rooms. Its committee was told that an advance would be made on the strict understanding that no grant would be made for the repayment of the principal and the interest. The Trustees were concerned that there was an over-concentration of higher level university teaching at Battersea and this may have affected their attitude. Woolwich Polytechnic asked for a grant to purchase the freehold of its site in 1913. The first reaction of the Trustees was to turn down the request but the Charity Commissioners had intimated that the acquisition of the freehold would make possible a re-building programme in which social activities could be better accommodated. The central governing body relented and agreed to lend £10,000 on the proviso that repayment instalments should be the first charge on the existing annual grant.[44]

The report of the Technical Education Board at the turn of the century included detailed lists of grants made by the Board under various headings including 'for instruction in science and art' and 'for the maintenance of buildings'.

For instruction in science and art:

Battersea Polytechnic Institute	£ 600
Birkbeck Institution	£ 650
Regent Street Polytechnic Institute	£1,520
South-Western Polytechnic Institute	£ 540
Woolwich Polytechnic Institute	£ 310

For maintenance of buildings:

Battersea Polytechnic Institute	£ 931
Borough Polytechnic Institute	£411
Northampton Institute	£411
Northern Polytechnic Institute	£36
Regent Street Polytechnic Institute	£ 113
South Western Polytechnic Institute	£289
Westminster Technical Institute	£19
Woolwich Polytechnic Institute	£ 446[45]

In order to appreciate the portion of income needed by individuals to pay their Polytechnic fees one should look at examples of the value of money in the 1890s. A headmaster of a Grammar School with 450 boys received a salary of £750 per annum while one of his assistant masters would have received £175. The wages for a daily domestic help would have been three shillings per week while a live-in servant might receive £5 per year plus board and lodging. An apprentice would get between seven shillings and sixpence, and 14 shillings weekly. The average rent for a working-class home would be two shillings weekly. (One shilling equals five present day pence.)[46]

A very detailed Prospectus of Day and Evening Classes for Battersea Polytechnic Institute for the 1894–5 session shows fees for 'membership' were: 16–25 years of age

Men: two shillings per quarter or six shillings per year

Women: one shilling per quarter or three shillings per year.

Above the age of 25 the Governing Body was able to admit a small number of students in this category but fees were different:

Men: three shillings per quarter or 10 shillings per year

Women: one shilling and six pence per quarter or five shillings per year.

It should be noted that these fees were paid quarterly, not termly, and that they made one a 'member' of the Polytechnic institute with entry to the building and to facilities such as the reading room which contained newspapers and periodicals and to the common room where members could play bagatelle, chess, drafts and other games. Being a member did not entitle you to attend classes without paying extra fees.

It is interesting to note that in 1894 smoking was not allowed in any part of the building either for students or staff, a rule that was re-introduced for the same building in 1995.

The cost of day classes varied. For two hours a week in geometrical and mechanical drawing fees were: Members two shillings and non-members three shillings per quarter.

For two and a half hours a week in carpentry and joinery members paid four shillings per quarter and non-members five shillings.

For evening classes in applied mathematics a one hour class for 30 weeks cost four shillings per session for a member and five shillings for a non-member. For two hours in the mechanical laboratory it cost: members three shillings for twelve lessons and non-members four shillings. For painters and house decorators work there was a weekly two and a quarter hour lesson (from 8 p.m. – 10.15 p.m.) for which members paid three shillings per quarter and non-members four shillings with a special concession for apprentices under 18 years who were admitted at two-thirds of the fee. Special courses for teachers were held in some subjects, for instance two and a half hour classes in woodwork each Saturday morning had a special quarterly fee of 10 shillings which included all materials used.[47]

The original aim of all polytechnics was to provide higher education for the working classes especially those who had been educated through the School Board for London and the apprenticeship system. It must be recorded however that for three consecutive years at Battersea Polytechnic the top students were in 1903–05 respectively A. Apted, A.S. Poncon and R. Mordin, all three having been educated at the private fee paying Alleyn's School in Dulwich, South London. This, of course, is only in the tradition of some of the great English Public Schools that started out as Charity Schools for poor scholars and ended up with parents paying substantial fees.[48]

Within three decades between 1880 and 1910 the Polytechnic Institutes had become a recognized part of the London educational scene. From a purely philanthropic start they had developed, with the aid of money from the City Parochial Foundation, into institutions that were attracting a great deal of money from appeals. Whisky money came at just the right time and then Government funding and grants from the rates established higher education in a permanent form. The institutions varied, their names varied, some were called Polytechnics, some institutes, some colleges and Birkbeck was even called an 'Institution'. Throughout this century they have all progressed in different ways and their designations have altered with the times. Some became Colleges of Technology and a large number became universities in their own right with funding from the Universities Grants Fund. Even so, appeals are still made to former students and sponsorship is sought from industry in order to supplement official income. Nothing changes!

CHAPTER EIGHT

The London polytechnics

John Izbicki

On 1 December 1992, The Rt. Hon The Lord Hailsham of Saint
Marylebone slowly climbed up into the pulpit of Westminster
Abbey and read the following extract from a letter written by his
grandfather, Quintin Hogg written more than a century earlier.

'There are several Polytechnics being formed, as you know, and
one thanks God for it,' Lord Hailsham's reading began and went
on: 'But I would say of all such work that to the extent God is
honoured in them mainly will depend their success'.[1] The occasion
of Lord Hailsham's reading was a Service of Thanksgiving and
Rededication marking the inauguration of the University of Westminster. The Abbey was packed with the great and the good, the
representatives of other universities in and around London, and
in particular the vice-chancellors of 'new' universities – those
which, until that year, had been polytechnics. They had assembled
to pay homage to the one institution which had originally inspired
what was to become a nationwide polytechnic movement.

As early as 1860, Hogg, the Eton-educated son of politician and
barrister Sir James Weir Hogg, had founded a school within a
stone's throw of Charing Cross. It was a ragged school[2] – for poor,
illiterate urchins of the area. His Of Alley ragged school was an
instant success and within a matter of months became too small.
He had to find bigger premises and moved the school by a few
streets to Covent Garden. It was reopened in what is now Long
Acre in 1871, and was expanded to include an evening institute at
which teenagers and adults could learn technical and recreational
subjects. Hogg had once again hit the right pulse of popularity and
the new school once more quickly outgrew its premises. Again
Quintin Hogg had to move. But where? In Regent Street, today
the very heart of London's West End, was a building which looked

appropriate enough for his requirements. Since 1838 it had been used as an exhibition and lecture centre for the industrial arts. It was called the Polytechnic Institution, a name that echoed the *Ecole Polytechnique*, a child of the French Revolution whose doors were first opened in Paris in 1795 by the National Committee of Public Safety. That *Ecole* taught students science as well as general subjects to the highest of standards and prepared them for employment at the most senior levels.[3]

But the Polytechnic Institute, unlike the French model whose name it had adopted, was a failure. Nothing helped, not even the presentation of a Royal Charter in 1839, along with a new title – the Royal Polytechnic Institute. It lost so much money it was forced to close. But the building proved ideal for Quintin Hogg's purposes and in 1881 he bought it. The only thing which remained for him to do was choose a name. Hogg immediately recognized the Regent Street building's great potential for secondary as well as further and perhaps even higher education. But he had no desire to ape Oxbridge. The monotechnic university, that is to say, an institution with only one single scholarly goal – pure philosophy, pure mathematics, pure science, as opposed to applied knowledge – was not for him. The Greek polus, for 'much' or 'many' and the number of *applied* vocational or technical subjects his institute offered, were contained in that one word *polytechnic*. The more he contemplated it, the more attractive the name became. Thus the Regent Street Polytechnic was born and became the prototype for other such institutions.

Making technical instruction available to the masses was not the only reason for the birth and growth of polytechnics. Education was seen as an influence on social cohesion – since the series of vitally important Acts passed between 1844 and 1889 – viz: the Factory Act (1844) which made it compulsory for parents whose children worked in the 'dark satanic mills' to send them to school for three full or six half days a week; Forster's great Education Act of 1870 making elementary education compulsory for all young children; The (Lord) Sandon Act of 1876 which made it the parent's duty to see that children received school instruction in reading, writing and arithmetic; it made the employment of children under the age of 10 illegal and allowed those aged 10–14 to be employed only if they passed an adequate standard in the Three Rs; the Elementary Education Act of 1880 made school boards produce byelaws on the compulsory school attendance of all children aged five to ten; and the Technical Instruction Act of 1889 which allowed a penny rate to be levied to pay for technical education.

Parliament was not alone in wanting to pour oil on potentially stormy waters. Numerous private organizations were also anxious to see that the volcanic rumblings of the poor should not erupt. Too much business, too many profits, were at stake. Education was seen as one way of ensuring appeasement. The Charity Commissioners were among the most active in this mission. A great deal of money (£161,000) had been spent on providing open spaces for Londoners, including Parliament Hill Fields, Clissold Park, Vauxhall Park, Brockwell Park, Peckham Rye and the Royal Victoria Gardens. The commissioners also turned their sights on education, particularly technical education. It was clear that far too few young people were given the opportunity of a further education between leaving elementary school and entering employment. There was a growing groundswell of criticism of the large stockpile of money Parochial charities in the City of London had managed to build over the years. It was time to use it on other things than the environment, important though open spaces and parklands were to the population at large (see Chapter five).

The Regent Street Polytechnic was originally opened as a Young Men's Christian Institute for artisans and apprentices. One of its main attractions was a 'new and elaborate' swimming bath.[4] Henry Cunynghame, a representative of the Charity Commissioners had been instructed to cross the Channel to attend a Congress on Technical Education at Bordeaux. Cunynghame took the opportunity of also visiting Paris and taking a look at the technical education being offered to French workers. On his return to London he wrote a report for the Commission which subsequently asked him to pay a visit to Mr Quintin Hogg's polytechnic. In 1887 he did just that. According to Quintin Hogg's daughter:

> No one knew his reasons for coming; he was merely a stranger who asked to be shown the place, and Mr Mitchell (the Secretary) took him all over it, unconscious that he was 'entertaining an angel unawares'. Mr Cunynghame was immensely struck with all he saw, brought other members of the Commission to investigate it also, and reported very strongly in favour of some of the money being spent in establishing or endowing similar conditions.[5]

As for Mr Cunynghame, he had this to say:

> I do not wish to appropriate more than my due. Quintin Hogg gave
> the idea and invitation, the Charity Commissioners took it up and
> threw into it the whole weight of their influence and experience,
> some of the City Companies stripped themselves bare to find the
> money to help – but the suggestion to institute Polytechnics was
> mine. The printed reports furnished by the Commissioners show
> this and I am not going to forgo the satisfaction and pleasure of
> thinking of the share I took in their splendid work.[6]

Cunnynghame's report certainly heaped lavish praise on the
Regent Street Polytechnic and said it provided the right model 'to
benefit the great mass of artisans and the poorer classes generally'.[7] He also proposed that a limited number of large institutions
(as opposed to a larger number of small ones) should be set up
along polytechnic lines. He costed the 'model polytechnic' at
£70,000 to build and equip. Operational costs, based on an
endowment, would come to £5,000 a year.

The consequences of Cunynghame's initiative were far reaching.
He could not possibly have dreamed that his work would last for
more than 100 years and that polytechnics would one day be
described by a prime minister as having 'come of age' and as 'the
success story of the twentieth Century'. Nor could Cunynghame
have ever guessed that they would one day become universities[9]
providing the vanguard of higher education and propelling it into
the twenty-first century. And where the Commissioners provided
the main initiative for the growth of the polytechnics, it was the
City Parochial Foundation, established by the Commissioners in
April 1891, that became tied, not always willingly, to the polytechnic principle for some 60 years.

Some while earlier, in October 1887, a lengthy feature article in
The Times presented a statement of accounts showing that the
various London parishes would be able to make certain monies
available for the foundation of 'working men's and women's
institutes'. The article which, according to Victor Belcher's centen-
nial work on the *City Parochial Foundation, 1891–1991*, was based
on 'what we would term today a press release', calculated that
£37,000 a year would be available 'for ecclesiastical ends' and
£57,000 for general charity purposes. It also made some play about
the £100,000 which had been promised for the development of

open spaces and free public libraries (see Chapter five for the origins of this money). *The Times* article also mentioned the Beaumont Institute in the East End. This became best known as the People's Palace which, according to Cunynghame, was ideal for spreading the polytechnic gospel further afield.

With the prompting of the Commissioners, committees of influential persons were formed and met regularly in and around south and north London. During one such meeting in December 1887 at the Royal Victoria Hall, later to become the Old Vic, it was announced that funds from City parochial charities could now be used for the 'endowment of institutions of popular education and recreation'.[10]

South London was first in developing voluntary support and, within a relatively short time, a target of £150,000 was set to fund three polytechnic institutions south of the river. Even the Prime Minister, Lord Salisbury, attended one meeting at Mansion House to support the motion: 'That this meeting being convinced of the urgent need in this country of technical and commercial education, approves of the scheme for the establishment in South London of polytechnic institutes.'[11]

Fund-raising for the founding of further polytechnics got into its stride, almost at the expense of all other considerations. Anyone who visited Gwydyr House to argue for the funding of free public lending libraries was steered along a different course to those who sought to fund more open spaces. Polytechnics became the veritable password of the day. Building costs of each were estimated in excess of £100,000. South-west London streaked ahead with a promised site for Chelsea College. But petty squabbles held back any plans for polytechnics in north London.[12]

THE POOR MUST COME FIRST

When the Commissioners produced their annual report for 1889, they were able to record that the South London target of £150,000 had been reached and plans for founding other polytechnics were well in hand. In some cases it was a matter of refurbishing and adapting existing premises; in others, the institutions were purpose-built. The Goldsmiths' Company offered help at New Cross; the Marquess of Northampton had also offered a site at Clerkenwell – today the City University. Other sites were at Borough Road, Battersea and Chelsea. Commissioners stressed the importance of technical instuction and made it clear that, by law, existing funds had to benefit the 'poorer classes'. Knowledge had to be spread not just to people in general but the teaching of technical and industrial skills had to be devoted mainly to artisans and labourers. Indeed, a body of trustees was to be set up for this specific purpose and to administer funds accordingly.[13]

When the Northern Polytechnic Institute opened to its first students in the Holloway Road on 5 October 1896, its mission was:

> to promote the industrial skill, general knowledge, health and well being of young men and women belonging to the poorer classes of Islington.[14]

The Charity Commissioners had stipulated that the City Parochial Foundation should produce mandatory annual grants to the polytechnics and 'kindred institutions'. In 1891 these grants worked out as follows: £5,350 to what was to be called City Polytechnic – an amalgamation of three institutions: Birkbeck Institution, which would receive £1,000; the City of London College, also £1,000; and the Northampton Institute, which had still to be set up, £3,350. Quintin Hogg's Regent Street Polytechnic would receive £3,500, as would the People's Palace on the Mile End Road; £2,500 went to Borough Polytechnic as well as to Battersea Polytechnic; £1,500 went to the South-Western Polytechnic; £1,000 went to both Morley College and the Royal Victoria Hall (now better known as the Old Vic); and £400 jointly to the Working Men's College and the College for Men and Women.[15]

Money was put aside for other still-to-be-established institutions and the Commissioners also earmarked up to £5,000 a year for any similar venture. An immediate £3,000 was at this time needed – £1,500 apiece for the proposed Northern and North-Western Polytechnics. At the interest rates then in force, an annual endowment of £1,500 was equivalent to a £50,000 capital grant – generosity indeed on the part of the Commissioners.[16]

When the Northern Polytechnic Institute opened, its coffers were not exactly bulging. Its only real asset was a compulsory scheme grant of £1,500. However, thanks to the Clothworkers' Company which owned considerable property in Islington and displayed more than a little interest in this north London parish, generous donations were promised. In 1892 they voted a grant of

£2,000 for buildings and equipment and later added a further £500 – double to £1,000 in 1901. The Company also later repaid a loan of £10,000 and also voted through numerous special grants.

There were meant to be two polytechnics in north London and it is worth looking at these in a little more detail to show that the birth and development of 'The Polys' were not one long fertile bed of roses. Certainly, all *seemed* to go well at first, when the representatives of the parishes of Hackney, Islington, Stoke Newington and St Pancras met in February 1888. Indeed, the meeting decided that four 'technical and recreative institutes' should be opened, one in each of the four boroughs. The following year, they launched an appeal for £200,000 to fund all four. But all did not go smoothly. Bureaucracy, petty squabbles and procrastination that seem to have become increasingly identified with this part of the capital city almost prevented the establishment of polytechnics in north London – had it not been for the power of the Press and the courage of an Islington resident, a simple vestry clerk.

In September 1889, under the headline *Technical Institutes for North London*, one newspaper asked the question: 'What has become of the fine scheme for planting technical institutes all over North London, which was so brilliantly launched many months ago?' It went on to name an imposing list of treasurers who were ready to gather together the necessary funds. The Charity Commissioners had generously offered to match all funds raised by local efforts, yet individual North London donors were conspicuous by their absence. What had succeeded so brilliantly south of the river, was failing abysmally north of it.[17]

This stinging leader was probably a reaction to a letter in the Old Thunderer itself on 21 September. This was written by W.F. Dewey, the Vestry Clerk at Vestry Hall, Upper Street, Islington. He wrote:

> Sir,- ... the draft scheme recently published by the Charity Commissioners ... provides for the application annually of £22,550, in sums varying from £150 to £5,350, for the maintenance of such institutes in the east, west, centre and south of the metropolis; but to my surprise the northern portion, with an area of 20 square miles, and a population of considerably over 1,000,000 appears to have been totally ignored. It is true that by Clause 44 the Commissioners reserve to themselves the power to devote a further sum of £5,000 annually to the maintenance of institutes yet to be

established and similar in character to those named in the schedule before mentioned, but no localities are specified and it may well be that these funds will be applied elsewhere than in the north.[18]

A response to *The Evening News and Post* leader (and possibly as a sideswipe at Mr Dewey, though he was never mentioned) appeared in *The Evening News*. Signed by J.H. Allen, Chairman of the Executive Committee: 'arrangements for establishing two out of the four institutes originally intended for North London are now being matured, and it is confidently hoped a satisfactory settlement will be arrived at before the end of the year. The executive committee deeply regret that they have been unable to do more than this, but the inhabitants of North London and the public generally have not responded to their appeals in the same generous way that has been done in South London'.[19]

The matter did not end there. Other newspapers jumped on the campaigning bandwagon. *The Islington Gazette* as well as the *Hackney and Kingsland Gazette* and *The Morning Post* all produced articles seeking to know why the Charity Commissioners were holding up the establishment of the four promised institutes in north London.

On 26 September 1889 *The Times* devoted almost eight columns to a report detailing the valiant six-year-long labours of the Charity Commissioners and the City Parochial Charities and faithfully recorded their draft scheme. Thus, for example, the following annual sums were to be paid out of the central Charity Commissioners' funds: To persons found to have vested interests or a 'moral claim to payments' out of parochial funds: £1,360.11s 11d; To Bishopsgate Free Library: £2,000; To specified polytechnics: £19,830; To other specified institutions and evening classes: £700; To polytechnics or institutions to be subsequently established by scheme of the Commissioners: £5,000.

In a lengthy report dated 26 September 1889, *The Times* criticized both the objectives and composition of the newly established London Parochial Charities Board: 'These funds are not educational endowments and, even in the scheme of the Commissioners are not, it is assumed, to be used for the advancement of learning in the University sense of the term, but in promoting skill in handicrafts and in furnishing the poorer classes with rational amusement. Why should bodies, necessarily not of a representative character, and charged with functions having no relation whatever to the objects to which the charity funds are directed to be applied by Parliament, be endowed with so potent a voice in their management? *There can be only one answer. The Commissioners have determined that the substance of these funds shall swell the long list of educational endowments,* and have constituted a Board which will finish their work and apply the funds in the way they desire. It is for London to say whether the decision on so important a matter shall be thus taken out of its hands.'[20]

As far as the polytechnics of north London were concerned, the report did little to advance the campaign in their favour. Mr Dewey, on the other hand, was inundated with what might today be known as fan mail, supporting the stance he had taken. In October, one newspaper, now defunct, published a long letter from a Mr Tom A. Cudlipp of Crayford Road, Tufnell Park, backing the Dewey line to the hilt.

> Mr Dewey must assuredly have the sympathy of every Islingtonian when he protests against the manifest wrong of depriving North London of all share of the £22,550 which is to be divided among the other divisions of the metropolis under the City Parochial Charities' Scheme of the Charity Commissioners. He ought to have more than sympathy – which, after all, is an unconscionably cheap sentiment – he ought to have warm and keen practical assistance.

Mr Cudlipp then goes on to argue at inordinate length the pros and cons of the Charity Commissioners' scheme as depicted in *The Times.* He ends with a serious suspicion concerning the wastage of funds and the disappearance of London's heritage, attacking the Commissioners for neglecting to devote funds to the education of north Londoners and, therefore, depriving the poorer classes of Islington in particular and north London in general of a decent education.

DECISIVE VESTRY MEETING

The matter certainly did not end there. On 7 November 1889, a deputation of members of the Central Executive Committee for the establishment of Technical Institutes in north London, a recently formed body, lobbied the Charity Commissioners and voiced their 'deep regret' in no uncertain terms at the Commissioners' failure to provide institutes in the boroughs of Hackney, Islington and St Pancras. They were told that the Charity Commission simply did not have enough money to set up three institutes. But the lobby, which included Sir A.K. Rollit MP as well as Mr Dewey, were presented with a proposal from the Commissioners. They were asked to choose between one large institute to serve the whole area and providing specialised instruction, or three minor institutes which could teach general science. The deputation decided to go away to consider this alternative and report back.[21]

A little more than a week later, there was a crowded meeting of the Islington Vestry, presided by the Rev. Dr W.H. Barlow, the local vicar. Mr Dewey, the Clerk, read out a lengthy letter from Mr D.R. Fearon, Secretary of the Charity Commission at Whitehall, in response to Mr Dewey's original protest. The Commissioners, it stated, had to consider the metropolis as a whole and

> so far as concerns the question of polytechnic institutes, it was already pointed out in a report to Her Majesty at the commencement of this year, the grounds on which they (the Commissioners) proceeded and the principles which have governed them. In conformity with these principles (they) thought it their duty to provide for the establishment on a firm basis of three polytechnic institutes in positions where they will be readily accessible to the inhabitants of a wide area and more particularly ... to those inhabiting the northern parts of the metropolis.

So far, so good. But the letter then went on to say that one polytechnic would definitely be established in the City, in Clerkenwell to be exact, and that this would straddle the southern boundary of Islington and would be within easy travelling distance from virtually anywhere within north London. The proposed polytechnic was of course the Northampton Institute which became one of the country's leading Colleges of Advanced Technology and is today the City University. But what of the Northern, the North Western or Hackney? Mr Fearon had this to say:

> The Commissioners had, indeed, at one time contemplated the establishment in Islington itself, at a distance of about two miles from the Northampton Institute, of a polytechnic of considerable

extent and importance; but the proposal proved not to be acceptable to those who represented the interests of Islington on the Executive Committee for Northern Polytechnics; and in the absence of any alternative proposal, and as a result of very advantageous opportunities presented to them, the Commissioners have been led to employ a larger share of the funds in question than otherwise they would have done in more developing the City Polytechnic.

The Commissioners, he added, regretted not being able to be more positive at this time, but they felt the money could be better used elsewhere. Furthemore, they felt that whereas other parishes had been most cooperative in coming forward with funds to assist with the establishment of colleges elsewhere, *'no proposition hitherto made to them from the parish of Islington has held out the prospect of any such assistance as would have justified them* [the Commissioners] *in the appropriation of funds to Polytechnic purposes within that parish'.*[22]

There was uproar. The Commissioners, the meeting felt, had totally evaded the issue and buried it under an avalanche of fine but meaningless words. When the chairman had managed to restore order, he called upon the Vestry Clerk to speak. Mr Dewey, still seething with indignation from the letter he had read, again made out a case for a polytechnic in Islington. The parish, he said, was bigger and more densely populated than any large provincial town, bar three or four, and had an excellent claim for the establishment of a polytechnic. The North London Polytechnics Committee, all present at the meeting, then passed a resolution declaring that, as there were not sufficient funds available to provide for fully equipped institutes in Hackney, Islington and St Pancras, the nucleus of an institute in each borough should be provided and gradually completed as and when funds permitted. It was proposed that between £10,000 and £30,000 should be appropriated for each of the three boroughs to secure sites and erect buildings. A sum of £1,500 should be applied for the endowment of the institutes. This was passed unanimously. It was further moved that the Fearon letter be referred to a special committee to respond to the inaccuracies, misconceptions and misstatements it contained and to prepare petitions. These could be lodged before the following February (1890). This, too, was unanimously carried.

A week later, the following brief report appeared in *The Daily Telegraph*:

> Islington is making an energetic protest against the scheme of the Commissioners in regard to the disposal of the funds of the City parochial charities and, as it would seem, with good reason. 'Merrie Islington', no longer a village, but an enormously populous borough, complains that it has been ignored by the scheme while £100,000 has been devoted to technical institutes and free libraries within the City, where confessedly population is declining, and £25,000 bestowed on City churches. A deputation representative of all political parties has been appointed to wait on the Charity Commissioners.[23]

The campaign to secure a polytechnic in Islington was reaching crescendo proportions. Meetings were held almost daily to ever bigger audiences and one deputation after another was elected to lobby the Charity Commissioners. What stuck in many an Islingtonian's throat was the Commissioners' allegation that Islington was unable to give pound for pound for what the Commissioners could give them. Islington, it was argued at protest meetings, could not give land as an equivalent for money even though there were landlords who were drawing colossal sums from the parish. One meeting was told (by a Mr A.R. Chamberlayne) that neighbouring Clerkenwell had produced land which had been 'over-estimated to the value of 300 per cent' and that is how Islington's neighbours got a grant. The slur on Clerkenwell produced raucous laughter at the meeting, which had taken place at the Primitive Methodist Chapel in the Caledonian Road. The meeting elected a working committee to take the campaign further.[24]

On 5 December, things were brought to a head, with a meeting at the Myddelton Hall, Islington. It turned out to be a long and noisy meeting and an exceptionally important one. For one thing, it brought together the various protest and organising committees and working parties that had been formed at the various previous meetings, and amalgamated them into one confederate body. Sir Albert Rollit MP chaired and was supported by another MP, Mr Bartley, and senior representatives of the LCC, the London boroughs and numerous important parochial bodies. The attendance and its temper were sufficient indication of the new zeal which has been born of the rather unexpected development of the agitation. A note had been received from James Anstie who, together with Sir Francis Richard Sandford had been appointed Commissioners under the 1883 Act. This note proposed a grant of £1,500 a year for the provision of a site and the erection of an 'adequate home'. This was turned into a motion and rapidly passed by the meeting. Commissioner Anstie was a QC and an examiner at the University of London. He was also a Nonconformist. His appointment by Prime Minister Gladstone had been made following pressure from Gladstone's Nonconformist supporters. All the Myddelton Hall speakers argued in favour of calm and a desire to co-operate amicably with all existing bodies. It was also stressed most strenuously that there was need to raise funds sufficient to purchase a central site. The figure proposed was £20,000. The work of other committees had already produced some funds and about £4,000 was in hand. A title for the new committee was chosen – the North London (Central) Technical Institute Committee – and Mr Dewey, the Vestry Clerk, was unanimously elected honorary secretary.[25] The way to north London polytechnics at last was clear and £1,500 was provided by the Commissioners to each of two parishes – Islington, for the erection of the Northern Polytechnic Institute, and St Pancras, for the foundation of the North-Western Polytechnic.

It had required a major campaign that had verged on the edge of violence – and might well have turned into a real battle had not the sense and sensitivity of the people of Islington and St Pancras prevailed. In August 1892, a glorious summer, according to contemporary records, Queen Victoria took a few minutes off her holiday at Osborne House on the Isle of Wight, to approve a scheme relating to the Northern Polytechnic Institute and on the 25 November that same year (cold and wet by all accounts) the Governing Body sat down to its first meeting in the Vestry Hall in Upper Street, Islington.[26] One of the governors was Richard Roberts. He later became the board's chairman. By 'strange coincidence', his son, Mr R.L. Roberts, CBE, MA, followed him as chairman, and by even stranger coincidence R.L.'s son, Mr Brian Roberts, MA, followed in his father's and grandfather's footsteps as chairman – a position he held until 1974. Brian Roberts held the added distinction of having been the first Editor of *The Sunday Telegraph*. So for 82 years, the chair of the Polytechnic's governance was held by the Roberts' Dynasty.

Although the Northern Polytechnic Institute's building with its distinctive clocktower was erected as planned and opened on the Holloway Road in 1896, the North-Western Polytechnic at Kentish Town was beset by one frustrating delay after another, so much so that the trustees grew thoroughly disgruntled and voted to transfer what funds the polytechnic possessed to the Woolwich Polytechnic (later to become Thames Polytechnic and, more recently, the University of Greenwich). However, the Charity Commissioners fortunately vetoed the move as being 'premature'. By 1898 even the Commissioners tired of waiting and decided to reduce the North-Western grant to £500. In the end, the Polytechnic was not opened until 1929 – but then it was a most festive occasion. The annual £500 had accumulated and grown; the buildings were most comfortable and the Prince of Wales drove into Kentish Town accompanied by tumultuous cheering from the local populace, to perform the official opening on the Prince of Wales Road, thus named after his grandfather who had chaired the funding campaign.[27]

By then, the Northern Polytechnic (it had shortened its name by deleting 'Institute' in 1924) was thriving. Indeed, it had long been so. Not only had it always kept to the original mission to educate the 'poorer classes of Islington' but it had added the following to its Charter shortly after its doors had been opened:

> The Northern Polytechnic was established to provide for the inhabitants of Islington and the neighbouring parts of north London, and especially for the Industrial Classes, the means of acquiring a sound General, Scientific, Technical and Commercial Education at small cost, and also to afford facilities for Physical Training and for Recreation.[28]

During the very first session in October 1896, this pledge was fulfilled to the letter and the following courses were delivered.

Mathematics, geometry, machine construction and drawing, steam, applied mathematics, building construction, builders' quantities, fitting and machine shop, metal plate work, carpentry and joinery, plumbing, brickwork, physics and electrical engineering, chemistry, botany, biology, physiology, hygiene, English and civil service, French, German, book-keeping, shorthand, typewriting, dressmaking, millinery, needlework, elocution and gymnastics.

All were held at elementary level and almost all were evening classes. In all, just 1,000 students had enrolled during the first year. They were taught by 34 members of staff. A student:staff ratio of 29.4 : 1! Far from complaining of overcrowded classes, more and more students registered and by 1900, the original 1,000 had doubled. And by 1920, almost a decade before the North-Western finally opened, the number had almost doubled again to a total of 3,800. By 1910 every department offered day classes and after that, the polytechnic offered what should now be called 'mixed mode teaching', including five-year evening degrees – and research on Saturdays.

The Northern trained domestic servants and awarded University of London degrees. There was a Women's Department which ran cookery classes, needlework, dressmaking and the like. Cookery classes developed rapidly into one of the capital's finest Hotel and Catering Departments with a Training Restaurant that many visitors regard as the only five-star restaurant in the Holloway area. The natural sciences, engineering and architectural and building studies were most quickly established and gained a high reputation for excellence, not only in London but throughout the country. The University of London was quick to approve the Polytechnic as an Institution with 'recognized teachers' for its internal degrees in science and this connection continued until the new Polytechnic of North London was designated in 1971 following the amalgamation of the Northern and North-Western Polytechnics, and the awarding of degrees and diplomas came under the jurisdiction of the Council for National Academic Awards (CNAA).

So what part did the University of London play in the early existence of the polytechnics? Until the passage of the University of London Act of 1898, the University's main function was that of an examining body. Under the Statutes of the 1898 Act, it became a teaching institution as well as keeping its other lucrative examining side. Under the Act, certain institutions within a radius of 30 miles of the University's Bloomsbury headquarters, could become recognized schools of the University. And Polytechnic teachers who had the proper academic qualifications could become 'recognized' as Teachers of the University. As such, their courses, if also approved, could count towards internal degrees of the University. The move, as might have been expected, created the first major row with some factions, including the intrepid Quintin Hogg, who was totally opposed to the idea. As he saw it, it moved the poly-technic away from its ethos of hands-on vocational, applied courses, and brought it too close for comfort to the uni-versity, a move he had always resisted. Other factions, including Sidney Webb, the Fabian Socialist chairman of governors of the 1895-founded London School of Economics, were among the first to rush forward in support of such recognition. A new map of London published by the University in 1906 – the first such map published since 1842 – pinpointed not only the 14 schools of the University and its 12 medical schools, but also the 31 institutions having recognized teachers. These included City of London College, the Northampton Institute, the Northern Polytechnic Institute, the Sir John Cass Technical Institute, the South-Western Polytechnic and West Ham Municipal Technical Institute.

The Northern Polytechnic, which leaned more towards the philosophy of Webb than that of Hogg, had been among the first to seek and obtain London University recognition and from the turn of the century and for many years to come – indeed, throughout the life of the old polytechnic, as opposed to the newly designated Polytechnic of North London in 1971 – the University of London approved it as an Institution with Recognised Teachers for the University's internal degrees in science. Prospectuses loudly and proudly proclaimed this 'recognized' status. Thus, for example, the Head of the Engineering and Metal Trades Department was *Herbert A. Garratt, Assoc.M.Inst.C.E., Recognized teacher of the London University.* The Physics and Electrical Engineering Department, had as its Head of Department *Victor A. Mundella, M.A., B.Sc., F.Ph.S.L., A.M.I.E.E. (Recognized Teacher in the University of London)*; and a lecturer called *J. Paley Yorke (Recognized Teacher in the University of London)*.[29] Even the Institute's first Principal, Reginald S Clay B.A., D.Sc. made a point of adding in brackets: *Recognized Teacher in the University of London for Mathematics and Physics.* It will be noted that institutions were still a long way from any form of corporate image. It did not seem to matter whether, within a few pages, one member of staff was simply a 'teacher', with a lower case 't' of the 'London University', while the others were 'Teachers' with a capital 't' of the 'University of London'.

From its very earliest days, the Polytechnic opened its classes to both men and women. And yet, it was felt that 'domestic subjects' should be directed exclusively at women. As early as September 1899, there was a School for Domestic Economy for Girls, open to girls over the age of 14, where 'cookery, dress-cutting and making, needlework and renovation, laundry-work, housewifery and hygiene drill' were taught. The complete course consisted of three terms, five days a week from 9.30 a.m. until 12.30 p.m. and from 2 p.m. until 4 p.m. and the fees: £2.7s.6d per term, with a goodly discount for the entire course – a snip, one might now think, at six guineas (£6.6s.6d) though in today's money it was not so much a snip as a hefty cut to the purse. Then from 1904 Miss Rowland Brown was put in charge of a Training School for Domestic Economy, which aimed to train teachers in these subjects. Here, applicants had to be over 18 and needed to pass an entrance examination in writing, English and composition. According to the Prospectus:

> Domestic Economy Teachers are being employed in increasing numbers by County Councils and other educational bodies in secondary and elementary schools, both in the day-time and in evening classes, so that at the expiration of the training, a student who has passed through her examinations successfully has no difficulty in obtaining appointments at a commencing salary of about £70 to £80 a year in elementary and other schools, in technical institutes or in peripatetic work.'[30]

Training was not exactly cheap, the entire course (two years and one term) costing £55. The cookery course on its own (35 weeks) cost £22; laundrywork (21 weeks) £12 guineas and housewifery ('not including cookery, science and education') cost a mere £13 for 'about 20 weeks'. There was also a Women's Department, a secondary school for girls under its 'Head Mistress' and a staff of nine women. They taught girls over the age of 15 dressmaking, tailoring, needlework, millinery, pillow lace, embroidery, cookery and laundry work. The girls could go on from there to the Training School of Domestic Economy for Teachers in connection with the National Union of Domestic Economy Teachers. Fees ranged from 7s6d a term to around 30s a session (year). Paper and chalk, in the case of tailoring, for drafting, cost a matter of pennies extra. And there was a rider in all cases: '*Domestic Servants are admitted at Half-fees*'. However, the Training School did not last long. In 1910 it was closed because

the LCC thought that three training schools (at Battersea Polytechnic, the National School of Cookery, and the National
Society's School) sufficed for London.

THE GREAT WAR YEARS

After the declaration of War in 1914, the Women's Department
was quick to put its first aid and home nursing classes to good use
and co-operate with the Hornsey Cottage Hospital in providing
relays of 12 nurses. Holiday classes were established in hospital,
convalescent and sick-room cookery, as well as in laundry, hygiene
and ward work. Sewing classes provided garments for hospitals
and special ambulance instruction and sick room classes were
organised.[31]

The Great War brought about some other changes, too. The
Gymnasium, which had been equipped with remarkable foresight
with a miniature rifle range, was put to immediate use and Mr
Nelson, the gymnastics instructor, was instructed to organise a
Volunteer Training Corps. In August 1915, just one year after war
had been declared, two classes were started to train munition
workers. They were restricted to men who were prepared to give
up their usual occupations and take on full-time munitions work.
to begin with the classes met on five evenings a week for six
weeks. Then, in February 1916 the Ministry of Munitions asked
that the course be reduced to four weeks (could this have been
the forerunner of accelerated qualifications?) and so, in order to
maintain high standards, the classes met on Saturday afternoons
as well.[32] Ordinary engineering classes were suspended and the
engineering shop entirely given over to munition classes and gauge
work. The manufacture of 100 fuse bodies was undertaken. In July
1916, the munition classes were suspended in order to increase the
output of gauges. The physics department was also put to good
use to help the war effort. The Ministry asked the polytechnic to
test a large number of delicate optical instruments. In all, 3,230
such instruments were tested.

Inevitably, there were many stories emanating from the war
years. The Northern provided a guard every evening to look out
for the arrival of German Zeppelins over Holloway and provide
assistance at times of Zeppelin raids. Soon the Polytechnic became
the centre where doctors, nurses and ambulance crews congre-
gated in cases of emergency. And Zeppelins there certainly were

and air raids caused the abandonment of evening classes from 27 September until 5 October 1917. Throughout these frightening nights, the Polytechnic became the official shelter for the residents of Islington with more than 1,200 taking refuge in its building regularly.[33] The Volunteer Training Corps continued with its drills and shooting practice and before the 1915 summer was out, the Corps constituted the Second Company of the Islington Battalion. Two members of the Polytechnic staff became its senior officers.

When the war was nearing its end and the full tragic truth started to be revealed of those who would never return and those who would come back maimed in body and soul, the Polytechnic tried desperately to provide at least some remedial help. Many soldiers were returning from the trenches literally deafened as a result of constantly pounding shells and bombs. In March 1918, the Polytechnic provided a room for a class, organized by the LCC, in lip reading. Twenty men came to the class but by the time autumn came, most of them had dropped out, their perseverance gone.

The war had disturbed the progress of the Polytechnic but it had not stopped it. It continued to grow and, although the distinctive London brick frontage on the Holloway Road with its four-sided folly of a clock tower remained modest in size, numerous extensions were added on sites behind the frontage. And as the prestige of its courses grew, so did the institution. Applications from students and their subsequent admissions rose steadily year by year and room had to be made for them.

The Principal's annual report for 1930–1 gives a brief but impressive review of the growth of the Polytechnic from 1902 to 1931. The report began thus:[34]

> When I was appointed in September 1902, the Polytechnic had been open about five years having been established with the other polytechnics under a scheme drawn up by the Charity Commissioners. It was then a comparatively small institution, its total income being about £10,000, derived in about equal amounts from endowment under the scheme, students' fees, a grant from the Technical Education Board, out of the old 'Whisky' money, and a payment from the Science and Art Department, as it was then called, which was based upon the number of student hours. Last year (i.e. 1929–30) the total income was £65,500. The Polytechnic's real work was in the evenings and was of a very varied character,

including engineering, building, science, commercial classes – short-hand, typewriting, languages etc – and women's classes. In the daytime there had been a training school for teachers and a commercial day school. The former was transferred the term I arrived and the latter became a mixed secondary school.[35] A Domestic Economy School for Girls was started in September 1899, which was originally intended to train girls for domestic service and similar work. In September 1916, under Mrs Adcock, its scope was altered and it became more of a secondary school with a domestic bias. This school was closed down in December 1930, to make room for more advanced work in the Women's Department.[36]

About 1913, Mr (later Sir Robert) Blair, the Education Officer of the LCC, in a detailed report advised polytechnics to stop duplicating and triplicating courses. There was, he felt, far too much overlap, with all polytechnics teaching more or less the same things: engineering, building, science, languages and so on. The Blair Report said each polytechnic should concentrate on a few special branches. The Northern gave up its engineering courses as a result of this advice. In the same year, the LCC set up Junior Trade Scholarships and the Northern founded the Junior Building Trades School to which an annual 25 scholarships were awarded. It became the best means of entering the building trade.

The Northern Polytechnic's governors arranged for the Principal to visit the 'Continent' in 1912. He went to France, Germany and Switzerland and wrote the following some years later:

We had at this time been hearing a great deal in the Daily Press of the great technical schools which had been set up in Germany, especially at Charlottenburg, and it was suggested that technical education in England was greatly inferior. I was, however, very much encouraged by my visit for, although the numbers attending German schools were much greater, I considered that the education itself was inferior, especially in engineering and building. The German students were given too much instruction and had little scope for using their own intelligence and initiative. My visit had one very important outcome. At Cologne I found a class in which instruction was being given in acetylene welding, and on my return I interviewed the heads of the British Oxygen Company, and the British Acetylene Association and persuaded them to set up a similar school at this Polytechnic. In the following year classes were also established at other centres with the result that when the War broke out and the process was required in the construction of aeroplanes, there was a large nucleus of skilled workers available.

As work of the polytechnic expanded, buildings needed to be enlarged. in 1902, there had been the front block with its clock tower, the Great Hall (later theatre; today The Rocket), a one floor building under the Women's classrooms and the block beyond that for the engineering and rubber workshops. The new building went up with a £15,000 grant from the ever-generous City Parochial Foundation, which thereafter provided enough each year to repay both capital and interest until the 'loan' was fully repaid in 1930.[37]

Once London had become well provided with polytechnics, their example spread rapidly throughout the country. And when the Robbins Report was published in 1963, they were to receive further promotion. Lord Robbins warned Sir Edward Boyle, the Conservative Education Minister of the day, that unless places were made available for 390,000 students in full-time higher education by 1973–4 and for 560,000 by 1980–1, the country would face an educational crisis of mammoth proportions.

The expansion Robbins wanted to see did not materialize fully but the principle enshrined in his committee's report – closer collaboration between higher education and industry, the expansion of universities and polytechnics to cope with growing demands from school leavers and giving colleges of advanced technology (CATS)[38] university status – remained.

Three years later, in 1966, Labour Education Secretary Anthony Crosland published a White Paper which gave life to a new breed of polytechnic. Existing technical colleges already providing courses to degree level were upgraded to Polytechnic status. They included the London polytechnics. In all, 30 polytechnics were thus born but it took three more years for another Labout Education Secretary, Edward Short, to designate the first of the 30. These became known as the New Polytechnics, just as they were to become the New Universities a further 20 years on.

The 'Polys' were an instant success, even though some of them were subjected to varying degrees of student unrest. But that was a phenomenon universally shared by higher education campuses at home and abroad during the late 1960s and early 1970s.

Polytechnics provided the exact formula outlined by Robbins. They concentrated on the vocational and gave their students the right amount of industrial, commercial and professional hands-on experience that had, until then, only been evident in countries like West Germany (where further and higher education were among the major ingredients responsible for that country's 'economic miracle'). Sandwich courses, combining academic lectures, seminars and laboratory work with direct (and paid) work experience were perfected in the polytechnics; modular courses – where students may pick 'n' mix from a lengthy menu of subjects – were widely adopted by the polytechnics.

Their popularity was reflected by the number of applications received. These came not only from school leavers but also from more mature students, particularly those who had missed out on higher education the first time round, or who were changing their professional direction or (and this applied particularly to women) who were returning to the world of work after several years' absence and who wanted to gain, improve or update their qualifications.

QUINTON HOGG AND THE NEW UNIVERSITIES

The total number of students attending polytechnics for degree and advanced non-degree courses soared from about 40,000 in 1970 when there were just eight polytechnics, to nearly 400,000 in 1991 when there were 34 such institutions in England and Wales and five in Scotland. And yet, despite their unquestionable success, something was amiss. Polytechnics were considered by a large proportion of parents as the Secondary Modern schools of higher education. They were 'not quite the same' as *the universities* (HE's 'grammar schools'). Teachers, particularly those in charge of careers education, were quicker to shed this kind snobbery and recognize the value of polytechnic degrees and other qualifications. Unfortunately, many employers took longer and, given the choice, opted for the university gradyuate even with a class of degree inferior to one held by a polytechnic graduate. The ('new') polytechnics had to wait until May 1991 when Prime Minister John Major declared: 'The Polytechnics have come of age' – and marked their 21st birthday by launching the White Paper that would in effect abolish once and for all the artificial distinction between universities and polytechnics and allow the latter to call themselves universities if they wished. And, regardless of title, they could for the first time award their own degrees instead of those of the Council for National Academic Awards.[39] The polytechnics' umbrella body, the Committee of Directors of Polytechnics, was to 'converge' with the universities' group – the Committee of Vice-Chancellors and Principals of the UK. The CVCP had been in existence for some 85 years. A group of management consultants was commissioned to advise on what changes in structure and organization would be required to accommodate and satisfy both groups. This advice was considered by members of the CDP and CVCP at their annual conferences and a date for convergence was tentatively fixed for April 1 1993. No such convergence took place. Instead, the CVCP enacted a straight takeover of the new sector. Alongside the 'old' and 'older' universities, the 'new' or 'modern' universities brought the national total to 115. London alone had 11 – and that does not count all the colleges – more than 40 – that form part of the giant University of London.

The old Regents Street Poly, which had replaced Quintin Hogg's Ragged School and Evening Institute well over a century before, had become the Polytechnic of Central London. Now it was the University of Westminster.[40] Lord Hailsham at that Thanksgiving and Rededication service at Westminster Abbey concluded his reading from his grandfather's letter with these words:

> We read that Christ 'taught the people many things', so he would not have neglected education; he had 'compassion for the leper', so he would have approved of our hospitals; he would, in fact, show that nothing that concerned his human brethren was a matter of unconcern to him; open spaces for people, football pitches for the young men, proper housing, free education, spiritual truth, one and all would find him a strenuous advocate.[41]

The question Lord Hailsham might have asked but perhaps did not dare to formulate: would his grandfather have been satisfied with this outcome? Quintin Hogg's dream was to bring education to the poorer classes. His Ragged School salvaged urchins from the backstreets of south London and provided them with the much-needed Three Rs. His Regent Street Poly and Evening Institute gave vocational education to generations of adults. It was a Christianity-based charitable system. The 'new' or 'modern' universities that London's polytechnics became in 1992–93 are anything but Christianity-based; as for providing free education, many of their students now suffer real hardship and are forced to beg and borrow enough to see them through their courses. Graduates face debts even before they can hope to start earning a working wage.

Above all, Quinton Hogg might have been shocked at the way in which some of his beloved polytechnics have been 'translated' from the highly reputable institutions specializing in bringing vocational scholarship to working-class men and women, to second-league universities. This had not been part of his dream.

When Leicester Polytechnic was designated a University along with all the other polytechnics, it adopted the title De Montfort University and sent huge clusters of balloons spiralling through the air. Each balloon carried the slogan: 'Only the name has changed!' One must now question whether each of the country's 38 polytechnics has upheld the same claim or whether some, if not all, are perhaps aping Oxbridge. This was certainly not what Quintin Hogg had intended.

CHAPTER NINE

Teacher training in London

Richard Aldrich

INTRODUCTION

It is difficult to do justice to the topic of teacher training in London during the nineteenth century in anything less than a volume, possibly a series of volumes. For this is a vast and disparate subject, characterized by a multiplicity of individual and institutional initiatives and experiences. These ranged from the monitorial school founded in 1798 in Borough Road, Southwark by a youthful Joseph Lancaster, through the numerous pupil teachers who provided so much of the teaching force in elementary schools in the second half of the nineteenth century, to the London Day Training College, established in 1902 following a concerted campaign waged by Sidney Webb, Sophie Bryant and others, and drawing upon the substantial resources and support of the London County Council and the University of London.

This chapter, therefore, can be no more than an introduction to the subject. Insofar as the title of this volume denotes a concern for 'establishment', emphasis will be placed upon the setting up of institutions of teacher training, rather than upon their subsequent development and the experiences of those who taught and studied within them, or upon more informal means of preparing teachers. This narrowing of focus, however, is complemented by a broad interpretation of the term 'higher education'. For very little of the teacher training that took place in London during the nineteenth century could be construed as higher education, either by the criteria of the times or by those of today. Such an approach may be justified on two grounds. The first is that although there were undeniable hierarchies in nineteenth-century education, this was a period of great development and change. For example, the University of London, as founded by royal charter in 1836, has been described as being 'in modern terms, an amalgam of an Open University and a Council for National Academic Awards'.[1] Contemporaries were not so kind, one Oxford critic declaring that 'This is a Government Education Board, not a University. Universities are bodies possessed of fixed privileges and rights, and of an independent internal government.'[2] A second justification is that although some institutions of teacher training no longer exist in any recognizable shape or form, others, including Borough Road itself, have survived to become integral parts of the map of higher education in London of the late twentieth century.

One further preliminary point should be made. In one sphere, teacher training (or teacher preparation) was already an integral part of higher education. As has been argued elsewhere, 'For much of English history the accepted method of preparation for holding the post of teacher or master in a grammar or public school, many private establishments, and indeed in the university itself, was a master's degree from the universities of Oxford or Cambridge'.[3] During the nineteenth century, many graduates from the University of London similarly proceeded to teaching posts, without any further qualification.

This chapter is divided into four parts. The first provides an overview of the foundation of the several institutions; the second, an examination of other dimensions of teacher training, including initiatives which emanated from central government. The third explores the university connection which developed from the later nineteenth century, the fourth the interventions of the London County Council. Finally some conclusions are drawn. Such divisions are not absolute and there is some overlap between the sections, as indeed with other chapters in the volume.

FOUNDATIONS

The modern origins of teacher training in England, and certainly in London, are generally traced to the work of the two founders of the monitorial system, Joseph Lancaster and Andrew Bell. The precise origins of this system are surrounded by uncertainties and controversy, principally because Lancaster and Bell, and their various supporters, proclaimed the superiority and prior establishment of their particular versions of the system. What is certain, however, is that by the first decade of the nineteenth century London was home to two institutions one of whose purposes was to instruct prospective or practising teachers in the operation of the monitorial system of instruction. The monitorial system was a pedagogical device whereby large numbers of children might be taught by monitors, senior pupils, all under the control of a single teacher. Naturally the monitors had to be instructed not only in the information they were to convey, but also in the methods by which they were to convey it.

By 1805, some £400 had been raised to enable Joseph Lancaster to attach a training department to his school, founded in 1798 in Borough Road, Southwark. Apprenticeship was still the traditional method of learning a craft, and in the training department senior monitors were apprenticed to Lancaster 'who undertook to board, clothe and train them as schoolmasters after his own system'.[4] Recruits to the training school, however, soon included not only senior monitors, but also older students who were attracted to the establishment in Borough Road both from other parts of the country and from overseas. Lancaster, who was guilty of financial mismanagement and other faults besides, was to fall out with the two committees established to support him, the Royal Lancasterian Institution and its successor from 1814 the British and Foreign School Society. Nevertheless, Borough Road continued to provide training for teachers and monitors on a non-denominational basis. It was unusual at this time in catering for males and females. Although it is unclear when the first female students arrived, the Annual Report of the British and Foreign School Society for 1814 declared that the institution at Borough Road would

> support and train up young persons of both sexes for supplying properly instructed Teachers to the inhabitants of such places in the British dominions, at home and abroad, as shall be desirous of establishing schools on the British system. It shall instruct all persons, whether natives or foreigners, who may be sent from time to time, for the purpose of being qualified as Teachers in this or any other country.[5]

Amongst the earliest trainees at Borough Road were Thomas Hood and John Pickton, who both subsequently returned there to become trainers of teachers themselves. Another pioneer was Ann Springman, both a monitor and apprentice teacher at Borough Road, who taught in schools in Birmingham and Chichester before returning to Southwark to take charge of the girls' school and female training institution in Martin Street. Springman, who married another of the early apprentices, Kenneth Macrae, was in charge of the women's department until its move to Stockwell in 1861.[6] Such in-breeding was to continue. The first principal of Borough Road College, James Cornwell, was a former student, as were his successors, Joshua Fitch and J.C. Curtis. Not until 1888 was an 'outsider', P.A. Barnett, appointed. Barnett, who was barely 30 when he became principal, boasted a first class degree in Greats from Oxford and had been Professor of English Literature at Firth College, Sheffield.[7]

The Anglican clergyman, Andrew Bell, whose own version of the monitorial system had been devised while he was superintendent of the Madras Male Orphan Asylum in India, was rector of Swanage in Dorset from 1801. His aim, of promoting Church of England schools organized on the 'Madras' plan, received substantial support from the National Society for the Promotion of the Poor in the Principles of the Established Church, founded in 1811. In the following year the Society opened a training establishment for schoolmasters at Baldwin's Gardens, off the Gray's Inn Road. Twenty years later it was relocated in Westminster.

Four characteristics of Borough Road and Baldwin's Gardens may be noted here. The first is that these institutions consisted essentially of schools to which a training department was attached. At Borough Road students lived on the site, while at Baldwin's Gardens they were boarded out. The second, that both schools and training were of an elementary nature. The monitorial system in which the teachers were drilled was specifically designed for the cheap mass instruction of the children of the poor. Third, the period of training was short, a matter of weeks, three months at the outside. The final point is that the whole process was one of training, rather than of education. Those who came to the establishments at Borough Road and Baldwin's Gardens were instructed in the craft of teaching. This was achieved by a combined process of studying manuals of method, and by working as monitors and teachers in the school.

In 1836 a quite different institution of teacher training was established in London. This was the college founded by the Home and Colonial Infant School Society in Holborn. The Society's purpose was to promote infant schools based upon the principles of Johann Pestalozzi, the Swiss educationist who had devoted his life to the schooling of the poor, and whose school at Yverdun had attracted considerable international attention. Elizabeth Mayo, one of the Society's chief promoters, wrote manuals on Pestalozzian methodology for use in the college. From the following year, the Home and Colonial Infant School Society's institution comprised a model school, residential hostels, and a 12 week course (extended to 15 weeks in 1838). Instruction was provided in a range of subjects – from natural history to elementary geography. The principles of teaching were based upon those of Pestalozzi and emerging theories of infant instruction, and by 1843 the college was training 100 infant teachers a year.[8] By 1846 the Home and Colonial Infant School Society had also added a second department for the training of governesses.

In 1839 there were three recognizable training colleges for teachers in England; by the middle of the next decade there were more than 20. The majority of these were diocesan colleges associated with the Anglican church in such cathedral towns as Canterbury, Durham and Winchester. Borough Road continued to flourish, and new buildings were opened by Lord John Russell in 1842. When, in 1890, Borough Road College was relocated at Isleworth, these buildings were acquired for a sum of £20,000 for the Borough Polytechnic Institute, formally opened by Lord Rosebery in October 1892.

Three important London foundations from this period were those of Battersea, and two National Society colleges in Chelsea: St. Mark's and Whitelands, Battersea and St. Mark's, which had 71 and 53 students respectively in 1845, and amalgamated in 1923 to form the College of St. Mark and St. John, were for men. Whitelands, with 54 students in 1845, was founded for the purpose of producing a '*superior* type of parochial school mistress'.[9]

Battersea, a Normal School (to use the terminology of the day) originally established by James Kay-Shuttleworth as a private institution, opened its doors in February 1840. Its first students, eight pupil teachers from the Poor Law schools training establishment at Norwood, who were apprenticed for seven years, were soon joined by older students who were admitted for one year courses. Life for the Battersea students was an unceasing round of activity, from 5.30 in the morning until 9.20 at night. Leisure time and holidays were unknown. In addition to their studies, the young men cleaned the college premises, tilled the gardens and looked after the livestock, for on financial grounds it was important that Battersea should be as self-supporting as possible. Kay-Shuttleworth believed that the main purpose of a normal school was 'the formation of the character of the schoolmaster'.[10] He argued that

> By this laborious and frugal life, economy of management is reconciled with efficiency both of the moral and intellectual training of the School, and the master goes forth into the world humble, industrious and instructed.[11]

In 1843 significant changes occurred at Battersea. In future no students would be admitted below the age of 18, while the maximum length of a course would be extended to two years. Financial and other pressures induced Kay-Shuttleworth to hand control over to the National Society.

In 1933, in his standard work on the training of teachers in England and Wales in the nineteenth century, R.W. Rich argued that 'Kay-Shuttleworth's experiment at Battersea is the most significant event in the history of the development of the English training college, for it was the type to which all subsequently founded training colleges conformed until the advent of the Day Training College.'[12] Rich's emphasis upon the importance of the residential element at Battersea has been questioned by Dent, who points out that 'Battersea was neither the first nor the only residential training college during the years 1840–43'.[13] The importance of Battersea, however, was not simply that of residence, but of ethos. At Battersea, residence and a minutely regulated corporate existence were designed to instill into prospective teachers a missionary spirit of lifelong service in schools for the poor. The further significance of Battersea was that it represented a personal experiment and commitment by a man who was the first Secretary of the Committee of Council on Education from 1839 until 1849, and whose name was closely associated with the introduction of an official pupil-teacher scheme from 1846. The pupil-teacher system, whereby elementary school pupils were apprenticed in their schools for five years before proceeding to training college at age 18, continued to emphasize the 'elementary' (as opposed to 'secondary' or 'higher') dimensions of nineteenth-century teacher training.

St. Mark's College, Chelsea was the main exception to this

emphasis. Its first principal, Derwent Coleridge, second son of the poet and philosopher, was a graduate of St. John's College, Cambridge. Ordained in 1825, he served as master of the grammar school at Helston, Cornwall from 1827 until his appointment to St. Mark's in 1841. Coleridge, who was declared by Dean Stanley to be the most accomplished linguist of his day, was fluent not only in classical and modern European languages, but also in such esoteric tongues as Hawaiian and Zulu. The three-year course at St. Mark's reflected Coleridge's belief in the importance of Latin as an instrument of education, and in the central role of the College chapel, which resounded to sung services. Many elements of the traditional 'Battersea' ethos were to be found at St. Mark's – the closely regulated and lengthy day, the sense of missionary zeal. But they were leavened by Coleridge's commitment to a literary and classical curriculum, and by his concern that the students should not be artificially limited. He found inspiration not in the rigorous training schools of Switzerland, but in the universities of Cambridge and Oxford. St. Mark's was to be 'an adapted copy, *mutatis mutandis*, of the elder educational institutions of the country . . . it must be attractive both to the student and to his friends. It must first attract, then elevate, refine, ennoble.'[14] Coleridge and St. Mark's were subject to numerous criticisms – that students were over-educated in academic subjects but insufficiently trained in the science and art of teaching, that they proceeded to ordination or to posts in middle-class schools, that 'popish' practices took place in the College chapel, that government money was being used for purposes for which it was not intended. Some of these criticisms were not without foundation. Many of those who were trained at St. Mark's did not live out their lives as elementary schoolteachers. Indeed, four of the first 10 students from 1841 were subsequently ordained. In 1864 Coleridge, who was appointed prebendary of St. Paul's Cathedral in 1846, himself left St. Mark's to become rector of Hanwell. By that date the alternative vision offered by St. Mark's had been overborne by policies emanating from central government.[15]

The second half of the nineteenth century saw the establishment of further training colleges under denominational control. In general, these foundations reflected the victory of the Battersea model of a training college over that of St. Mark's. Anglican foundations included St. Katharine's College at Tottenham in

1878, and St. Gabriel's in Camberwell in 1899. St. Katharine's was the product of a joint venture by the National Society and the Society for Promoting Christian Knowledge, and Edwin Hobson, then vice-principal at St. John's, Battersea, was appointed principal at an annual salary of £300 plus a house.[16] Roman Catholic colleges were represented by St. Mary's, which began at Brook Green, Hammersmith in 1850, and a college founded in 1874 in a wing of the Convent of the Sacred Heart at Roehampton, which experienced a peripatetic existence in Wandsworth and Kensington (where it was known as St. Charles) before returning to Roehampton as Digby Stuart College. The Methodists sited their college in Westminster, with Southlands, a further college for women established in Battersea in 1872.

The Congregational College of Homerton is of particular interest in respect of its former associations with higher education. Its origins lay in the academies founded or supported by the Congregational Fund Board in order to provide a supply of educated ministers. These included the Homerton Academy in east London, which dated from 1768. In 1823, with the completion of new buildings, the name was changed to Homerton College, while in 1840 it was designated as one of the 'Institutions, approved by the Secretary of State, whose students, having matriculated, could become candidates for degrees in Arts and Laws of the University of London.'[17] In 1851 the theological work of Homerton was transferred via an amalgamation with Highbury College to New College in the Finchley Road.

The Congregational Board of Education was established in 1844. Initial attempts to train teachers relied upon the simple expedient of sending students to Borough Road, but dissatisfaction with the training provided there, and a determination to adhere strictly to the voluntary principle (Borough Road was in receipt of government grants) led to a decision to establish separate facilities. Training for women began in Rotherhithe in 1846, and for men in Liverpool Street in 1848. In 1850, Samuel Morley, the wealthy textile manufacturer who was treasurer both of the governing body of Homerton College and of the Congregational Board of Education, secured the transfer of the College premises to the Board. The new Homerton College, dedicated to the education and training of teachers to serve in Congregational schools, and with William Unwin as its first principal, opened in

March 1852. It catered for male and female students, though elaborate rules and devices were employed to keep them apart. Since neither Congregational schools nor the college received government aid, they were not subject to central regulations, and more progressive ideas might flourish. For example, between 1854 and 1869 Homerton appointed, 'six successive tutors from Switzerland, "for the purpose of getting a more complete knowledge of the system pursued there, to aid in introducing the plans employed by Pestalozzi"'.[18] In 1868, however, the Congregational Board of Education accepted government aid for the College, and it began to conform more closely to the training college norm. Between 1870 and 1895 20 of the 39 appointments to the College staff were made from former students.[19] In 1893 Homerton College moved to Cambridge where it occupied the premises of the former Cavendish College. Three years later the decision was taken to admit only females. Nevertheless, in the early years of the twentieth century Homerton, with its 200 students, was the largest training college in England.

In 1861 the female students from Borough Road College were transferred to a new college (again opened by Lord John Russell) some one and a half miles to the south at Stockwell, while in 1890 Borough Road College itself was relocated at Isleworth. There, in the spacious accommodation and grounds of Spring Grove, and under the energetic leadership of the youthful Bartlett, a metamorphosis began. From 1890 the Education Department allowed students in residential colleges, as well as those in the new day training institutions, to take university examinations, including those for London matriculation, intermediate and general degree. By 1893 more than a third of the Borough Road students were preparing for university examinations. Another development from this period, initiated by Bartlett and continued under his successor from 1893, H.L. Withers, was an emphasis upon sport and physical fitness. This emphasis reflected not simply a concern for the health of elementary school children and their teachers, but also that celebration of the games cult and of manliness which was so prominent in the boys' public schools and ancient universities of the day.[20] All students were required to participate, for belief in the moral (even religious) as well as the physical, value of sporting endeavour was almost universal. From 1914, the sporting prowess honed at Isleworth was tested on a sterner field, and no fewer than 111 former students, students and staff of Borough Road College lost their lives in the First World War.[21]

Although the London School Board, in common with other boards established under the Elementary Education Act of 1870, was not empowered to create teacher training colleges, three initiatives from the last 30 years of the century can be noted. These three colleges were disparate in some senses – one being concerned with training for secondary age pupils, another with a particular area of the curriculum, the third with young children. But all three owed their foundation to the efforts of women, rather than of men, and none was under religious control.

The first was Maria Grey (for the first 10 years Bishopsgate) College, begun in 1878 by the Teachers' Training and Registration Society, a group associated with the Girls' Public Day School Company, and committed to the education and training of women for work in girls' secondary schools. Although for the first two years the college had to issue its own certificates, in 1880 the Senate of Cambridge University approved the appointment of a Teachers' Training Syndicate with the authority to arrange courses of lectures and to conduct examinations for certificates in the theory of education and in practical teaching. The examination of June 1880 was a triumph for the Bishopsgate students:

> Out of 27 successful candidates 24 were from Bishopsgate and 17 of these (15 present and 2 former students) passed in both parts of the examination. Only the Bishopsgate students, in fact, qualified for the practical efficiency certificate.[22]

The second was the Bergman-Österberg Physical Training College, founded in 1885 in Broadhurst Gardens, Hampstead by the Swedish-born Martina Bergman-Österberg. In 1888, Bergman-Österberg gave up her post of Lady Superintendent of physical exercise in girls' and infants' schools for the London School Board, to devote herself to the work of the College, and to introducing her courses on Swedish gymnastics to other colleges such as Whitelands and Maria Grey. The regime at Hampstead was not for the faint hearted; each day began with a cold bath. Anatomy, physiology, hygiene, physiotherapy, gymnastics, fencing, swimming, cricket, tennis and dancing featured in the curriculum. By 1895 the College had outgrown its original home and was transferred to more spacious premises and surroundings at Dartford in Kent. Cycling now became a further activity, while netball was developed from American basketball, introduced during the Hampstead era, with the first set of rules printed in 1901. Another invention was the 'gym slip', designed in 1897 by a student and subsequent member of staff, Mary Tait.[23]

The third college was the Froebel Educational Institute, begun in 1892 on the initiative of Mrs Salis Schwabe. The teachings of Friedrich Froebel, who had worked under Pestalozzi at Yverdun, and opened his first kindergarten at Keilhau in 1837, had been known in England for many years. Froebel's 'gifts' and 'occupations', were not simply playthings for developing dexterity in young children, but representations of the child's growing understanding of the world. There was a kindergarten in Bloomsbury from 1851, and a variety of groups and institutions, including the Home and Colonial Infant School Society and the Girls' Public Day School Company, established kindergartens and began to address the issue of training teachers for them. The Froebel Society for the Promotion of the Kindergarten System was founded in 1875, and four years later the London Froebel Kindergarten Society opened a training school and college. The Froebel Educational Institute was based in West Kensington, but the original scheme for a training college with model kindergartens and other schools, both fee-paying and free, had to be modified. By 1894 the training college was in existence; the fee-paying establishments were under construction, but the free schools had been postponed.[24]

The colleges of Maria Grey, Bergman-Österberg and the Froebel Institute may be identified with two important and interrelated developments of the last decades of the nineteenth century. The first was the increasing role of women in teaching. At the beginning of the nineteenth century the model teacher, even in an infant school, was a male. By 1900, female teachers were in the majority in all types of infant and elementary schools. Girls' secondary schooling, moreover, was beginning to emerge from the private into the public sphere, a movement soon to be spurred on by the founding of 'county' secondary schools under the provisions of the Education Act of 1902. In consequence it was necessary to train more women teachers.

The second development reflected an increased concern for

specialization in the secular curriculum, and for secular control. Maria Grey and Bergman-Österberg colleges and the Froebel Institute were not named after saints of the Christian church. They bore the names of three nineteenth-century educational pioneers: one English, one Swedish and one German. Their particular concerns, moreover, reflected the development of curriculum and age-phase specialisms. Not that development of the secular curriculum was necessarily antithetical to religious control. Berridge House, founded with a bequest from Richard Berridge for the purposes of promoting 'technical and sanitary education', was placed under the direction of the National Society. Indeed this National Society's Training College for Domestic Subjects began in 1893 as a cookery school in the disused brew house of Lambeth Palace. Training and charitable work were combined. One-year courses were provided in the teaching of cookery and other domestic subjects. At the same time thousands of free or penny dinners were provided to the poor of Lambeth. In 1964 Berridge House, which by that date was located in Hampstead, was amalgamated with St. Katharine's, Tottenham, to form the College of All Saints.[25]

OTHER DIMENSIONS

During the nineteenth century, although teacher training in London took place in colleges controlled by religious bodies and by other voluntary associations, other influences were at work. This section focuses upon three of the 'other dimensions': as represented by the role of central government, the Department of Science and Art and the particular problems of providing teachers for technical subjects, and the College of Preceptors.

Central government played a significant role in teacher training. This role was exercised in various ways. For example, in 1839 the Whig government of Lord Melbourne tried, unsuccessfully, to establish a State Normal School for the training of teachers in elementary schools. The failure of this plan was one factor which, in the 1840s, induced subsequent governments to establish and develop a pupil-teacher scheme. During their five years of apprenticeship pupil-teachers would receive payment from the Committee of Council, while further sums would be paid to those teachers to whom their training was entrusted. On the basis of performance in an annual examination, Queen's Scholarships would be awarded to some pupil-teachers, who might thus be supported at public expense while at training college. Successful completion of a pupil-teacher apprenticeship gave entitlement both to enter the Queen's scholarship examination and to teach in a grant aided elementary school, albeit as an uncertificated teacher. Successful completion of a training college course was rewarded not only by a government teaching certificate, but also by an entitlement to supplementation of salary. Training colleges were eligible for government grants in respect of all their students.

Clearly this package of reforms, whose operation was scrupulously monitored by Her Majesty's Inspectors, produced a system of training and of teaching superior to that which existed under the monitorial system. Whether these reforms should be interpreted as a significant step towards making teacher training part of higher education, or whether such government control, in itself, precluded teacher training from becoming part of higher education, is less certain. What is evident, is that from 1854 central government intervention in respect of the training college syllabus placed increasing emphasis upon elementary subjects, a process confirmed under the terms of the Revised Code of 1862. This Code introduced a system of 'payment by results' into schools, with severe consequences for the system of grants to pupil-teachers, students, teachers and colleges. Numbers of pupil-teachers and college students rapidly declined, and not until the Elementary Education Act of 1870 was the situation restored. Over the next decade, the numbers of pupil-teachers in England and Wales more than doubled, from 14,612 to 32,128, while certificated teachers nearly trebled, from 12,467 to 31,422.[26]

By 1874, however, the London School Board was becoming increasingly concerned about the deficiencies of pupil-teachers, both in respect of their role as teachers and of their training. After considerable arguments between the Board and the Education Department, which centred on the Department's insistence that pupil-teachers should be instructed by the headteacher in whose school they were apprenticed and worked, some modifications were secured. These allowed the establishment of pupil-teacher centres, some 11 by 1887, instructing 1636 pupil-teachers.[27]

The members of the Cross Commission, appointed in 1886 to inquire into elementary education, gave general approval to the pupil-teacher centres, whose products soon came to dominate the examinations for the Queen's Scholarships. They were more divided, however, on the extent to which teacher training might become a function of universities. The majority adhered to the existing system, with its emphases upon residence and the formation of character. Nevertheless, following the Commission's report in 1888, the Education Department drew up regulations under which day training colleges, unconnected with any denomination but attached to universities or university colleges, might be established. The effect of this decision will be considered in the next section.

The drawbacks of so much central government intervention in the training and certification of teachers, and the need for a university connection, were widely remarked upon during the nineteenth century. For example, in 1861 in an address to the United Association of Schoolmasters of Great Britain, Harry Chester, former Assistant Secretary to the Committee of the Privy Council on Education, asked

> Why should there not be, say, a University of South Kensington? All training colleges might be incorporated colleges of the University, which would grant degrees and licences to teach. Such institutions as the Royal Academy of Art, the Royal Academy of Music, the School of Mines, the College of Preceptors, and Schools of Science and Art might also be incorporated into the University.[28]

Chester's reference to a University of South Kensington, much canvassed as the best central site for the University of London, leads to a consideration of the training of teachers in scientific and technical subjects, particularly under the auspices of the Department of Science and Art. Throughout the nineteenth century little attention was paid in training colleges to practical and technical subjects, although Chester College proved to be an honourable exception. In the 1840s some training of teachers in practical art began at the Central School of Design at Somerset House and continued following the move to Marlborough House. By the 1850s it was frequently referred to as the 'National Art Training School'. In 1853 the schools of design came under the aegis of the newly-established Department of Science and Art. The Department operated a system of payment on results according to the performance of students in examinations. Examinations were also provided for teachers. In 1881 a Normal School of Science, with

Thomas Huxley as Dean, was established at South Kensington, principally 'to train teachers of science classes'.[29] Students, who normally undertook a three years' course, received free instruction and maintenance grants. From 1884 the training of technical teachers also took place at South Kensington, under the auspices of the City and Guilds of London Institute. In a report of 1878 the Institute had resolved that its Central Institution would 'supply competent Teachers for the Local Trade Schools'.[30]

Nevertheless, throughout the nineteenth century, in a society in which the former systems of apprenticeship had become largely outmoded, the shortage of teachers for scientific, technical and trade subjects remained acute. This shortage hindered the establishment of trade schools of the type which were being developed in some other European countries. In commenting on the difficulty of finding suitable teachers for trade classes in polytechnics, the Technical Education Board of the London County Council declared in its report for 1902–3:

> Ten years ago it was extremely difficult to start such instruction owing to ... above all, the extreme difficulty of obtaining teachers who (i) had a practical knowledge of the trades ... (ii) understood the scientific ... principles involved ... (iii) possessed the ability to teach.[31]

One body from within the teaching profession which sought to supply good teachers for all schools was the College of Preceptors, initially an association of teachers of schools for the middle classes, founded in 1846 and granted a Royal Charter in 1849. In January 1847, the College began its series of examinations for teachers, and throughout the century urged upon central government the need for a training college for teachers for middle-class schools and for the registration of teachers. In 1873, the College appointed Joseph Payne, a former founder and headmaster of two private schools, and Vice-President both of the College of Preceptors and of the Scholastic Registration Association, to be its Professor of Education, the first such appointment in Britain. Payne's lecture courses, first delivered in that year, comprised the Science of Education, the Art of Education and the History of Education. They were subsequently published, together with others of his lectures and writings, in two volumes edited by his second son, Joseph Frank Payne. Joseph Payne, who chaired the Committee of the Women's Education Union, and served on the Council of the Girls' Public Day School Company and the Committee of the Froebel Society, also chaired the foundation meeting of the Society for the Development of the Science of Education. In so doing he brought together many of the elements which were to link the worlds of teacher training and of higher education. The great majority of those who attended his classes were prospective or practising female teachers in secondary (middle-class) schools for girls. Indeed, Payne worked closely with such leading female educators as Frances Buss and Beata Doreck, who were prime movers in the establishment of the Professorship. Payne's students included Sophie Bryant, who in 1895 succeeded Frances Buss as headmistress of the North London Collegiate School, and served on the Bryce Commission on Secondary Education and on the Senate of the University of London. In 1873 Payne's pamphlet on *The Importance of the Training of the Teacher* was published as the fourth in a series produced under the auspices of the Women's Education Union. After his death in 1876, Frances Buss and Maria Grey established a Joseph Payne Memorial Prize which was awarded annually to the most successful student at the Maria Grey Training College.[32]

THE UNIVERSITY CONNECTION

William Taylor has summarized some of the early connections of the University of London with the subject of education. In the 1830s these included a course of lectures on education given at Gower Street by the Revd James Bryce, Principal of the Belfast Academy, and an unsuccessful proposal by the London philanthropist, J.H. Morgan, to establish and endow a chair in the subject. In 1881, following a succession of recommendations from the College of Preceptors, Frances Buss and Joshua Fitch, that the University should establish a degree in education so that teaching might rank on a par with other professions, the University of London instituted an examination in the 'Theory and Practice of Teaching' which would lead to the award of a Teachers' Diploma.[33]

From the 1890s clear connections between teacher training and the world of higher education were established with the advent of the day training colleges. The government's original intention was that the new colleges should supplement existing provision by providing two-year courses for day students intending to teach in elementary schools. Residential facilities, however, soon developed, while three- (from 1911 four-) year programmes were constructed for those wishing to pursue concurrent or consecutive courses for a degree and a teaching certificate. One-year programmes were supplied for those who already held advanced qualifications. By 1902 there were some 20 institutions in England and Wales of university rank, providing more than a quarter of the 5,000 students then in training. Notwithstanding the university connection, however, the vast majority of these students were prepared for, and destined to teach in, elementary rather than secondary schools.

In 1890, King's College was the first in London to establish a day training department, and in October of that year some 25 Queen's Scholars, former pupil-teachers, began a two year course. John William Adamson, himself a former pupil-teacher who had studied at Cheltenham Training College and as an evening student at King's, was appointed head of the training department and 'normal master'. His annual salary was £180 per annum. In 1900, a conference representing University, King's and Bedford Colleges and the College of Preceptors, recommended to the commissioners making new statutes for the University of London, that a new board of studies and a one-year postgraduate course of training should be introduced. In that year Adamson was duly appointed secretary to the newly established University Board of Studies in Pedagogy, and in 1901 to a lectureship in education.[34] There were many early difficulties. As Adamson, himself acknowledged, 'The ablest and best-equipped students continued to go to the old-established residential training colleges of good repute'.[35] In 1894 the day training facility established two years earlier at University College was closed, and its two remaining students transferred to King's. At King's, proposals of 1892 for the addition of a group of 50 female students, and of 1895 for the training of teachers for secondary schools, both came to nothing.[36]

Both King's and University College departments were for men; that established at Bedford College in 1891 was for women. Bedford College had been founded in 1849 in Bedford Square by the wealthy Unitarian widow, Elisabeth Jesser Reid. From 1878 it concentrated upon preparing women for degree examinations of the University of London. The Bedford Training Department, which began with five students, reaching a peak of some 60 in 1914–15, survived until 1922.[37]

In contrast, the London Day Training College (Institute of Education from 1932), founded in 1902, took both male and female students. John Adams, its first principal, was a former pupil teacher who had studied at the Glasgow Free Church Training College and at the Universities of Glasgow and Leipzig, and taught in schools and training colleges in Aberdeen and Glasgow.[38] The breadth of Adams' experience was beyond question; while his academic reputation depended upon a seminal work, *The Herbartian Psychology Applied to Education*, published in 1897. Adams personified the link between teacher training and higher education. Appointed by the London County Council as Principal of the Day Training College, Adams was simultaneously appointed by the University of London as its first Professor of Education. His status was confirmed by a salary of £800 a year, whilst his two deputies, Margaret Punnett and D.R. Harris, received £400 each. In the following year, Adamson of King's was also appointed to a chair.

The establishment by the University of a Board of Pedagogy and of the chairs in education to which Adams and Adamson were appointed, marked a most important development in the relationship between teacher training and higher education in London. During the nineteenth century, the primary concern of teacher training colleges, even those like St. Mark's or Maria Grey, which showed an appreciation of higher culture, and whose students might proceed to teach in middle-class rather than elementary schools, was to train teachers how to teach. The London Day Training College and King's College were also centrally concerned with training teachers how to teach in elementary schools. The great majority of their early recruits were former pupil-teachers, financed by an Education Department which insisted upon the appointment of a master or mistress of method, and upon exercising some control over the professional curriculum. But the day training colleges were essential to the process whereby teacher training was enlarged into teacher education. Some students achieved degrees in subjects other than education, concurrently with their teacher training. Some were prepared for secondary schools. Some took the diploma or other advanced courses in education, the MA from 1914, the Ph.D. from 1919. For these students were not only members of day training colleges, they were also members of university departments headed from 1902 and 1903 by professors whose responsibility was to advance the subject of education as a field of study or discipline. For example, Adamson's academic interest was in the history of education. Thus his pamphlet of 1904 entitled *Our Defective System of Training Teachers* was followed in the next year by *Pioneers of Modern Education, 1600–1700*; *The Practice of Instruction* (1907) by *The Educational Writings of John Locke* (1912). Adams' concerns centred rather upon psychology and philosophy. His most ambitious work, *The Evolution of Educational Theory*, was also published in 1912. T. Percy Nunn, who succeeded Adams as principal of the London Day Training College in 1922, vice-principal from 1905 and appointed to a second chair in 1913, continued in this tradition. In 1907 he contributed a chapter to Adamson's *The Practice of Instruction*, but his most famous and highly influential work was *Education: its Data and First Principles*, first published in 1920, a volume which 'shows the close link between his epistemological and psychological interests'.[39] In 1925, the Departmental Committee on the Training of Teachers for Public Elementary Schools looked back to 1890 and declared that 'At that point, for the first time, the arrangements for the education and training of Elementary School teachers touch the main current of higher education, and the long period of separate development is seen to be drawing to a close'.[40]

LONDON COUNTY COUNCIL
From 1902, the London Day Training College provided the clearest link between teacher training, higher education and the new local authority established in 1889. This link caused some resentment. For example, Adamson observed that 'King's Scholars from the County Council's college, who themselves paid no fees, sat side by side with King's Scholars of King's College, who paid £10 per annum in the faculty of arts and £20 in that of science'.[41] Margaret Tuke, principal of Bedford College, 1907–29, even attributed the demise of the Bedford Training Department in 1922 to 'the policy of the London County Council in the direction of concentrating graduate training at the London Day Training College'.[42]

Similar problems were caused for the residential denominational colleges by such new foundations as Goldsmiths' College and Avery Hill. As Michael Boyd in his administrative study of the Church of England training colleges, 1890–1944, has shown, the foundation of local authority colleges

> was to cause the Church colleges considerable anxiety, an anxiety not generally displayed in the course of the establishment of the early day training colleges. It is true that the number of local authorities who took advantage of the situation was few, and by 1914 there were only twenty local authority colleges. But in terms of facilities provided, especially after the original building grant of 25 per cent had been increased to 75 per cent in 1906, the Church colleges could barely compete.[43]

Just as the schools of the London School Board came to outmatch those of the voluntary societies, so, too, the training colleges of the London County Council might outmatch those under religious control. Further provision was certainly required. In 1902 the London School Board appointed 891 new teachers, only 330 of them from colleges in the London area.[44]

No uniform pattern for the new colleges, however, was immediately apparent. In 1904, on assuming its responsibility for education in the capital, in addition to the duly constituted London Day Training College 'the London County Council inherited what was in effect an illegal training college'.[45]

This was Graystoke Place, a training facility established by the London School Board where, since the 1890s, ex pupil-teachers and others who did not want to attend residential training colleges, had been instructed under the supervision of W.T. Goode, former head of the Training Department at Owen's College, Victoria University, Manchester. These students, men and women, attended classes half time over a period of two or three years, during which they prepared for the Acting Teachers' Certificate. Some even took an external degree from the University of London. During the other half of their time they were employed in the Board's schools. In 1904, Graystoke Place with its 58 students, was officially recognized by the Board of Education, and continued in existence for another 30 years.

Goldsmiths' College was another anomalous institution. Opened in 1891 at New Cross in south-east London, in the former buildings of the Royal Naval School, the Goldsmiths' Company

Technical and Recreative Institute was originally intended for the 'promotion of the individual skill, general knowledge, health and well being of young men and women belonging to the industrial, working and poorer classes'.[46] In 1904, the Institute was offered to the University of London. The University, however, whilst establishing a Goldsmiths' College Delegacy responsible to the University Senate, concurred with the general view that Goldsmiths' should become a training college for students taking the two-year certificate course, and serving the local authority sector. The first of such students arrived in 1905. Places were reserved for nearby authorities: 183 for the LCC, 92 each for Kent, Surrey and Middlesex County Councils and 39 for the Borough of Croydon.[47] Clearly Goldsmiths' represented a link between teacher training and higher education, but repeated attempts to secure independent college status and an extension of degree work were unsuccessful. There was a particular crisis around 1910 with the threatened loss of the Goldsmiths' Company's original subsidy, and the LCC's decision not to nominate students for the 183 reserved training places.[48] Not until 1988 was Goldsmiths' admitted as a full School of the University of London.

Other foundations of the first decade of the twentieth century included Shoreditch College, established in 1907 in Pitfield Street for the training of handicraft teachers, and Fulham Training College, founded in 1908 and amalgamated with Clapham Training College under the name of Furzedown in 1915. But the showpiece was Avery Hill.

In 1902 the London County Council acquired a mansion with some 85 acres situated in Eltham in south-east London. The mansion had been built in 1890 for the nitrate millionaire, Colonel North, and was purchased by the LCC for recreational purposes for the very low sum of £25,000. In 1904, a full meeting of the LCC agreed to transfer the mansion and four acres of land to the Education Committee for the purpose of establishing a residential training college for women. Avery Hill College opened in 1906 with Mary Bentinck Smith MA, D. Litt, a former director of studies at Girton and lecturer in Medieval and Modern Languages at Cambridge, as principal. Smith's subsequent ill-health and that of her successor, A.B. Collier, meant that in leadership terms Avery Hill was off to a shaky start, but in 1907 stability was restored when the redoubtable Philippa Fawcett forsook her post at County Hall to become the College's acting principal for a year. The third principal, Emily Maria Julian, held office from 1908 until 1922. Some 160 students began a two-year course for the certificate in 1906, although in the first year only 45 were resident, with 67 in lodgings in Eltham and another 48 living at home.[49] Though threatened with closure in 1976, Avery Hill, unlike many other London colleges, survived, to be incorporated in 1985 into Thames Polytechnic, subsequently the University of Greenwich.

CONCLUSIONS

Three points may be made in conclusion. The first is that in many ways London was at the forefront of teacher training during the nineteenth century, its leadership exemplified by the foundations of Borough Road at the beginning of the period and of the London Day at the end. But, in numerical terms, it was often at a disadvantage. During the Victorian era the ownership and control of teacher training colleges was predominantly in the hands of the Anglican Church. The location of such colleges reflected the Church's diocesan organization. Teachers, of course, did not necessarily continue within the schools of the locality or denomination within which they had been trained, but one of the greatest weaknesses of the large urban school boards, a weakness particularly apparent in the case of London, was that they were not empowered to establish training colleges. Not until the first decade of the twentieth century, therefore, with the assumption by the LCC of a general responsibility for education, including the training of teachers, was it possible in a coherent way to identify and supply sufficient trained and certificated teachers for London schools. Accordingly, one of the first acts of the Council's Education Committee was to establish a subcommittee on the training of teachers. In 1904 only some 56 per cent of the nation's teachers were certificated and only 30 per cent of them had been trained.[50] As Sidney Webb declared, if the LCC wished to ensure that only trained teachers were to be employed in all London schools the capital would require 'more than 40 per cent of the entire annual output of all the training colleges in England and Wales put together, and [or?] more than twice that of those situated in the London area'.[51] In January 1905, William Garnett confirmed such calculations when he reported to the teacher training subcommittee that London needed some 1,500 new teachers each year. While half of these might be supplied from voluntary colleges, by 1909 the Council was overseeing an annual output of 900 teachers from seven colleges.[52]

A second point is to confirm that in this period teacher training was essentially for those proceeding to employment in elementary schools, schools for the poor. Those who taught in grammar or public schools or in the universities did not receive training in the science and art of teaching. They continued to be qualified, as they had been for centuries, by virtue of their university degrees. Some individuals, however, excluded by poverty, birth or sex from access to such institutions, undertook a pupil-teacher apprenticeship as a substitute for secondary schooling, and a training college course in place of study at a recognized institution of higher education. Their experiences, moreover, led them to champion the expansion both of better facilities for teacher training and of higher education and of the connections between them. Joshua Fitch provides a classic example both of personal upward mobility and of commitment to the causes of greater educational opportunity and interaction. Born in Southwark in 1824, the son of a clerk, Fitch was a pupil-teacher and assistant at Borough Road College. By 1856 he occupied the post of principal. Following posts as an inspector of schools and assistant commissioner to the Schools Inquiry Commission, in 1885 he was appointed chief inspector of training colleges. Fitch was particularly aware of the limited educational opportunities available for women. He was a promoter of two colleges for training women teachers for secondary schools – Maria Grey and the Cambridge Training College, and two of university rank – the College for Women at Hitchin which became Girton College, Cambridge, and Royal Holloway College, Egham. Fitch served on the Senate of the University of London and was a member of the local committee appointed in 1902 to oversee the new London Day Training College. He was knighted in 1896.

Upward mobility and creativity for teachers, however, was not merely to be found within the sphere of education. London offered a myriad of opportunities for those who had tasted the fruits of knowledge, albeit in bleak and grudging surroundings, and whose spirits could not be confined within the classroom walls. For example, H.G. Wells, born in 1866 at Bromley in Kent, failed both as a draper's and chemist's apprentice. A scholarship to the

Normal School for Science at South Kensington, however, led him to a career as a teacher, first at Wrexham, and then in London. After an initial failure in geology, Wells obtained a London B. Sc. degree in 1890, but his personal and professional development took place within the context of the College of Preceptors. Wells was a prizewinner in the College's Licentiateship and Fellowship examinations, a contributor to its journal, the *Educational Times*, and in December 1894 lectured in its College Hall in Bloomsbury Square on 'Science Teaching – an Ideal and some realities'. Gradually, as Vincent Chapman has observed, 'The science writer took over from the science teacher'.[53]

Finally, it should be noted that the place of teacher training within metropolitan higher education which was clearly problematic in the nineteenth century, has continued to be so in the twentieth. Not until the 1970s was the principle of an all-graduate teaching profession secured. In the 1980s, moreover, non-graduates entered London classrooms once again, while in the 1990s a new pattern of school-centred initial teacher training was introduced, albeit for graduates, whose students might have no contact with higher education whatsoever during their training. The establishment of the Teacher Training Agency in 1994 (in succession to the Council for the Accreditation of Teacher Education of 1984) showed not only the increasing intervention of central government – as in the establishment of a national curriculum for teacher training – but also that the very term 'teacher education' had reverted to its former designation as 'teacher training'.

Note

I am most grateful to Sean Glynn for his comments on an earlier version of this chapter, and to Lynda Woodroffe for her help in the location of sources.

CHAPTER TEN

Technical and scientific education in London

Richard G. Williams

The history of higher technical and scientific education in London before the present century is largely the history of institutions which have since become absorbed or transmuted into other bodies, mainly but not solely within the University of London. Almost nothing, except the learned societies, has avoided a major sea-change to this day, and it is the purpose of this chapter to trace that process and its underlying causes.

THE BEGINNINGS OF EDUCATION IN SCIENCE

The first successful formal attempt to introduce scientific education into London can be traced back to the foundation of Gresham College in 1579. Among institutions, it is one of only a few actually to have been sited within the City of London before the middle of this century – a curious rejection by the City of the values of higher education in spite of its owning a school (City of London School) and providing a home for others, some of which, such as Christ's Hospital, are no longer within the City, and one discussed at greater length in Chapter five. Until Elizabethan times, there had been no education at higher level in London other than that provided by the monasteries and by the Inns of Court (which would certainly have been lacking in scientific content) – curious that the capital should so little value the higher education available then only in Oxford, Cambridge, and the older Scottish universities. While other European capitals like Paris had long had universities, it was not until about 1570 that the first serious suggestion of educational opportunities in London were first raised, by Sir Humphrey Gilbert, navigator and explorer. The emphasis then proposed was to be practical, in terms of equipping students both for peace and war, the first of many largely abortive proposals over the next two centuries, before the beginnings of initiatives which were at last to bear permanent fruit. Gresham College was the only institution actually to be founded, out of the will of Sir Thomas Gresham (1519–79), founder of the Royal Exchange, and based in his city mansion in Bishopsgate. Among the seven professorships endowed there were those in astronomy, geometry and physic, and the College was under the control of the City Corporation and the Mercers' Company. The College gave one well-attended lecture a week in each of the subjects and attendance was free to all comers – hardly a formal course of study with a demonstrable outcome for the student. Gresham's heyday was little over a century long, a decline setting in after 1710, culminating in the disposal of the by-then-decayed building in 1768 by trustees so desperate that they even paid the Government to demolish the building. Gresham's Royal Exchange then provided a poor home of sorts until the erection of a more modest building in 1842, the institution then continuing an existence of sorts, unrelieved by an attempt in 1892/3 by a Royal Commission to incorporate the link with the City by enfolding it within the proposed 'Albert University', until its connection to the new City University in 1966. Nevertheless, as Negley Harte has pointed out, 'neither the University of London nor the City University owed anything in their origins to Sir Thomas Gresham's imaginative but squandered foundation.'[1]

Scientific learning in London long centred round the Royal Society and the Royal Institution, both bodies made up of eminent scientists dedicated to the furthering of scientific knowledge. There is a linear link with the first endeavours to develop scientific instruction in that the first meeting of the Royal Society, founded by King Charles II early on his return from exile in 1660, was held at Gresham College, where the Society continued to meet until 1710, when its departure set in motion a decline in the College's fortunes from which it never properly recovered. The Society's aims for a formal 'Colledge for the Promoting of Physico-Mathematicall Experimentall Learning', proposed in the year of its foundation, came to nothing, like so many other plans and dreams of the seventeenth and eighteenth centuries, unless one counts the teaching of medicine, which has a long history, stretching back to Rahere's foundation of St Bartholomew's Hospital at Smithfield in 1123 and to the origins of St Thomas's Hospital of obscure, probably late eleventh or early twelth century date. To this was added a group of other hospitals in the eighteenth century – Westminster in 1716, Guy's in 1726, St George's in 1733, the London Hospital in 1740 and the Middlesex Infirmary in 1745, at about the time when the hitherto obscure teaching methods were evolving into more formalized and coherent teaching practices. The Royal Society, however, was more a forum for the meeting of scientists who elected each other to membership and who had achieved eminence, in spite of the long tradition of permitting the election of distinguished, and especially royal, non-scientists, a place for the publication and dissemination of the results of research to their fellows. While the distinction of the scientists and their work should not be underestimated, this was not the place for the wider teaching of science, any more than was the Royal Institution in Albemarle Street, founded in 1799 to promote the value of 'useful knowledge', that is to say, technology, rather than the purer science tended by and large by the Royal Society. The Institution was, however, influential, spawning other similar bodies away from the metropolis, and it was influential largely because it was timely, coinciding in its *foundation* with a period of unprecedented social and industrial change. It would have been more so had it not, under Faraday and Davy, become 'a tiny focus of pure and applied scientific research', contrary to its founders' aims.[2]Perhaps this points to reasons for the lack of success of previous educational ventures in London, and perhaps it is indicative that it succeeded (and still does) at a time when technological change was so pervasive and so fast.

THE BEGINNINGS OF TECHNICAL EDUCATION

Technical education was a different matter entirely, closely associated with craft. The City Guilds had long histories of tending the development of their specialities through apprenticeships and guild memberships – hardly a coherent pattern of training and education, though undeniably effective. Apart from the learned societies, the first directions in development took an entirely different form, among the working-men's institutions set up in large numbers all over the British Isles at the very end of the eighteenth century and in the early nineteenth. The one which one should perhaps look at as the real precursor was the Andersonian Institution in Glasgow, set up by an eccentric and wealthy philanthropist, James Anderson, in 1796, and one of the forebears of Strathclyde University. This institution appointed a young medical doctor, George Birkbeck (1776–1841) as a science instructor in 1800. Birkbeck found the instructional equipment so poor that he designed his own and went out in search of craftsmen to make the equipment he needed. A famous account tells how he entered a tin-worker's shop in Glasgow with his designs and found such an interest in what he was doing and a hunger after knowledge that he realized the need to provide instruction for the working classes targeted to their needs.[3] As a direct result he established in this rather genteel establishment in the autumn of 1800 what became known as the Mechanics' Class, attracting over 500 workers by the end of the first term. It success owed much to Birkbeck's skill as a lecturer – like Huxley later in the century – and to his tailoring of the classes closely to the technical work of his audiences. Birkbeck left the Institution in 1804 but the success continued, leading to a more ambitious scheme of the establishment of the Glasgow Mechanics' institution in July 1823. It had direct results in London almost immediately. A report of the Glasgow venture which appeared in September 1823 in the *Glasgow Free Press* was sent to the editors of the newly-founded *London Mechanics' Magazine*, whose editors, J.C. Robertson and Thomas Hodgskin, began to plan for the foundation of a similar institution in London. On 11 October 1823 the editors appealed to the mechanics of London to found a London equivalent, and among the letters received in support were one from Birkbeck (who had been working as a physician at the Aldersgate Dispensary in London since leaving Glasgow in 1805) and another from the radical tailor Francis Place. On 2 December 1823, following a preliminary meeting on 11 November at which Birkbeck had been asked to take the chair, a General Meeting of more than 2,000 persons was held in the Crown and Anchor Tavern, opposite St Clement Dane's Church in the Strand, whose memorable outcome was the establishment of the London Mechanics' Institution on the Glaswegian model. Among the number of supporters present were 'numbers of respectable mechanics'.[4]

This was not the first such effort to establish education for working men in London, and indeed there was a clear movement towards foundations for this purpose. One such was the Mechanics' Institution set up by Timothy Claxton in 1817 with a membership entirely of working men and the drawback that it had to meet in their houses; it lasted a mere three years. Many such met their doom in the hostile political climate of the time, when it could be said in all seriousness that knowledge of mathematics could be claimed as the cause of the attitudes which fomented the French Revolution.[5] This same journal claimed that danger lay in the dissemination of too much knowledge: 'What is wanted is practical mechanics – instruction in trades . . . Science, in the very nature of things, must be confined to a few.' Much hostility to the London Mechanics' Institution and other bodies of the kind came from the fact that the intention was to provide more than mere technical training, thus raising for many the spectre that it would therefore be associated with dangerous and politically destabilising views. Equally revolutionary was the concept of provision of education for adults, since the whole thrust of the institution was to provide for working men, and even, from as early as 1830, to admit women to attendance at lectures (it should be remembered that the earliest provision in London for higher education of women was made with the foundation of Queen's College, Harley Street, in 1848 and of Bedford College in the following year).

The London Mechanics' Institution survived because it was able to tap into support from wealthy middle-class liberals (such as Birkbeck, Brougham – later to be the prime mover in the first establishment of the University of London, Francis Place, T.C. Hansard and the editor of the *Morning Chronicle*), rather than just relying on the still-essential support of its working students when other similar attempts went under, especially in the troubled and uneasy times between the French Revolution and the year of revolutions in 1848, years of Chartist and so many other agitations; indeed the varying political stances of the founders soon led to Robertson and Hodgskin severing their connections with the infant institution because of political differences over the support of the new body. They had considered that the middle-class funding militated against the aims of leaving the institution entirely supported by those from whose teaching it benefited, and rapidly lost out to supporters of a wider range of benefactors. Certainly the resulting institution was not as radical as these and other initial supporters wished, but that would have ensured its failure to survive in the early years of its foundation. Even so, the institution had from the outset a guiding tenet that it should be organized by an association of working men. There was always a strong element of student involvement in the governance of the institution in all its varying manifestations, the student body continuing until as late as 1992/3 to elect four of its members to the governing body via a Court of Electors comprised of the whole student body.

The aims of the institution were stated in the initial plan entered in 1824 in the Minute Book: 'The principal object will be to make them acquainted with the facts of chemistry and of mechanical philosophy and of the science of the creation and distribution of wealth' – in other words of the physical sciences and of economics, which was in fact to be taught here, first among London institutions, later in the century. Indeed, the Institution's first public lecture, by George Birkbeck (who had been invited to become the Institution's first President), was on the subject of steam power. The teaching range of the institution rapidly widened, and it is difficult to say whether the widening was the cause or the effect of the diversification of its teaching as it moved increasingly away from the sciences, which were always more expensive to support and to teach; by 1843, there was nevertheless a regular chemistry class with 24 experimenting members and 12 others.

The new Institution had no immediate permanent home but lost little time in establishing itself in premises in Southampton Buildings, part of which it shared with the Birkbeck Building Society and Bank (established by Ravenscroft and unconnected with the Institution), whose foundation stone was laid, to donations from Mill, Ricardo, Grote, Cobbett, Place, Bentham, J.C. Hobhouse and Sir Francis Burdett, at the end of 1824. Opened in 1825, it rapidly organized itself with the creation of such supporting facilities as a library. It remained there until its move to Fetter Lane in 1885, still within the City of London, where it remained in Bream's Buildings until bombed out in 1941 and moved immediately after the war to its present home in Bloomsbury.[6] Growing and broadening in focus, it survived a serious crisis in 1866, owing its re-foundation to its own members and in particular to Francis Ravenscroft, a member of the family of proprietors of Ede and Ravenscroft (robe-makers to the University of London and to the law courts), becoming in that year the Birkbeck Literary and Scientific Institution and, after the recommendations of the Haldane Commission in 1913 and the gap of the war years, a constituent college of the University of London as Birkbeck College in 1919, a recognition that for over 20 years it had become a part of the London higher education system in the sense that an increasing number of its students now sat for University of London degrees.

The new Institution was soon imitated elsewhere in London and beyond, with Dr Birkbeck prominent in the establishment of the Mechanics' Institutions at Spitalfields, Hackney, Deptford, Rotherhithe and Bermondsey, and Hammersmith and Chiswick, all in 1825. Student numbers at the London Institution consisted in 1830 of 1,144, of whom 800 were classed as mechanics, and in 1839 of 883 members, 174 students, 13 members' sons and apprentices, and 11 ladies, a total of 1,081; in 1839 'two-thirds of the members consist not of mechanics but of a different class of men, viz. Merchants and attorneys' clerks, etc.',[7] a shift which with time became increasingly more marked as the local resident population changed, with mechanics increasingly being replaced by commercial and legal clerks. The students whose names appear in the early registers range from 'gentleman' to a wide range of skilled artisans and small businessmen, and with it came change to a more varied and less science- and technology-centred curriculum; by 1843, two years after George Birkbeck's death, most of the teaching was outside the area of science and technology (only mathematics and chemistry remained constant in the curriculum, although the range was again extended following its rescue from near-bankruptcy and near-collapse in 1866), and the institution had become and was to remain multi-disciplinary. Costs were not negligible: six shillings per quarter with 2s.6d. entrance fee, both for adults and youths under 18 (students), members' sons or apprentices being allowed to attend classes or lectures at half the quarterly rate. Women were charged 5s per quarter to attend lectures and have use of the library but could not attend classes. Teaching quality was variable, with some early teaching in arithmetic described as poorly delivered, a possible reflection on the remuneration of lecturers, ranging from the good to little or nothing. Teaching was of two kinds: general education for working men and mechanics in return for payment and from paid teachers, and a more general attention to broader public interest in science and its industrial applications, with lectures delivered by competent but voluntary teachers. This was the pattern for most such institutions, with the London Mechanics' Institution leading the way and by some margin the largest in numbers of students.

One possible cause of the near-collapse of the London Mechanics' Institution (not helped by fraud on the part of the then Secretary) and of the demise of other similar institutions may have been the development of the University of London, following the foundation in 1826 and opening in 1828 of its first manifestation, under a council of 24, one of whom was George Birkbeck. As so often the inspiration was German, this time the University of Bonn and in particular its religious toleration. The curriculum included mathematics, physics and medicine, and a particular innovation was the inclusion of experimental sciences. A rival college, again including teaching of the sciences, was founded as King's College in 1829. From 1836 onwards it had a charter and was able to award degrees, a charter renewed in 1858 and revised in 1863. As early as the 1850s the Institution's members were beginning to look for qualifications, and some sat for the examinations of the Society of Arts. It was only when the need to compete was addressed that the institution was again able to develop and flourish, although student numbers, having gradually risen by 1879 to 3,526, remained fairly constant until well into the present century.

In 1889, a proposal was submitted to the Charity Commissioners for a new institution, to be named 'The City Polytechnic', formed out of an amalgamation of the City of London College, Birkbeck and the proposed Northampton Institute. In some ways the concept of the Polytechnics was similar to that which resulted in the foundation of the London Mechanics' institution, nearly 60 years before the establishment in 1880 by the City merchant Quintin Hogg of the Regent Street Polytechnic, that pulling together of his courses in many parts of London designed more clearly for social intercourse and recreation even though aimed at 'technical' knowledge in engineering and allied trades and in commerce. The polytechnics are discussed more fully in Chapters five and eight. Birkbeck never really formed part of the polytechnic movement but had a clear sense that at this time financial support for institutions was flowing towards vocationally oriented study. Birkbeck indeed became in theory part of the City Polytechnic at a time when it was being pulled away from the ethos of the Polytechnic because so many of its students were now working for

University of London degrees, towards the mooted Albert University. Ultimately the City Polytechnic took its own various routes, more firmly wedded to science and technology than Birkbeck now was; Birkbeck had become and was to remain truly a multi-faculty institution.

THE ROLE OF PRINCE ALBERT

One man in mid-century had a particularly strong effect on developments in science and industry, Prince Albert, Queen Victoria's Prince Consort; had he not succumbed at an early age to typhoid, then it would be interesting to speculate where the course of scientific and industrial development and of the education to support it would have led – certainly to far more positive and swifter results than actually occurred, in spite of the suspicion with which in some quarters his endeavours were greeted. Prince Albert's great gift was the bringing to bear on English life of a truly international understanding and approach. At this time the German state of Prussia led Europe and the world, as the dominant power in Europe. It perceived education as a force to be centrally directed because of its importance to the direct interests of the state and therefore evolved a centrally controlled and shaped educational system, not least in science and technology. It was fortunate for Britain that Albert was German; as a German, he was particularly aware how far in advance of British achievement German, and particularly Prussian, scientific education lay. The Great Exhibition of 1851 in Hyde Park owed its inception largely to him, a major endeavour to demonstrate to the world how good British products were and to stimulate further improvement by exposing British industry, industrial design and taste to competition with the products of other lands. The very considerable profits of the Great Exhibition were devoted, by the wish of the Prince Consort, to furthering the aim of the Great Exhibition, the use of science and technology to develop and improve industrial technique and design and to enhance Britain's manufacturing wealth. To that end the Department of Science and Art was set up as a government department to guide and control the development of education in those fields which Prince Albert saw as relevant to the improvement of the design and production quality of British industry, work which it continued to oversee and support to the end of the century, both at school and at higher education level. We have already seen examples of the influence of German (especially Prussian) models on the development of British, and particularly, London, higher education, and with the German-born Prince Consort taking a keen interest in the field, that influence became particularly strong and was to remain so until after the Great War. His was not only the drive to improve British industry and the educational support which it needed, but also the concept, not fully realized until after his early death, of a concentration of teaching institutions and instructive museums on or close to the site of the Great Exhibition, still there to this day, for the furtherance of education in this field.

HE ESTABLISHMENT OF SCIENCE

Most started elsewhere. The Royal College of Chemistry was founded in 1845 under the patronage of the Prince Consort, as President of its Council, in Hanover Square and with an impressive frontage onto Oxford Street. The costs of its founding, £6,000 in the first seven years, came from private donors – chemists and druggists, landowners and chemical manufacturers. It drew its students from agriculture, industry and medicine and attained immediate academic prestige – yet another example of German influence – by the appointment of August Wilhelm von Hofmann, from Liebig's renowned laboratory in Giessen, as Professor. It is interesting to see that, in spite of the huge sea-change of the Industrial Revolution which had swept Britain first among nations, this initiative should have come because of interests from land-owners concerned to improve agriculture by bettering soil fertility just as much as from industry. Further impetus came from a decision by the Society of Apothecaries in 1835, which required candidates applying for their licence to practise medicine (the most sought-after method at the time of entry into the profession of physician) to demonstrate competence in practical chemistry. Though chemistry, like botany, had long been taught in a very generalized way in British and other European universities to medical students, practical teaching in chemistry was then very difficult to obtain for the large numbers of medical students at the London teaching hospitals. Among the 356 students enrolled, mostly for a year or less for courses which were actually more theoretical than the donors would have liked, was G.D. Liveing (1827–1924), who spent a month learning how to mount courses before returning to Cambridge to do just that and proceed eventually to a professorship there.

Similar land-owning interests provoked government attention to the needs of mining, with the potential for exploitation of minerals considered a major potential resource for landlords. Geology, therefore, was the one and only branch of science to receive any support at all from government sources before 1840, the Ordnance Survey having made a grant to Henry de la Beche (1796–1855) to make a new geological survey of Devon; this led three years later to his appointment, under a committee of senior geologists (Buckland, Lyell and Sedgwick), as director of a Geological Survey of Britain at a princely salary of £500. This opportunity would not have happened even then had it not been for de la Beche's urgent need to re-establish his personal fortune, which he had lost as a consequence of the collapse of the West Indian sugar trade. A sum of £500 was a very modest cost indeed to the Government for what was actually the very beginning of official civilian science in Britain. de la Beche was again an excellent choice for the appointment, a strong advocate of practical science education. The Director made it an urgent priority to establish a public educational collection of minerals, maps and mining equipment, opened in 1841 near Scotland Yard as the Museum of Economic Geology. From the very start the Museum offered teaching in analytical chemistry, metallurgy and mineralogy, teaching which expanded when the Museum moved in the year of the Great Exhibition from Craig's Court to Jermyn Street, as the Government School of Mines Applied to the Arts. In 1863 this became the Royal School of Mines, which moved piecemeal to South Kensington between 1874 and 1891. It attracted almost immediately teaching staff of high calibre: the palaeontologist Edward Forbes (1815–54), the chemists Richard Phillips and Lyon Playfair (whose emigration to Canada Sir Robert Peel had personally prevented at Richard Buckland's insistence because of his high potential usefulness to British science) and Darwin's friend J.D. Hooker (1817–1911), whose father William Jackson Hooker created a Museum of Economic Botany in Kew Gardens in 1847. If this had been a German institute, it would have focused on scientific research as of intellectual importance; being British it focused on the utility of science.

The Royal College of Chemistry always had a shaky financial

base and lasted independently a mere eight years before amalgamation with the School of Mines under the title of Metropolitan
School of Science, although it continued for another twenty years
on its Oxford Street site, granting its own diplomas. A less than
ideal union, the College always aspired to be a German-style
research institution, while the School's function was to deliver
only elementary instruction in science. This tension was never
really resolved until the move of the institutions in the 1870s to
the site at South Kensington bought out of proceeds of the Great
Exhibition, but the record of the Metropolitan School was to
provide even further promise and distinction. Under de la Beche's
successor Sir Roderick Murchison (1792–1871), one of the three
great geologists of the century, a first-rate team of teachers was
formed, of whom the greatest was, without doubt, Thomas Henry
Huxley (1825–1895), 'Darwin's bulldog'.

Huxley succeeded the great Edward Forbes in 1854 as Lecturer
in Natural History at the School of Mines and Palaeontologist to
the Geological Survey. He, Playfair and Haldane tower above
their many distinguished contemporaries and colleagues as the
most influential shapers of science education in the capital and,
indeed, in the country as a whole. Huxley was a man of many
talents, medically qualified (1845), a former serving naval officer
converted to a zoologist by his participation in the scientific voyage
of the *Rattlesnake*. The recipient of a Royal Medal from the Royal
Society in 1852, he was totally committed to the work of the
School, teaching not just advanced science but also popular science
in regular School-based 'lectures to working men'. He became a
staunch advocate of properly conducted public examinations in
science, which he called 'the most important engine for forcing
science into ordinary education'. H.G. Wells, one of Huxley's last
students at what was by then the Normal School of Science, came
in 1883 with the award of one of the science scholarships awarded
to 'a teacher in training' (tenable for a year at a time in whatever
science discipline had spare places); he remembered Huxley as
'the great teacher, the most lucid and valiant of controversialists'.[8]
Huxley held the post of Dean of the Normal School of Science (as
the merged Royal College of Chemistry and Royal School of
Mines was then known) from 1881 to 1895. A great friend of the
pathologically shy Charles Darwin, he was the chief protagonist of
Darwin's ideas, and it is said of him that Darwin used to listen to

his lectures on the origin of species, hidden from view by curtains at the back of the theatre; it was Huxley, too, who so memorably riposted to 'Soapy Sam', Bishop Wilberforce of Oxford on his attack on Darwinism about ancestry from apes and intellectual honesty.[9]

THE RISE OF TECHNICAL EDUCATION

When basic technical education along the lines pioneered by the London Mechanics' Institution came back again into the forefront of attention, it was under the auspices of the City of London, whose livery companies in 1878 set up the City and Guilds of London Institute. Failing for the moment to find a site for their Central Institution in the overcrowded City, they concentrated first on creating feeder institutions local to the homes of workers (a necessity for success, as T.H. Huxley pointed out). Only one of these ever made it off the ground, the Finsbury Technical College, a brilliant success under the Institute's director and secretary Phillip Magnus (1842–1933) which ran from 1878 to 1926. Within two years of opening its doors it had 400 students from all sorts of trades in Islington, Shoreditch, Hoxton and Clerkenwell, following two types of instruction in a day school, the one 'to prepare boys for work in factory or engineering shops and [the other in] a night school for those already at work'.[10] Magnus appointed two brilliant young teachers, Henry Edward Armstrong (1848–1937, regarded as the father of chemical engineering in Britain)[11] and William Edward Ayrton (1847–1908), the one to teach chemistry, the other physics, both of them in courses intended to pave the way for higher-level courses in the future Institution, and he sent them off to Germany in 1881 to investigate teaching methods – once again the influence of German scientific teaching on the London scene. In 1885 Silvanus Thompson was appointed Principal and Professor of Applied Physics and Engineering at Finsbury, another strong appointment, this time of a pioneer in the development of applied electricity and an exceptional teacher with 'unusual experimental and inventive skill and the true instinct of an engineer' as well as strong interests in the history of science and technology. The City Companies wanted their Institution to be in the City but were unable to find a site. They were eventually persuaded by General Sir John Donnelly, Secretary of the Science and Art Department, to found it on the 87-acre site at South Kensington bought by the

1851 Commissioners for £342,500 for 'purposes of art and science' in perpetuity. Ayrton and Armstrong then moved across to take charge of the Institution, where they were joined by the engineer W.C. Unwin (1838–1933), the Institution's first Dean, and the brilliant mathematician Olaus Henrici (1840–1918). There were interesting and unusual features of the teaching, which covered not just engineering but also the 'pure' sciences of chemistry and mathematics and also languages; the significant departure was teaching principally by experiment rather than by verbal lectures, a new departure in England though the norm by then in Germany and one which encountered hostility because of its greater expense. The Institution became in due course incorporated into the New Imperial College in 1907, under the still-current name of City and Guilds College.

We have already seen the key role played by the working-men's institutes and also the similar role of the Normal School of Science in the delivery of scientific instruction to working men. To this should be added the foundation in 1887 of one further institution, the People's Palace in the Mile End Road, founded, according to Queen Victoria, 'for the benefit of the people of East London, whose lives of unceasing toil will be cheered by the various opportunities of rational and instructive entertainment and of artistic enjoyment here afforded to them'. The People's Palace is more fully discussed in Chapter Three; here it is sufficient to point out that technical schools were attached to the Palace, which grew in 1896 into the East London Technical College and in 1905 into the East London College, which in turn became part of the University of London in 1907, assuming the name of Queen Mary College in 1934.

One other legacy from the Prince Consort and from the Great Exhibition was the foundation within the Board of Trade in 1853 of the Department of Science and Art, to oversee the development of technical education at all levels. It should be clearly understood that the teaching of art was, for the department, an extension of the science teaching; the concentration was on the teaching of design for industrial use, and there was very little, if any teaching of art solely for art's sake – this was not the teaching of aspiring painters and sculptors. Much of its work concentrated on elementary teaching, and by 1855 it was already supporting science teaching in 33 parochial schools (including specialist schools such as the London Navigation School), with relatively small numbers of students and the teaching drawn from a central Training School. The Department lasted until 1900 before being subsumed elsewhere in the civil service, but at least it set a solid basis for technical education at the most basic level and encouragement for some teaching at a higher level. It also enabled constructive thought on future development to emerge through the various Government commissions which, in the latter art of the century, turned their attention to improvement of British scientific education.[12]

THE ADVANCEMENT OF SCIENCE

An early concern for adequacy of scientific equipment for teaching was addressed by the foundation by the Department of a loan collection of such equipment, listed even from the first report of 1853.[13] This enlightened move was an answer to the perpetual concerns about the cost of science education, running fairly consistently throughout the nineteenth century at around double the cost of non-scientific education. This received further strengthening following the setting up in South Kensington of a Government Solar Physics Observatory as a result of a recommendation from the Royal Commission on Scientific Instruction and the Advancement of Science (1870–75). The Commission's Secretary, Sir Norman Lockyer (1836–1920), there assembled a loan collection of scientific instruments which eventually became the core nucleus of the collections of the Science Museum.

Something should certainly be said of the Observatory and of its Director, since in its day it was second only in importance to the Royal Observatory at Greenwich, having nevertheless an educational function in a way that Greenwich never really had. It became part of the Royal College of Science in 1890 and remained in London, with Lockyer as its director until its transfer to Cambridge in 1911. Lockyer is an important figure in scientific education and would have been such had he been merely the founder of the scientific journal *Nature* in 1869. A civil servant and Secretary to the Royal Commission on Scientific Instruction and the Advancement of Science, he was seconded from the War Office to South Kensington in 1875 to direct the new observatory and was appointed Lecturer and later Professor in Astronomical Physics at the Normal School of Science in 1881. He was the discoverer in the sun's spectrum of the then unknown gas which was to become known as 'helium' and a pioneer in observation of sunspots.[14]

Lyon Playfair (1818–98)is one of those commanding figures in the history of higher education in London whose influence was pervasive. A prominent chemist who attracted the attention of Sir Robert Peel and of Prince Albert, he had an interest in the practical application of chemistry to agriculture and was a leading exponent of technical scientific education. He was asked to intervene in the London Mechanics' Institution's problems in 1857, producing a damning report of mismanagement and academic incompetence which made proposals for radical change acted upon by the institution, to such an extent that when he came to give the 70th anniversary address in 1892 he was able to refer to 'the prominent position which Birkbeck occupies among the evening colleges'.[15] Playfair was that dual figure of leading civil servant and science teacher, and it was inevitable that his influence as Secretary of the Department of Science and Art should be profound, right from the first clear-sighted summary of needs and recommendations in the Department's first report. He was a Member of Parliament, significantly for the Universities of Edinburgh and St Andrews from 1868 to 1892 and Postmaster General in 1873. His influence can be felt again and again in the development of scientific education in this country, a clear and focused, if rather cold and chilling, mind backed by an iron determination and contacts in all the influential quarters, not least with the Prince Consort. He was an ever-present figure in the deliberations of all the commissions on education in the nineteenth century – the Select Committee on Scientific Instruction of 1867–8, to which Huxley also gave significant evidence,[16] the Royal Commission on Scientific Instruction and the Advancement of Science in 1871–4,[17] and the abortive Gresham University Commission of 1894[18] which nevertheless shaped the directions for the later Haldane Commission, and, as his final work, the Select Committee on Museums of the Science and Art Department of 1898.[19]

It is in Richard Burdon Haldane (1856–1928) that we see perhaps most clearly the influence on English, and particularly London, scientific education of German models. Haldane, the first Labour Lord Chancellor after having held office as Secretary for War in Asquith's Liberal administration until unwarranted accusations of pro-German sympathies drove him out of office at the beginning of the Great War, had been educated in philosophy at Edinburgh and Berlin and was striving to create in Britain a similar scientific and technical institution to the outstanding Technische Hochschule at Berlin-Charlottenburg, the ideal behind his vision for what was to become the University of London's Imperial College in 1907, an institution which can justly be called Haldane's own personal creation.[20] Other elements of German influence in the development of scientific education may be seen, for instance, in the foundation of the British Association for the Advancement of Science in 1831, based on the model of the Gesellschaft der Naturförscher und Aertzte, founded nine years earlier in Leipzig; this association never had any direct function in the development of scientific teaching although its role in the dissemination and encouragement of scientific knowledge and study was and is of major importance. Haldane's great vision indeed bore productive fruit, but his influence was wider than this, since it was he who presided over the Royal Commission on the future of university education in London which bears his name. It finally reported in 1913, giving the University of London the shape which it assumed after the war and has borne, give or take some changes both minor and major, ever since.[21]

And there, until the rise of the polytechnics and their eventual transformation into universities in their own right, lay the scientific educational patterns of London. The great influences were the ideals of German scientific education and a desire to bring British technical education up to standards which then led Europe, the influence of the needs of the new industrialized nation, particularly as focused by the Prince Consort and especially through the Great Exhibition, the working-men's educational movement (as the earliest significant development in the field), and the influence of a number of exceptional men who shaped and fought for scientific education in the Metropolis – where it bore its most obvious fruits – and in the nation as a whole.

CHAPTER ELEVEN

Higher education and the visual arts
W. Vaughan

THE RISE OF LONDON AS A CENTRE FOR THE VISUAL ARTS

Britain is not a country traditionally considered to be pre-eminent
in the visual arts. In the mid eighteenth century, however, it rose
to prominence in this field and sustained a distinctive character
throughout the following century. This is the period that witnessed
the 'classic' phase of British painting – reaching from Hogarth to
the Pre-Raphaelites and including major portraitists such as Gains-
borough and Reynolds and landscapists such as Turner and
Constable. Architectural standards remained high through this
time. It was also a period in which Britain made leading contributions in engraving and sculpture, and initiated directions in design
and the applied arts that culminated in the Arts and Crafts
movement in the later nineteenth century.

As the capital of Britain, and as a growing metropolis of
increasing world importance, London played a decisive part in this
artistic flowering. It was the place where the majority of the most
prominent artists lived and conducted their business. London also
became a leading centre of the art trade, rivalled only by Paris. In
the nineteenth century, London also expanded strongly as a centre
for education in the visual arts. There were limits to its reputation,
however. The metropolis never became one of the leading European places for studying the fine arts. There was no time in which
it attracted aspirant painters, sculptors and architects from abroad
in the way that Paris, Rome and Munich did. But it did witness a
huge expansion in art education and systematic training. Furthermore, while it may not have cut a big figure in the area of the fine
arts, it did experience dramatic developments in the areas of
design, craft and art manufactures.

It was concern about these areas, and the ways in which they had been affected by the processes of industrialization, that triggered a new level of state intervention. During the 1830s the Government began to accept responsibility for art education. In the area of design, in particular, it was felt to be a matter of national importance to ensure that standards were maintained and developed. In 1836 a Government School of Design was set up in London. This grew in the 1850s to become the monitor of a national system of art training practised at branch schools throughout the country. Later in the century there was a shift towards devolving the responsibility for these schools onto local authorities. This was part of a general concern for the provision of technical education through local authorities at the time. The result was a network of schools of art and design – sometimes independent, but frequently associated with the polytechnics that were being established at that time. Aesthetics and politics mixed curiously here, with a pooling of interests between those who desired a recovery of medieval craft traditions and those who sought to ensure that practical instruction was given to young artisans working in a modern industrialized society. This mixture parallelled the amalgam of philanthropic idealism and technical instruction that made the British polytechnics quite unlike the equivalent colleges of higher technology that could be found on the continent. The British model was, indeed, to become an inspiration for art educators abroad, particularly in Germany and Scandinavia.

The pattern of art education that emerged at that time set up a structure that has continued to have an impact to this day. With the exception of the Royal Academy schools, all the principal schools of art and design in London had their origins in this process. A great number of them, too, retain practices that relate to their origins, despite having sometimes changed their name, institutional affiliation, and even location.

PROBLEMS OF DEFINITION AND CLASS; BETWEEN CRAFT
AND ACADEME

With the exception of the Slade School of Art – established as part of University College London in 1871 – all art education in nineteenth century London fell outside the university system. Only in 1905 did another art school come under the aegis of a University. This was the art school at Goldsmiths' college. However, the ambivalence revealed by the University of London to this college underlines the problems that traditional academic institutions had at that time in acknowledging forms of education that involved the visual arts.

The relationship between training in the visual arts and that for more traditional academic subjects has always been a complex one. On the one hand fine art is held to be one of the highest of human achievements, an experience exhilarating and life-enhancing. On the other hand it is seen as something not quite intellectual, not to be considered in the same light as those disciplines that can be seen to train the mind for any activities. It was not a 'liberal' art in the traditional sense, and was normally seen as a kind of specialist training. Yet prior to this century such a view was vigorously opposed by artists themselves. They were keen to emphasize the more learned side of the art. It was for this reason that they felt a great need to make a distinction between themselves and those other specially-trained people who practised crafts. This was as much a question of social as of aesthetic status. In the later eighteenth century the Royal Academy had been established, an organization that could claim to put the fine arts on the level with other intellectual pursuits. Significantly the Royal Academy had a strict delineation between the fine artist and the craftsman. Not even engravers were allowed to join as full academicians, and other forms of art workers were completely excluded. The move towards incorporating design and the applied arts into art education was opposed by the Academy when it occurred in the nineteenth century.

One result of this situation was that two quite distinct types of art schools grew up in the period. On the one hand there were the specialist schools for the fine arts – such as the Royal Academy and the Slade. On the other there were those institutions that taught applied art and design, such as the Government Schools of Design. The schools of fine art were usually independent. The schools of design and industrial art were usually attached to places of technical instruction. Architectural schools might fall into either camp – depending on whether the practice was seen as a profession (as it was in the Architectural Association), or as a superior kind of craft (as it was in the Central School for Arts and Crafts).

ART EDUCATION IN LONDON PRIOR TO 1835

Prior to the nineteenth century training in art took place largely at a practical level, through being apprenticed to a master of the particular skill the initiate wished to acquire. The determining factor here was as much economics as ability. The fine artist charged more to take on an apprentice than did engravers and other practitioners of the applied arts. It was for this reason that both William Hogarth and William Blake – Londoners coming from impoverished backgrounds – were apprenticed to engravers rather than to painters.

However, in the eighteenth century apprenticeship in the fine arts became supplemented increasingly by instruction offered in academies. The first significant one was set up by Sir Godfrey Kneller, the royal portrait painter in the early eighteenth century. It was succeeded by a number of others – notably the St. Martin's Lane Academy that was run by Hogarth. These academies were relatively liberal in nature, and operated largely as self-help organizations. The situation changed with the establishment of the Royal Academy in 1768. This operated a school run on regulated principles, in emulation of the Academies of France and Italy.

It should be stressed that these academies did not set out to provide a full training in the practice of one of the arts. They provided instead those 'intellectual' sides of art training that could not be provided by apprenticeship. This was, in particular, drawing from the antique and from the nude, and instruction in anatomy, perspective, ancient literature and other pursuits that were felt necessary to turn the artist into a man of sense and knowledge. Instruction was, for the most part, in the evening, so that the students could pursue a practical training in a studio or workshop simultaneously. Thus the Royal Academy school taught drawing, but not painting, sculpture or architecture. It was not until 1815 that a painting department was established – significantly for the copying of the old masters.

The limited nature of the Academy's practical instruction came under increasing attack in the nineteenth century. The Academy did gradually make concessions, and expanded the scope of teaching in the fine arts. But it remained opposed to the teaching of the applied arts. Involvement in such commercial matters, it was felt, would compromise the quality of fine art without leading to improvements elsewhere. Only by spreading good taste through the practice of fine art, it was claimed, could the climate be created in which the applied arts would improve. As Sir Joshua Reynolds, first President of the Academy, put it:

> An institution like this has often been recommended upon consider-ations merely mercantile; but an Academy founded on such prin-ciples, can never effect even its narrow purposes. If it has an origin no higher, no taste can ever be formed in manufactures; but if the higher Arts of Design flourish, these inferior ends will be answered of course.[1]

However convincing this argument may have sounded when it was put by Reynolds in 1769, it certainly carried less weight in the 1830s. Sixty odd years of the example of good taste as practised by the Academy had not had a beneficial effect on the quality of art manufactures; quite the reverse, in fact. It was the continued resistance of the Academy to involvement in technical training of any kind that finally convinced the Government that there would have to be state intervention in this area. As has already been said, the impetus was more commercial than aesthetic. It was the fear that British goods would become unsaleable through being poorly designed that finally spurred them into action.

The mechanics' Institutes
The need for practical art education had already been recognized in the Mechanics' Institutes which sprang up in the early nine-teenth century. These institutions – established to address the growing demand for education and training amongst artisans and working people – were to form the basis of later colleges of art and technology. It was the common practice of the Mechanics' Institute to offer instruction in drawing as part of the curriculum, it being recognized that this was a practical and useful form of training, particularly for artisans. In fact, the mechanics institutes were the only places where skilled workers were offered the chance of learning to draw, prior to the establishment of the Government Schools of Design.[2] Dr Birkbeck's Institute in London – the flagship of the movement – was exemplary from this point of view. It offered instruction in the 1830s from no less a person than historical painter Benjamin Robert Haydon. Haydon was at the heart of the public debate about art education in the

1830s.[3] He was one of the most vociferous campaigners for Government intervention in this area. A persistent lobbyist, he gained first of all the ear of William Ewart, the reformist MP for Liverpool, and eventually gained an audience with the Prime Minister, Lord Melbourne. He opposed the elitist position of the Academy and held that art training was an important part of the education of anyone involved in design and manufacture. It was his wish that a National Art School be established which would replace the Royal Academy schools and introduce a system of instructing which would include proper technical training in both design and in the fine arts. In the end his wish was not to be realized. Yet his lobbying did set in motion the events that led to the setting up of the first Government sponsored school of art instruction.

THE CASE FOR STATE INTERVENTION: THE SETTING UP OF THE
GOVERNMENT SCHOOLS OF DESIGN, C.1835–53

'God Help the Minister that meddles with Art' declared Lord Melbourne, when confronted by Haydon in 1834 on the subject of establishing a national system for promoting the arts.[4] Yet within a year of making this pronouncement he had set up a Select Committee to investigate the matter. This in itself is a sign of how serious the situation had become by this time.

The Select Committee of 1835 was set up by the Government to enquire 'into the best means of extending a knowledge of the Arts and the Principles of Design amongst the People (especially the Manufacturing Population)'.[5] It looked both at the problem of the quality of existing design and at the existing provision of art education, particularly that provided by the Royal Academy. After much earnest investigation of witnesses – both native and foreign, the committee came to the conclusion that foreign excellence in design was indeed due to the state-promoted training in design that was common in continental Europe – particularly in France and in the German States. The committee also came to the conclusion that promotion of Fine Art was an altogether different matter. State intervention here was seen as being a matter of exemplary patronage, of setting a good example. The occasion for this soon came to hand, in the commissioning of mural decorations for the Houses of Parliament.[6] At the same time it was determined to set aside more state funds for the promotion of the National

Gallery and similar institutions. In the field of education they decided to keep away from the tricky business of training the fine artist. This was left in the hands of the Royal Academy and whatever other private institutions might be set up for the purpose. In the case of design training, however, they determined that state intervention was necessary to fill the gap left by the collapse of apprenticeship systems. They therefore recommended that a Government School of Design be established for the purpose.

This decision was a momentous one for the whole future history of the teaching of art in this country. For, as has already been said, most of the present art schools are direct descendants of those design schools set up as a consequence of the decisions of the recommendations of the Select Committee of 1836. Perhaps the most striking feature about the decision was the way in which it isolated design as a separate practice. Because it was not 'fine' art, it was held that its practitioners should be trained differently to painters and sculptors. They should be made to focus directly on practices thought relevant to industrial design. They were to be taught accuracy of draughtsmanship, but not to be given instruction in those parts of art suitable for higher callings. This meant that the study of the human figure – that talisman of the art academy – was to be expressly excluded. This was one of the most hotly disputed decisions made and it caused Haydon to set up his own rival institution in protest.

It is striking, too, that the committee decided not to build on the art practice already existing in the Mechanics' Institute. Much criticism was made of the standard of teaching here – perhaps unjustly. But the main point was that it was felt that design training was something exclusive that was best taught in a specialist institution rather than in one that dealt with a wide variety of subjects and training schemes. As in the case of fine art, design became isolated from other forms of education. This has remained the norm up to the present day.

The first school – called the 'School of Design in Ornamental Art' was established in Somerset House in the Strand, in the premises recently vacated by the Royal Academy schools which had been moved to join the National Gallery in Trafalgar Square. It was set up under the Board of Trade – a sign that it was seen largely as a venture relating to commercial enterprise. The first director for the school was the architect J.B. Papworth, and the committee governing it had many Royal Academicians amongst its members. There seems to have been considerable confusion about what a school of design should do. It was agreed that design should be taught, but nobody knew how to define this except by saying that it did *not* involve the study of the human figure. There was also an amazing lack of consideration for the School's potential audience. It was intended to provide instruction for artisans. But the hours of instruction were set from 10 a.m. to 4 p.m. – when working people would have been unable to attend. Furthermore the fees were set at four shillings (20 pence) a week – a prohibitive sum for any mechanic in those days. (It is interesting to contrast this with the policy of the Academy, where instruction was offered free of charge.)

However, such blunders began to be ameliorated. Within two months evening classes between 6 and 9 p.m. were introduced. They rapidly outstripped the day courses in membership. After a dismal report at the end of the first year Papworth was replaced by the artist William Dyce. Dyce was a much travelled artist who had a thorough knowledge of continental systems of education. Furthermore he had a great sympathy for the cause of the art worker, being one of those reformist artists who looked with admiration at the vanished craft world of the middle ages. In this sense he shared the views of the revivalist architect A.W.N. Pugin, and was a precursor of Ruskin and William Morris. Dyce recommended that training should follow the lines of the German workshop (Werkstatt) system of training he had observed in Bavaria. He introduced life drawing – arguing that artist and workman should be united in their understanding of form. He also attempted to link design to practical training by introducing a loom for weaving.

Following the German model, Dyce also supported the notion of systematized instruction. He himself designed a progressive drawing book. This was to become the model for future instruction in the decades to come. The school of design flourished under Dyce. Numbers rose rapidly and branch schools were set up elsewhere. In 1841 a school was established at Spitalfields, and a female school of design was set up. In 1842 the city of Manchester petitioned to have a school of design, partly funded by the Government and partly by the City.

Despite his success Dyce left the school in 1843 – largely because the governors would not accept the fact that he wished to continue his successful career as a painter at the same time as administering the school. The next nine years were to be stormy ones, in which there were a succession of unsatisfactory directors (there was even a student revolt in 1845). The whole venture might, in fact, have collapsed had it not been clear that there was an intense need for such institutions. In the end the project was saved by the rise to power of a man who came to dominate the whole field of design education for the next two decades. This was Henry Cole.

THE REIGN OF KING COLE (1852–73)

Cole was a forceful and able civil servant, a man of vision and managerial prowess who had a genuine interest and involvement in practical design. Amongst other things he can be credited with having invented the Christmas card – a prime example of providing a commercial application for art. More importantly he had, under the pseudonym 'Felix Summerly', made designs for practical and effective pottery in the 1840s.

Cole came to the problem of the management of the Government Schools of Design with considerable authority, after having been the triumphant administrator behind the Great Exhibition of 1851. This not only reintroduced the issue of the need for more practical instruction in design. It also provided the funds to do something about the matter from its profits. The immediate outcome was the establishment of the South Kensington Museum (later the Victoria and Albert Museum), which became a repository of examples of design from all countries and all ages for the edification of British designers. The association between this collection and the Government Schools of Design became increasingly intimate – particularly after the school moved to occupy an adjacent site in 1857.

Cole saw that the Government Schools of Design would only be able to flourish and fulfil their purpose if they became part of a much more powerful structure. He therefore only accepted the post of Head of the School of Design after he had engineered significant changes in its status. He turned it, in effect, into a Government department. This was the Department of Practical Art, a separate department within the Board of Trade, with responsibility only to the President or Vice-President. Cole became the General Superintendent of the Department of Practical Art in 1852. A year later the Department received the even more prestigious name of Department of Science and Art. While this meant that he did in fact run the school of design, he also became responsible for overseeing the instruction in all the satellite schools that were rapidly springing up over the country.

In the ensuing years Cole introduced a highly centralized form of art education. He established a National Curriculum in which the work done at the South Kensington School became the model for the country. He brought together a team of able artists and designers who helped in his scheme of standardization. These included Owen Jones whose *Grammar of Ornament* (1856) became the standard reference work on the subject and is still in print today. But the most influential figure at the time was the artist Richard Redgrave who devised the whole of the National Curriculum in Art. This was a course in 23 stages which included 10 stages of drawing (ranging from 'linear drawing with instruments' to freehand study of the human figure), six of painting, four of modelling and two of design. This national system was applied in all Government Schools of Art. It was further supported by a National Competition. Instigated in 1852, this lasted until 1915.

Although figure study was included within the curriculum, it was given a relatively limited role and was only introduced after a rigorous training in copying geometrical and ornamental forms. In that sense Cole and his assistants moved design training further away from fine art practice, thus reversing the tendency towards their integration that had been introduced by Dyce. Cole was also able to use his powers to gain important commissions for the school, such as the designing of the funeral car for the Duke of Wellington and the commission from the post office to design and construct the pillar box. This was designed by Richard Redgrave – admittedly in a rather flowery form. But it became the model for the modern pillar box.

There was no doubt that Cole' regime was immensely effective. It gave design a new status in official circles and ensured the spread of effective schools throughout the country. By 1864, the year in which a further Select Committee was set up to review art education, there were 90 in the country, teaching about 16,000 students.[7] Among those in the London area that were to survive to become noted art schools were the South Kensington school, which became the National Art Training School in 1864 and finally the Royal College of Art in 1896; St. Martins (1854); Lambeth (1854); West London (1862); and Islington (1873). Furthermore the movement continued beyond him, with Government schools set up in Blackheath and Kennington in 1880, Hornsey, Chelsea and Stoke Newington in 1882, Holloway in 1883 and Bayswater and Putney in 1884.[8]

As well as becoming the leading institution for the teaching of design, the South Kensington School also assumed importance as a centre for training art teachers, particularly after 1863, when it became the National Art Training School. Indeed, by the end of Cole's regime it's principal function seems to have been the training of instructors to teach in the other schools of design. This might have been a logical development in some senses, but it was also a symptom of a rather over-ordered system. There was, in fact, increasing criticism of the methods employed at South Kensington. The highly ordered system of education certainly developed precise skills, particularly in drawing and design. Students were well-informed, too, about the principal styles of different countries and the past. But there was little encouragement for creativity, and also little direct contact with practical manufacture. Increasingly the students seemed to come not from those artisan classes for whom the schools had been set up, but from the middle classes. Also, the students were mainly middle-class women, and increasingly so.

Amongst the most vociferous critics of the South Kensington structure was the art critic John Ruskin. Ruskin saw the ordered methods of South Kensington as mirroring the mechanization which, in his eyes, had been the soul-destroying effect of industrialization.

> Drawing may be taught by tutors; but design only by Heaven; and to every scholar who thinks to sell his inspiration, Heaven refuses its half.[9]

His lone if powerful voice against such art instruction was listened to with increasing enthusiasm by artists and designers of a younger generation; notably by William Morris who set up his own firm of artist-craftsmen as a practical critique of the methods employed. On a practical level it was felt that too much centralization was taking place and there was not enough contact with local industries. Such thinking was to become central in the post-Cole period, and fitted in with the wave of concern for the spread of education symbolized by the education act of 1870. But it was not until the Technical Instruction Act of 1889 that the system set up by Cole finally became dismantled and the course for instruction devised by Redgrave ceased to be followed by schools of art.

DIVERGENCES, C. 1870–1914

The dismantling of Cole's empire was part of a more general move towards devolution. Art instruction, along with other kinds of technical training, increasingly became the responsibility of local authorities. There was also increasing fragmentation and variety in what was being offered. This movement can be seen as part of the spread of the polytechnic system at this time, and indeed, many of the art schools became attached to, or were actually started up by the new polytechnics. The main artistic force behind this was the Arts and Crafts Movement, a movement that combined a romantic yearning for the medieval craftsman with radical politics. The web of influences that included Ruskin, the Pre-Raphaelites and the Aesthetic movement led to arguments for a more individual and less mechanistic approach to art instruction and training.

The most powerful strand at work was the claim that arts and manufactures had become fragmented as part of the process of industrialization. The seminal publication was Ruskin's *Nature of Gothic*, in which the image of the medieval craftsman was evoked as a person who both designed and made his product and was able to live creatively fulfilled. Ruskin's message was given a more definite Socialist slant by William Morris, who proclaimed the *Nature of Gothic* to be the most important publication of the century apart from Marx's *Capital*. The movement was symbolized by the founding of a succession of art workers' guilds – the Century Guild was established by Macmurdo in 1882, the Art Workers Guild by Lethaby in 1884, and the Guild of Handicraft by C.R. Ashbee in 1884.[10] This case was put most powerfully by the artist and designer Walter Crane in his book *The Claims of Decorative Art* in 1892.[11] Crane attacked Richard Redgrave's syllabus, which he thought was spuriously scientific and reiterated the Ruskinian message that artistic creativity and originality could only be stimulated through direct experience of the handicrafts.

Crane was one of those art educators who triumphed after the collapse of Cole's system as a result of the changes brought about by the Technical Education Act of 1889. In 1893 he became director of the Manchester School of Art, and in 1898 he was appointed Principal of the Royal College of Art – the heart of Cole's former empire – where he introduced practical classes in enamelling, book-binding, handicraft and similar activities. By the time of Crane's triumph, however, the case for this kind of educational approach had already been demonstrated in London with the establishment of the Central School of Arts and Crafts by the London County Council in 1896.[12]

A highly important part of the reason for the triumph of the Arts and Crafts Movement in education in London lay in the fact that its message had become so thoroughly absorbed by those wielding political power in the LCC. For after the Technical Education Act local authorities were empowered to levy a rate specifically to support technical higher education in their area. This led throughout the country to a tendency for municipal authorities to take over their local schools of design and introduce more vocational training. A prime mover in the case of the LCC was Sidney Webb who, after his election as a member for Deptford in 1892, became a leading figure for progressive reform. As part of the scheme for reforming higher education in London through the LCC's Technical Education Board established in 1893, Webb set out to provide the kind of education for workmen and artisans that was felt to be widely lacking in the country in general and in London in particular. This concern was heightened – as indeed it had been in the 1830s – by the fear of foreign competition. This time there was a greater urgency to the situation since Britain had now passed its peak as an industrial nation and was beginning to fall behind in competition to its major rivals, in particular the United States of America and Germany. London was a particularly important site for art manufactures. The high rents in the capital meant that it was not a suitable site on the whole for large scale industrial concerns, which were still concentrated largely in the North. On the other hand the proximity to the luxury trade of the West End made it a particularly favourable site for the promotion of specialized, fancy and high-skilled goods and services, such as jewelry, watchmaking, clothes and printing.[13] These were precisely the areas in which traditional craftsmanship had lasted longest and which were now beginning to succumb in a way that lower quality goods production had done earlier in the century (see Chapter two).

THE POSITION OF ARCHITECTURE

In the case of art manufactures Webb relied to a large extent on the advice of the architect W.R. Lethaby, who was appointed art inspector to the Technical Education Board in 1894. Lethaby – a confirmed Fabian and Ruskinite – saw the re-integration of arts with crafts as the key to the revival of art manufactures. He grouped training in these areas with that of architecture, emulating a practice that he believed had existed in the middle ages. He held that this art – which had increasingly become a separate practice in the nineteenth century needed to be re-integrated with craft practice.

Since the eighteenth century there had been a progressive tendency to professionalize architecture. Traditionally architects had been trained in an office, under the 'pupillage' system. This system had become increasingly abused in the nineteenth century. Just as apprenticeship systems had declined in the crafts, so 'pupillage' had degenerated into employing aspirants to the profession as menial draughtsmen in an office without any concern for their wider training. This system is satirized by Dickens in his representation of Mr Pecksniff's office in *Martin Chuzzlewit* (1844).[14] While the Royal Academy schools notionally included architects amongst their students, there had been scant attention paid there to specific training for architects. It was the sense of the lack of instruction in this area that had stimulated the architect Sir John Soane – himself an academician – to establish a personal collection in his house in Lincoln's Inn Fields as a museum and place of instruction for young architects in 1835.[15] Concerns in this area parallelled those expressed about design, which had led to the establishment of the Select Committee on arts and manufactures in 1835. The Institute of British Architects was established in 1834 to provide 'uniformity and respectability of practice in the profession'.[16] Its progress towards this goal was slow. In 1866 it became the Royal Institute of British Architects, and in 1887 it instituted professional exams. But by 1900 no more than 10 per cent of the profession were members, and it was not until the early twentieth century that it became obligatory to take the RIBA exams to qualify as a professional architect.

While raising the issue of professional standards, the RIBA was not directly involved in architectural education. In 1842, however, the Association of Architectural Draughtsmen was set up to promote the interests of junior and apprentice architects. This eventually became the Architectural Association and began to run its own courses. In the mid-Victorian period, however, it remained the practice for architectural students to be articled to an architect and to attend an educational institution for their wider training. It was Lethaby's initiation to make this training one that involved a close association with the crafts. As art inspector to the technical education board he introduced a scheme for architectural students to study craft in the central London institutes of higher education. Attempts to have a scheme involving the polytechnics (notably Westminster and Chelsea) providing workshop-based training for architects foundered, and it was this that led eventually to the establishment of a separate school for this purpose, the Central School for Arts and Crafts. In response to Webb's call for 'specialist art teaching in its application to particular industries in close relation with the employers and workmen in those industries'.[17] Lethaby devised a curriculum in which architecture was taught as 'experimental building' including practical building crafts and the design of modern building, and where the decorative arts would include such crafts as stained glass, lettering, silversmithing and enamelling. When the Central School was set up as a result of this Lethaby took care to institute well-equipped workshops so that the practical involvement with craft was thorough and exacting.

However, it should be born in mind that Lethaby saw this school as a 'higher' polytechnic in which students were to be taught who had received basic training elsewhere. In recognition of the particular needs of the building industry in this respect he went on to establish the School of Building in 1904. There had indeed been something of a crisis in the London building industry prior to this. For with growing commercialization and competition in London there had been increasing building activity and decreasing opportunities of training. London youths found it harder and harder to acquire skills, and there was a growing tendency to employ skilled men from outside London, from areas where a healthier system of apprenticeship still survived. It seems that the response to this opportunity was immense. In 1897–8, According to Swenarton, over a third (3548) of the 10,269 students enrolled in the nine polytechnics supported by the TEB, were in the building trade.[18]

Lethaby entertained a considerable idealism towards the building worker, as can be seen in the paper he delivered to the RIBA on 'Education in Building' in 1901. Following Ruskin's vision of the medieval craftsman in 'The Nature of Gothic' he called upon architects to learn from and respect, not despise the building workers:

> These rough, tired men ... are after all the true artists in building, the representatives of the medieval architects.... I never go on a building which I call my own but I want to beg their pardon for my vulgarity, pretentiousness and ignorance. It is they and only they who sufficiently know what stones are sound.[19]

But while he continued to promote such ventures, Lethaby had himself moved on. In 1901 Lethaby moved to the Royal College where he extended the introduction of craft practice that Walter Crane had initiated.

CITY OF LONDON INVOLVEMENT; CITY AND GUILDS;
GOLDSMITHS' COLLEGE

The concern for increasing technical art education had also become a concern of the City of London (see Chapter five). The Lord Mayor of London called in 1872 for a movement 'for the encouragement of Art, Manufacture and Technical education in connection with the City of London'.[20] This eventually led to the City and Guilds of London Institute, established in 1878.

Following the lead established by the Mechanics' Institutes earlier in the century, other organizations integrated art instruction into their curricula. This was all the more important in a London context, as has already been noted, because of the prevalence of art manufactures in the city. It was also particularly notable in connection with the building trade. The City and Guilds incorporated art training within its structure from the start, acquiring the Lambeth School of Art (formerly a Government School of Design) in 1878.[21] This became the Kennington art school, and proved to be remarkably successful. Its evening classes attracted a vigorous following from amongst the local artisans, including those who worked in the local pottery, the high quality Doulton Works and sculptors and carvers employed in the building trade.[22] This was a highly specialized group of workers who formed a major part of the Victorian building trade.

In contrast to the principles that had pertained in the Government Schools of Design, it became the principle of those running the Kennington Art School to give artisans a full art training. As a report in 1882 said,

> Your Council feels that too much importance cannot be attached to good instruction in Design and Ornament, in the training of those who are engaged in the application of Art to industrial work, and they are therefore endeavouring to give prominence to this branch of Art teaching in the Schools connected with the Institute.[23]

It is probably for this reason that Kennington Art School remained a lively art centre in which artists and craftsmen mixed. Many fine artists began their careers there.

From the late 1880s a number of polytechnics were established which included art instruction in their curricula. Also, a number of key art schools were set up, including Camberwell, which was opened in 1898 as a full art school, after having run evening classes successfully for a number of years.[24] Probably the most notable of these new creations was Goldsmiths' college, established as a 'Technical and Recreative Institute' by the Goldsmiths' Company in 1891.[25] Its aim was typical of the mixture of philanthropy and technical instruction that has been noted in the polytechnical movement as a whole. As the clerk of the company said in his inaugural address, the college was intended for the

> Promotion of technical skill, knowledge, health and general well-being among men and women of the industrial, working and artisan classes.[26]

Goldsmiths' College received an enthusiastic local welcome – perhaps because institutes of higher and adult education were less frequent in that part of London than in some of the more central and northern parts. The school of art – ably led in the early years by Frederick Marriot – was from the start one of the most successful parts. As in polytechnics generally, it offered a wide and liberal range of instruction, reaching from life drawing, design and modelling to wood carving art needlework and metalwork. What makes the history of Goldsmiths' curious, however, is the particular way in which the institution was supported by the Goldsmiths' Company. Perhaps because of the very eminence of its position, the Company kept the College as a privately funded venture at a time when similar organizations were seeking partnerships with local authorities. After the London Education Act of 1903 the Company decided to call an end to this independence. But instead of passing the College over to the authority of the LCC as would have normally been expected, they gave it to the University of London. While appreciative of the gift of a thriving institution, the University experienced continuing problems in viewing it in the context of university education. Such problems had been anticipated locally at the time when the Goldsmiths' Company was making its decision. As the *Kentish Mercury* complained in March 1904:

> if the University should take over the Institute for its own purposes it will be goodbye to the Art School – the best in London – and goodbye to the great engineering classes (with thousands of students) ... unequalled by any of the Polytechnics.[27]

In fact the University's solution was to accept such activities, but only at arm's length. As a report of 1910 made clear, the College was 'incorporated' within the University, but it was not to be deemed a 'school'. Its strengths in areas not normally covered by the University – such as teacher training, technical instruction and the visual arts – were recognized, but they were to remain distinct from mainstream university activities. The position of the school of art is particularly interesting, since the University had since 1871 run the highly successful Slade School of Art at University College. But the Slade – itself a daring innovation within British University practice – was at least a place where fine art alone was taught, rather than the wide range of subjects of a more craft and technical nature that were also offered by Goldsmiths'. Despite this situation, Goldsmiths' continued to flourish as one of the best art schools in London – a tradition that it has maintained right up to the present. Final full recognition of Goldsmiths as a college of the University did not occur until the 1980s at a time when the widescale revision of the university structure within the country was under way.

FINE ART EDUCATION; THE SLADE

While art and design education moved so decisively in the direction of craft, the training in the fine arts also became more firmly based on practice. Here, by the middle of the nineteenth century, practice was lagging badly behind the systems that had developed on the Continent, particularly in Paris. While in the eighteenth century Academies had only been involved in the 'intellectual' sides of art training – that of drawing from the antique and the model and the acquisition of historical and scientific knowledge appropriate for the practice of history painting – there had been an increasing tendency for the actual practice of painting, sculpture and other fine art activities to be included in the curriculum. In Paris this had developed as an 'atelier' system, in which an established artist would run a studio in which students would gain such practical training. In the absence of such instruction at the academy in London there had grown up a series of private schools, most notable that of Henry Sass. Established in 1817, this private academy was noted for the care it gave to students, so much to be contrasted with practice at the Royal Academy. As the painter David Wilkie observed, Henry Sass could have taught a stone to draw. Sass himself was a man of radical sympathies who was genuinely committed to the spread of art education. Unfortunately he lost his mind in later years. But his academy was taken over by another able teacher, Carey in 1840 and continued to provide an introduction to art studies in London for years to come. A rival establishment was set up by James Matthew Leigh, a pupil of Etty's in 1845 which became Heatherley's in 1860. Originally intended as 'preliminary' schools for the Royal Academy (as well as for training drawing masters and educating amateurs) these increasingly began to offer a full training of their own. Later distinguished examples were the school established by the painter Hubert von Herkomer at Bushey in 1883, and the Byam Shaw School, established in 1910. At the same time many of the most ambitious art students went abroad to study in Paris, and as these returned, they brought with them the desire to introduce the French atelier system into Britain. After a Government enquiry in 1863 the Royal Academy itself instituted some changes of practice, following the recommendation that they should adopt the French atelier system. But the changes made were far less substantial than this and the Academy schools still continued to seem repressive and anachronistic. In 1871, however, a new art school was established which brought the French atelier system into the heart of London. This was the Slade School of Art, which was set up at University College London with money from an endowment by Felix Slade.

The setting up of the Slade School was a remarkable innovation. The first surprise is that such a school should be set up as an integral part of a university, rather than as an independent body or as part of an institute of technical instruction. University college showed itself to be thoroughly progressive in making such a move. Similar funds bequeathed by Felix Slade to the Universities of Oxford and Cambridge for art instruction were simply used to inaugurate a series of lectures by distinguished visiting professors – Ruskin being the first and the most distinguished of the succession in Oxford. University College made thorough investigations before setting up their school and took advice from a wide variety of artists and art authorities of the period. It was as a result of this that they became convinced that the atelier system was the best one to establish. They were also convinced that art education could be an appropriate activity for young gentlemen – but only if it were clearly distinguished from any kind of craft training. There was, therefore, nothing but fine art taught at the Slade. The first principal was the history painter Edward Poynter, who had studied in Gleyre's studio in Paris after having spent no more than a year at the Royal Academy schools in 1854–5. Poynter set up the school on the basis of the atelier system that he had himself experienced. The French model was firmly established by Alphonse Legros, an immigrant French artist, who took over from Poynter in 1875.[28]

It was also part of the liberal principle of the Slade that women students were admitted. Women students had, of course, played a large role in the Government Schools of Art and Design, but the Academy resisted their regular enrolment until the 1880s. The importance of the Slade's position was that it recognized the case for providing education for women in 'fine' art as well as in the lower spheres of applied art and design. It was rewarded with a series of brilliant students, of whom the most notable was Gwen John.

The Slade School, with its emphasis on a modern, French-orientated system of art training, rapidly put the Royal Academy

Schools in the shade. In the late Victorian and Edwardian period it produced a succession of the most talented of British artists – figures like Augustus and Gwen John, Paul Nash, Mark Gertler, David Bomberg and Stanley Spencer. They benefitted from the liberal instruction of the likes of Wilson Steer, Fred Brown and Tonks. Eventually the Slade system triumphed for the teaching of fine art. Already by 1875 it was having its impact at South Kensington. Here the painter Edward Poynter – himself trained in Paris – had taken over upon the retirement of Richard Redgrave in 1875. He reorganized the school more in the direction of fine art education as offered in the Parisian atelier system and at the Slade. There was a shift back towards the crafts in 1898 when first Walter Crane and then W.R. Lethaby became Principal. The Royal Academy schools also altered their practice after conducting an internal review in 1887. Many of the other schools retained their arts and crafts mix – in particular the Central school. But in 1920 with the appointment of Rothenstein, the Royal College of Art moved once more strongly in the direction of fine art. This is a too-ing and froing in the history of the Royal College which has continued up to this day – often with great creative result.

By 1914 the complex web of London art schools that exists today was more or less in place. Art and Design was still being taught in specialized schools or colleges, even if these were sometimes nominally under the aegis of a wider institution. There is no doubt that the polytechnic movement had had a major impact on the provision of art education in London. 'We have to note' wrote Sydney Webb proudly in 1904 'that the school of art is an important department of every Polytechnic institute. Its work ranges from the elementary drawing, which every technical student is urged to learn, up to the highest development of "fine art" and design.'[29] According to Webb 'more than a third' of art teaching in London was provided by these institutions at that date. Webb also noted the high success of polytechnic students in the National Art Competition and in exhibiting societies. Yet while some notable fine art schools – such as Chelsea – emerged as a result of the establishment of polytechnics in the last decades of the nineteenth century, it was by and large in the area of design that they had their greatest impact. After the First World War, at the same time that art schools like the Royal College were veering towards specializing in fine art, there was a new sense of professionalism beginning to emerge in those places dedicated to design education. This was now seen to be aimed at providing skilled workers for the commercial and industrial sectors. Craft training, by contrast, became more marginalized and tended to move across to be taught more in those institutions traditionally more associated with 'fine' art.

Yet these divisions have never been complete. Moreover, if there has sometimes been confusion, this has often led to a productive and fruitful situation. London's eminent position in the world of design is certainly due in part to the high quality of training that has continued to be provided by the varied art institutions of the city. It is gratifying, too, to see that the recent changes in the University system has finally brought art education securely within the orbit of integrated higher education. It is to be hoped that both artists and non-artists will benefit from this new degree of proximity.

Notes

Chapter One

1. S.F. Cotgrove, *Technical education and social change,* 1958.
2. Asa Briggs, 'The development of higher education in the United Kingdom; the nineteenth and twentieth centuries', in W.R. Niblett (ed.), *Higher education: Demand and response,* Tavistock, 1969.
3. Sidney Webb, *London education,* 1904.
4. Robbins Report, *Higher education* Cmnd. 2154 (1963) p. 14.
5. F. Sheppard, *London 1808–1870: The infernal wen* , 1971.
6. Rosa L. Pincus, 'The conception and development of metropolitan London, 1800–1855', Ph.D., Buffalo, USA.
7. K. Young and P. Garside, *Metropolitan London. Politics and urban change, 1837–1981,* 1982, p. 1.
8. Heather Creaton, *History of education in London: a bibliography,* Centre for Metropolitan History, 1993.
9. T. Kelly, *A history of adult education in Great Britain from the middle ages to the twentieth century,* 3rd edition, Liverpool, 1992.
10. B. Simon, *Studies in the history of education, 1780–1870,* 1960; M. Bryant, *The London experience of secondary education,* London, The Athlone Press 1986.
11. N. Harte, *The University of London 1836–1986. An illustrated history,* London, The Athlone Press 1986.
12. J.W. Hudson, *The history of adult education,* 1851. New impression, Woburn Books, 1969, Preface, p. 5.
13. Kelly, op. cit.
14. H.J. Burgess, *Enterprise in education. The story of the work of the established church in the education of the people prior to 1870,* 1958.
15. Hudson, op. cit.
16. Census 1851. pp lxviii–lxix: M.E. Sadler (ed.) *Continuation schools in England and Wales,* 1907: Kelly, op. cit., p. 155.
17. Bryant, op. cit.
18. R.D. Anderson, *Universities and elites in Britain since 1800,* 1992.
19. F.M.L. Thompson (ed.) *The University of London and the world of learning 1836–1986,* 1990.

20. James Bowen, *A history of western education. Vol. 3. The modern west*,1981.
21. William Cobbett, *Rural Rides*, ed. by G.D.H. and M. Cole, 1930; G. Stedman Jones, *Outcast London. A study in the relationship between classes in Victorian society*, Oxford, 1971.
22. R. Price-Williams, 'The population of London 1807–1881', *Journal of the Royal Statistical Society,* 48, 3, 1885.
23. H.A. Shannon, 'Migration and the growth of London, 1841–91', *Economic history review*, April, 1935.
24. L. Hollen Lees, *Exiles of Erin. Irish migrants in Victorian London*, Manchester, 1979.
25. H.J. Dyos, *Victorian suburb: a study of the growth of Camberwell*, Leicester, 1961.
26. J.R. Kellett, *The impact of railways on Victorian cities*, 1969.
27. K. Hoggart and D.R. Green (eds) *London. A new metropolitan geography*, 1991.
28. R. Floud and D. McCloskey, (eds) *The economic history of Britain since 1700. Vol.1. 1700–1860*, Cambridge, 1994.
29. S. Pollard, 'The decline of shipbuilding on the Thames', *Economic history review*, 3, 1950–51.
30. Stedman-Jones, op. cit.
31. E.J. Hobsbawm, 'The nineteenth century London labour market', in Centre for Urban Studies, *London: aspects of change*, 1964.
32. Hudson, op. cit.
33. idem.
34. W.A. Robson, *The government and misgovernment of London*, 1939.
35. Young and Garside, op. cit.
36. Sheppard, op. cit.
37. Young and Garside, op. cit., p. 21.
38. D. Owen, (ed. R. MacLeod), *The government of Victorian London, 1855–1889*, Cambridge, Mass., 1982.
39. Watson Foster, *Beginnings of the teaching of modern subjects in England*, 1909.
40. Quoted by Bryant, op. cit., p. 62.
41. W.K. Jordan, *The charities of London 1480–1660*, 1960.
42. F.M.L. Thompson, op. cit., preface, p.x.
43. Hudson, op. cit., p. 166.
44. idem, p. 170.
45. idem.
46. W. Devereux, *Adult education in inner London, 1870–1980*, 1982.
47. Hudson, op. cit., p. 52.
48. Kelly, op. cit., p. 126.
49. idem, pp. 140–142.
50. J.F.C. Harrison, *A history of the working men's college, 1854–1954*, 1954.

51. H.J. Edwards, *The evening institute*, 1961.
52. Kelly, op. cit., p. 129.
53. M. Argles, *South Kensington to Robbins. An account of English technical and scientific education since 1851*, 1964; D.E. Thoms, *The history of technical education in London, 1904–1940*, 1976.
54. ibid, p. 7.
55. D.S.L. Cardwell, *The organisation of science in England*, 1957.
56. Education Department, *Annual Report*, 1858, pp. 40, 82.
57. Newcastle Commission, *Royal Commission on the state of popular education in England*, Report, vol.1, 1861.C.2794.
58. Devereux, op. cit., p. 24.
59. Webb, op. cit.
60. I.G. Doolittle, *The City of London and its Livery Companies*, Dorchester, 1982.
61. *Report of the Royal Commission on City of London Livery Companies*, 1884. Cmd.4073.
62. P. Stevens, *City and Guilds of London Institute. A short history 1878–1992*, 1993.
63. V. Belcher, *The City Parochial Foundation 1891–1991. A trust for the poor of London*, Aldershot, 1991.
64. *Royal Commission appointed to inquire into the condition and administration of the Parochial Charities of the City of London*, 1880. C.2522.
65. Belcher, op. cit.
66. *Royal Commission on Technical Instruction*, Second report, 1884. C.3981.
67. *Times*, 3 October, 1887.
68. Belcher, op. cit., passim.
69. H. Llewellyn Smith, *Report to the Special Committee on technical education*, LCC, 1892.
70. P. Thompson, *Socialists, Liberals and Labour. The struggle for London, 1885–1914*, 1967.
71. See Chapter five.
72. See Chapter six.
73. Devereux, op. cit.
74. Harte, op. cit.
75. Anderson, op. cit., pp. 14–15.
76. M. Sanderson, *The university and British industry,* 1972, pp. 106–120.
77. A.E. Firth, *Goldsmith's College. A centenary account*, London, The Athlone Press, 1991.
78. V.A. McClellend, *English Roman Catholics and higher education, 1830–1903*, Oxford, 1973.
79. Gresham University Commission, *The Report of the Commissioners to consider the draft charter for the proposed Gresham University for London*, BPP, 1893–94, 31, 24 January, 1894.

80. Harte, p. 40.
81. R. Dahrendorf, *LSE. A history of the London School of Economics, 1895–1995*, 1995 pp. 32–35.
82. Webb, op. cit.
83. ibid, p. 51.
84. Devereux, op. cit., p. 80.
85. S. Marriot, *University extension 1873–1914*, 1985.
86. A. Briggs and A. McCarthy, *Toynbee Hall. The first hundred years*, 1984.
87. Kelly, op. cit., p. 224.
88. TEB, *Annual report*, 1897, p. 18.
89. Webb, op. cit., pp. 46 and 157.

Chapter Two

1. Schultz, T. (1961) 'Investment in human capital' *American Economic Review*, 51, 1–17.
2. Harbison, F. and Myers, C. (1964) *Education, Manpower and Economic Growth*, New York, McGraw-Hill.
3. Mace, J. (1984) 'The economics of education: a revisionist's view', *Higher Education Review*, 10, 3, spring, 39–56.
4. Denison, E. (1962) *The Sources of Economic Growth in the United States and the Alternatives before us*, Washington DC, Committee for Economic Development.
5. Psacharopoulos, G. (1981) 'Returns to education: an updated international comparison', *Comparative Education*, October.
6. Musgrave, P.W. (1970) 'Constant factors in the demand for technical education, 1860–1960', in Musgrave, P.W. (ed.) *Sociology, History and Education*, London, Methuen, pp. 143–57.
7. Roderick, G.W. and Stephens, M.D. (1978) *Education and Industry in the Nineteenth Century: The English Disease?*, Harlow, Longman.
8. Green, D.R. (1991) 'The metropolitan economy: continuity and change 1800–1939', in Hoggart, K. and Green, D.R. (eds) *London: A New Metropolitan Geography*, London, Edward Arnold, p. 11.
9. Lawrence, J., Martin, D. and Robert, J.L. (1992) 'The outbreak of war and the urban economy: Paris, Berlin and London in 1914', *Economic History Review*, XLV, 3, 566.
10. Royal Commission on Local Government in Greater London (1960) *Report*, London, HMSO, Cmnd 1164, 20.
11. Green, 1991, *op. cit.*, p. 12.
12. Quoted in Johnson, P. (1996) 'Economic development and industrial dynamism in Victorian London', *London Journal*, 21, 1, 27.
13. For example, Stedman-Jones, G. (1971) *Outcast London*, Oxford, Clarendon Press.
14. Green, 1991, *op. cit.*, pp. 8–9.

15. Hall, P.G. (1962) *The Industries of London since 1861*, London, Hutchinson.
16. Green, 1991, *op. cit.*, p. 14.
17. Green, 1991, *op. cit.*, p. 15.
18. Green, 1991, *op. cit.*, p. 24.
19. Green, 1991, *op. cit.*, p. 14.
20. Johnson *op. cit.*
21. Johnson, *op. cit.*, p. 34
22. Stedman-Jones, G. (1974) 'Working-class culture and working-class politics in London 1870–1900: notes on the remaking of a working-class', *Journal of Social History*, VII, cited in Johnson, 1996, *op. cit.*
23. Johnson, *op. cit.*, p. 36.
24. Green, D. (1996) 'The nineteenth-century metropolitan economy: a revisionist interpretation', *London Journal*, 21, 1, pp. 9–26.
25. Green, 1996, *op. cit.*, p. 20.
26. Green, 1996, *op. cit.*, p. 24.
27. Hall, *op. cit.*, p. 21.
28. Roderick, G.W. (1967) *The Emergence of a Scientific Society in England 1800–1965*, London, MacMillan, p. 39.
29. Sheppard, F. (1971) *London 1808–1870: The Infernal Wen*, London, Secker and Warburg, pp. 166–8.
30. Wardle, T. (1884) 'Report on the English silk industry' in Royal Commission on Technical Instruction. (Second Report), III [c-3981-II], p. xxxi.
31. Wardle, *op. cit.*
32. Shephard, *op. cit.*, p. 168.
33. Pollard, S. (1950) 'The decline of shipbuilding on the Thames', *Economic History Review*, III, 3, 89.
34. Burgess, T., Locke, M., Pratt, J. and Richards, N. (1995) *Degrees East: The Making of the University of East London 1892–1992*, London, Athlone, p. 31.
35. Weightman, G. and Humphries, S. (1984) *The Making of Modern London 1914–39*, London, Sidgwick and Jackson, p. 58.
36. Deane, P. (1973) 'Great Britain' in Cipolla, C.M. (ed.) *The Fontana Economic History of Europe: The Emergence of Industrial Societies – 1*, London, Fontana, p. 172.
37. Hounsell, D.A. (1984) *From the American System to Mass Production 1800–1932*, Baltimore, Johns Hopkins University Press.
38. Broadberry, S.N. and Wagner, K. (1996) 'Human capital and productivity in manufacturing during the twentieth century: Britain, Germany and the United States', paper presented at the Economics of Education Group seminar, London.
39. Harley, C.K. (1974) 'Skilled labour and the choice of technique in Edwardian industry', *Explorations in Economic History*, 2, 391–414.
40. Broadberry, S.N. (1993) 'Manufacturing and the convergence

hypothesis: what long run data show' *Journal of Economic History* (cited in Broadberry and Wagner op. cit.).

41. Broadberry and Wagner, *op. cit.*
42. Floud, R. (1984) 'Technical education 1850–1914: speculations on human capital formation', Centre for Economic Policy Research, Discussion Paper No. 12.
43. Floud, *op. cit.*, p. 10.
44. Purvis, J. (1991) *A History of Women's Education in England*, Buckingham, Open University Press, p. 107.
45. Pollard, S. (1989) *Britain's Prime and Britain's Decline: The British economy 1870–1914*, London, Edward Arnold, p. 116.
46. Hudson, J.W. (1969) *The History of Adult Education*, (First published in 1851), London, The Woburn Press, pp. 222–38.
47. Kelly, T. (1957) *George Birkbeck, Pioneer of Adult Education*, Liverpool, Liverpool University Press, p. 265.
48. Hudson, *op. cit.*, p. vi.
49. Kelly, T. (1992) *A History of Adult Education in Great Britain*, Liverpool, Liverpool University Press, p. 127.
50. Roderick and Stephens, *op. cit.*
51. Quoted in Argles, M. (1964) *South Kensington to Robbins*, Harlow, Longman, p. 8.
52. *Mechanics' Magazine*, XLII, Jan-Jun 1845, p. 236.
53. Crossick, G. (1978) *An Artisan Elite in Victorian Society*: *Kentish London 1840–1880*, London, Croom Helm, p. 137.
54. Hudson, *op. cit.*, pp. 214–16.
55. Quoted in Argles, *op. cit.*, p. 12.
56. Kelly, 1992, *op. cit.*, p 114.
57. Quoted in Argles, *op. cit.*, p. 5.
58. Ministry of Education (1951) *Education 1900–1950: The Report of the Ministry of Education and the Statistics of Public Education for England and Wales for the Year 1950*, London, HMSO, Cmnd 8244, 47.
59. Roderick, *op. cit.*, p. 18.
60. Quoted in Roderick, *op. cit.*, p. 14.
61. Roderick, *op. cit.*, p. 11.
62. Quoted in Roderick, *op. cit.*, p. 23.
63. Quoted in Roderick, *op. cit.*, p. 24.
64. Quoted in Roderick, *op. cit.*, p. 26.
65. *ibid.*
66. Simon, B. (1974) *Education and the Labour Movement 1870–1920*, London, Lawrence and Wishart, p. 72.
67. Argles, *op. cit.*, p. 39.
68. Simon, *op. cit.*, p. 82.
69. Simon, *op. cit.*, p. 85.
70. Quoted in Argles, *op. cit.*, p. 22.

71. Foden, F. (1982) 'The technology examinations of the City and Guilds' in MacLeod, R. (ed.) *Days of Judgement*, Driffield, Nafferton Books, p. 81.
72. Ministry of Education, *op. cit.*, p. 47.
73. Foden, *op. cit.*, p. 80.
74. Saint, A. (1989) 'Technical education and the early LCC' in Saint, A. (ed.) *Politics and the People of London: The London County Council 1889–1965*, London, Hambledon Press, p. 73.
75. *ibid.*
76. Saint, *op. cit.*, p. 74
77. Ministry of Education, *op. cit.*, p. 47.
78. Quoted in Argles, *op. cit.*, p. 26.
79. Ashworth, W. (1972) *An Economic History of England 1870–1939*, London, Methuen, p. 226.
80. Maclure, S. (1970) *One Hundred Years of London Education, 1870–1970*, London, Allen Lane The Penguin Press, p. 69.
81. Quoted in Maclure, *op. cit.*, p. 69.
82. Quoted in Argles, *op. cit.*, p. 37.
83. Ministry of Education, *op. cit.*, p. 47.
84. *Ibid.*
85. London County Council (1912) 'Return of occupation of students attending evening classes in the administrative county of London during the session 1908–9' (appendix b) in *Eight Years of Technical Education and Continuing Education Schools*, Report by LCC Education Officer, p. 12.
86. MCC (Middlesex County Council) (1912) *Higher Education in the Administrative County of Middlesex*.
87. Burgess *et al., op. cit.*
88. Information supplied to the authors by Croydon Local Studies Library and Archive Service, 1997.
89. MCC, *op. cit.*
90. *Ibid.*
91. Burgess, *et al., op. cit.*, p. 72.
92. Marriott, J.W. (1988) 'West Ham: London's industrial centre and gateway to the world', *London Journal*, 14, 1.
93. Davis, J. (1995) 'Modern London 1850–1939', *London Journal*, 20, 2, 61.
94. Smith, D. (1969) 'The industrial archaeology of the lower Lea Valley', *East London Papers*, 12, 2, 112.
95. *Thames Ironworks Gazette* (1895), 1, January, p. 19.
96. Science and Art Department (1891), *Reports of the Department of Science and Art*, p. 67.
97. Burgess *et al., op. cit.*, p. 53.
98. Adamson, J.W. (1930) *English Education 1782–1902*, Cambridge, Cambridge University Press, p. 346.

99. *Stratford Express* (1896), 31 October, p. 5.
100. *Stratford Express* (1898), 8 October, p. 5.
101. Burgess *et al., op. cit.*, p. 84.
102. Board of Education (1921) *Report of HM Inspectors on the West Ham Municipal Technical Institute, for the Period Ending 31st July 1921*, p. 1.
103. Pollard (1989) *op. cit.*, p 116.
104. Royal Commission on the Depression of Trade and Industry (1886) *Final report*, para. 97.
105. Sanderson, M. (1972) *The University and British Industry 1850–1970*, London, Routledge & Kegan Paul, p. 187.
106. Hewins, W.A.S. (1929) *The Apologia of an Imperialist*, Vol i, in Sanderson, M. (ed.) (1975) *The Universities in the Nineteenth Century*, London, Routledge & Kegan Paul, p. 24.
107. Saint, *op. cit.*, p. 83.
108. Sanderson, *op. cit.*, p. 188.
109. Saint, *op. cit.*, p. 83.
110. Sanderson, *op. cit.*
111. Saint, *op. cit*, p. 85.
112. Sanderson (1972), *op. cit.*, pp. 114–15.
113. Sanderson (1972), *op. cit.*, p. 115.
114. Sanderson (1972), *op. cit.*, p. 117.
115. London County Council (1904–5 to 1914–15) *London Statistics*, 15–25, Lists of schools of the University and number of internal students in each faculty.
116. LCC (1912), *op. cit.*
117. Pratt, J. and Burgess, T. (1974) *Polytechnics: A Report*, London, Pitman.
118. Quoted in Burgess *et al., op. cit.*, p. 143.
119. Royal Commission (1913) Royal Commission on University Education in London, 1910–1913. Final Report, London, HMSO, p. 17.
120. Royal Commission (1910) Royal Commission on University Education in London, 1910–1913. First Report, London, HMSO, p. 26.
121. Board of Education (1935) Memo from Mr Savage to Mr Eaton, 11/12/35. Cited in Burgess *et al.*, op. cit.
122. Deane, *op. cit.*, p. 168.
123. Bronowski, J. (1973) *The Ascent of Man*, London, BBC, pp. 260ff.
124. Musgrave (1970), *op. cit.*
125. Roderick, *op. cit.*, p. 9.
126. Hobsbawm, E. (1969) Industry and Empire, Harmondsworth, Penguin Books. (First published by Weidenfeld & Nicolson in 1968, p. 169).
127. Pollard, S. and Robertson, P. (1979) *The British Shipbuilding Industry, 1890–1914*, Cambridge, Mass, p. 130.
128. Pollard (1989) *op. cit.*, p. 207.

129. Pollard, *op. cit.*, p. 130.
130. 'London's higher education institutions "unknown and under-util-ised"', Focus central London TEC, Press Release, 18 April 1997.

Chapter Three
  1. The first three definitions are dated between 1700 and 1727, the second two are dated 1888, all are from *The Shorter Oxford English Dictionary*, 1978 ed., Oxford, OUP, vol. l, p. 379.
  2. The title working class is a nomenclature which itself benefits from further definition. E.P. Thompson in his seminal work *The Making of the English Working Class*, refers to class as 'a historical phenom-enon, unifying a number of disparate and seemingly unconnected events ... when some men, as a result of common experiences (inherited or shared), feel and articulate the identity of their interests as between themselves, and as against other men whose interests are different from (and usually opposed to) theirs.' See E.P. Thompson, *The Making of the English Working Class*, Harmondsworth, Pen-guin, 1977 ed., p. 9. However, there were many divisions amongst those who manifestly were of the working class, for example, skilled workers in regular employment had little in common with the casual labourer or member of the residuum, the sweated alien tailor with the bricklayer.
  3. As is described below, the People's Palace became East London Technical College, then East London College, Queen Mary College and today is Queen Mary and Westfield College, University of London.
  4. For details on the nature of immigration into London see C. Holmes, 'Cosmopolitan London', in A.J. Kershen (ed.), *London the Promised Land?*, Ashgate, Aldershot, 1997, Chapter Two, pp 10–37, and N. Merriman (ed.), The *Peopling of London*, London, Museum of London, 1993.
  5. See C. Booth, *Life and Labour of the People of London*, London, Macmillan, 1889 and A.J. Kershen, H. Mayhew and C. Booth 'Men of Their Time?' in G. Alderman and C. Holmes, *Outsiders and Outcasts*, London, Duckworth, 1993, pp 94–117.
  6. For a detailed account of the structure of industry in outcast London, see G. Stedman Jones, *Outcast London*, Harmondsworth, Penguin, 1984 ed., Chapter 1.
  7. S. Maclure, *History of Education in London 1870–1914*, London, Allen Lane, 1970, p. 23.
  8. L. Gartner, *Jewish Immigrant in England 1870–1914*, London George Allen and Unwin, 1960, p. 230.
  9. In 1822 the Jews' Free School opened its doors to girls as well. Details from G. Black, *The Largest School in the World, a History of JFS 1732–1997*, forthcoming.

10. V. Lipman, *History of the Jews in Britain since 1858*, Leicester, Leicester University Press, 1990, p. 29.
11. M. Bryant, *The London Experience of Secondary Education*, London, The Athlone Press, 1986, p. 376.
12. Ibid., p. 377.
13. J.W. Adamson, *English Education 1789–1902*, London University Press, 1930, p. 432.
14. For a detailed account of the development of technical education in London see this volume Chapter five.
15. Though the accusation was the immigrants were taking the jobs of Englishmen there were instances where they were doing work that Englishmen were not trained for. One example of this is to be found in the ladies tailoring trade, where in the early 1880s there was a paucity of English ladies' tailors. See A.J. Kershen, 'Morris Cohen and the origins of the women's wholesale clothing industry in the East End' in *Textile History*, vol. 28, no. 1, June 1997.
16. Deed of the People's Palace Committee, dated 20 May 1885. Queen Mary and Westfield College (QMW), London, E1.
17. By the closing decades of the nineteenth century the East End of London was regarded by some journalists and writers as 'a city of darkest night', an abyss, a jungle; its inhabitants as savages.
18. Reverend Samuel Barnett speaking abut the activities of Toynbee Hall in June 1888. Quoted in W.J. Fishman, *East End 1888*, London, Duckworth, 1988, pp 246–8.
19. Beaumont Square was certainly not an area of poverty but one which housed the lower middle and artisan classes.
20. Quoted in G.P. Moss and M.V. Saville, *From Palace to College*, London, 1985, p. 19.
21. Ibid., p. 21.
22. W. Besant, *All Sorts and Conditions of Men*, London, 1894, p. 18.
23. Ibid., p. 135.
24. *Jewish World*, 5 February 1886.
25. The Decennial Census never has, to this date, included a question on religious affiliation, thus the only method of determing religious background in terms of the Jewish community is by synagogue affiliation and name association – the latter certainly not foolproof but one which provides a guide to ethnic origin.
26. Deeds of the People's Palace, loc.cit.
27. *London Evening Standard*, 27 May 1885.
28. *East London Leader*, 6 February 1886.
29. *Jewish Chronicle*, 12 February 1886.
30. *The Times*, 23 February 1886.
31. QMW archives, loc.cit.
32. *Echo*, 18 May 1887.
33. Details on attendance from the People's Palace Institute Report to

the Beaumont Trustees. May 1888, and Hay Currie's Annual Reporty to the Trustees of the People's Palace, 1888–89 both in the archives of QMW, loc.cit.

34. *Daily Telegraph*, 16 May 1888.
35. Moss and Saville, op.cit., p. 31.
36. Letter dated 15 August 1888m Box 19/misc. QMW Archives, loc.cit.
37. Ibid.
38. Except during the period of the dock strike in August 1889, when these did not take place. See E. Hay Currie, 'The Working of the People's Palace' in *Nineteenth Century*, February 1890, pp 344–55.
39. Charity Commissioners Recommendations for the People's Palace Scheme, 1892, archives of QMW.
40. Ibid., p. 350.
41. Clearly recruitment efforts were not, at that time, being extended towards the female members of the local community, though they were accepted and did register for courses.
42. *Nineteenth Century*, op.cit.
43. Tailors' cutting was the most skilled element of the tailoring trade and the most highly paid. See A.J. Kershen, *Uniting the Tailors*, Frank Cass, Ilford, 1995, Chapter Four, pp 97–125.
44. Calendar of Evening Classes held at the People's Palace, 1890–1, archives of QMW, loc.cit.
45. Box 21, QMW Archives, loc.cit.
46. Letter to Edmund Hay Currie, undated, Box 11, QMW archives, loc.cit.
47. *Palace Journal*, vol. 1, no. 1, 5 February 1895.
48. There were some notable exceptions, see below, p. 126.
49. Information from interviews carried out by the author in May and June 1988.
50. *Magazine of Art*, May-October, 1897, p. 252.
51. At a cost of between £1. 11s. and £3. 3s. per course.
52. Moss and Saville, op.cit., p. 43.
53. Calendars of the People's Palace, 1890–1900, QMW archives, loc.cit.
54. Minutes of the Vestry Committee, East London College, 16 May 1907, QMW archives, loc.cit.
55. The term used by Eric Hobsbawm to describe the skilled worker and artisan.
56. K.C.T. McDonnell, 'East London College and its Students', *East London Papers*, vol.13, no. 2, Winter 1970–1, pp 89–96.
57. Mc.Donnell, op.cit., p. 91.
58. List of Matriculated and Registered Internal Students East London College, 1912–13, QMW Archives, loc.cit.
59. East London College Record Book of Those Killed in World War One, QMW archives, loc.cit.
60. List of Day and Evening Students attending University Courses at

East London College During the Session 1922–23, QMW Archives, loc.cit.

61. *Daily Telegraph*, 15 May 1928.
62. List of Day and Evening Students Attending University Courses at East London College During the Session 1930–31, QMW Archives, loc.cit.
63. *East London College Magazine*, vol. V111, no. 2, March 1928.
64. *Jewish Guardian*, 6 March 1931.
65. Author's interview with some 60 residents of Nightingale House, London SW12 who had previously lived in the East End, 7 May 1997.
66. A *chazan* is a Jewish religious singer
67. See note 65 above.
68. *East London Advertiser*, 7 March 1931.
69. *East London Observer*, 21 November 1931.
70. See article in the *East London Advertiser*, 15 May 1932, on the proposed location of the new People's Palace and the building of a replacement for the burnt down Queen's Hall.
71. Of course it should not be assumed that all the poor were unambitious, there were those keen to grasp all that was available and work all hours to improve their lot, but they were the minority.

Chapter Four

1. This chapter is based on my inaugural lecture given on 7 November 1990. I gave the first and only inaugural professorial lecture at what was then South Bank Polytechnic. I was also the first and only woman to be awarded the title of Professor at South Bank in that inaugural round in the academic session 1988–9 in which eight professors, mainly male scientists, were seen as meriting the academic honour. Recently (THES, 6 June 1997) SBU boasts 30 per cent of professors being women and is top of these league tables.

    More intriguingly, the initial round of conferments of the title of professor on existing meritorious members of the academic staff was presided over by the first woman head of an academic institution of higher education in the public sector. Mrs Pauline Perry subsequently became the first woman to be awarded the title of vice chancellor when South Bank became incorporated as a University in the first round after the passing of the Further and Higher Education Act of 1992. Moreover, her own origins paralleled, but did not mirror, those of the institution of which she was then director, since she had come to South Bank from a career as one of Her Majesty's Inspectors of Schools (HMI) as had one of her nineteenth century illustrious predecessors as I document.
2. G. B. Shaw *Man and Superman*, 1903. Emphasis added.
3. A. Tropp *The School Teachers*, London, Heinemann, 1957, p. 11.

4. M. E. David *The State, the Family and Education*, London, Routledge & Kegan Paul, 1980.
5. H. C. Bartle *A History of Borough Road College*, Dalkieth Press, 1976.
6. Tropp op.cit., p. 23.
7. In David op.cit.
8. See note 1. above.
9. In David 1980, op.cit.
10. ibid.
11. J. E. Brennan *Education for National Efficiency: The contribution of the Webbs*, London, Longman, 1975, p. 13.
12. ibid.
13. In David, 1980, op.cit.
14. Brennan op.cit.
15. Brennan op.cit.
16. ibid., p. 15.
17. O. Banks *The Sociology of Education*, London, Batsford, 1976, p. 3.
18. M. Argles *South Kensington to Robbins*, London, Longman, 1964, p. 40.
19. ibid.
20. Sir Phillip Magnus 'The New Polytechnic Institutes' in D. Macleod (ed.) *Good Words for 1889*, London, Isbister and Co., 1889, p. 622.
21. ibid., p. 622.
22. Brennan op.cit., p. 24.
23. Introduction, Bayley op.cit.
24. Bayley ibid., p. 10.
25. F. G. Evans *Borough Polytechnic 1892–1969*, London, Borough Polytechnic, 1979, pp. 14–15.
26. C. Dyhouse *Girls Growing Up in Late Victorian and Edwardian England*, London, Routledge & Kegan Paul, 1981.
27. Evans op.cit.
28. C. Booth *Life and Labour of the People in London*, 1889, vol. 1.
29. J. Purvis *Hard Lessons: The Lives and Education of Working Class Women in Nineteenth Century England*, Oxford, Polity Press, 1989 and C. Dyhouse *Feminism and the Family in England 1880–1939*, Oxford, Blackwell, 1989.
30. A. M. McBriar in M. Cole (ed.) *The Webbs and their Works*, London, Mueller, 1949, p. 88.
31. F. G. Evans *Borough Polytechnic 1892–1969*, London, Borough Polytechnic, 1969.
32. ibid., p. 26.
33. M. E. David *Reform, Reaction and Resources: The 3Rs of Educational Planning*, NFER Pub. Co, 1977.
34. Webb in Bayley op.cit.
35. Beveridge Report *Social Insurance and Allied Services*, HMSO, Cmd 1942.

36. H. Glennerster and G. Wilson *Paying for Private Education*, 1976.
37. David 1980, op.cit.
38. O. Banks *Parity and Prestige in English Secondary Education*, London, Routledge & Kegan Paul, 1955, p. 8.
39. ibid., p. 248.
40. M. E. David *Parents Gender & Education Reform*, Cambridge, Polity Press, 1993.
41. ibid.
42. David 1977, op.cit.
43. M. E. David and D. Woodward (eds) *Negotiating the Glass Ceiling: Senior Women in Academe*, London UCL/Taylor & Francis, 1997.
44. T. Burgess and J. Pratt *The Polytechnics: A Report*, London, Pitman, 1974.
45. Robbins committee's Report *Higher Education*, 1963.
46. David 1980, op.cit.
47. A. Halsey, A. Heath and J. M. Ridge *Origins and Destinations: Family, Class and Education*, Oxford, Clarendon Press, 1980.
48. David 1993, op.cit.
49. ibid.
50. ibid. and P. Brown 'The "third wave": education and the ideology of parentocracy, *British Journal of the Sociology of Education*, 11/1, 65–68, 1990.
51. S. Gewirtz, S. Ball and R. Bowe *Markets, Choice and Equity in Education*, Buckingham, Open University Press, 1995.
52. A. Edwards, J. Fitz and G. Whitty *The State and Private Education: An Evaluation of the Assisted Places Scheme*, Lewes, Falmer Press, 1989.
53. R. Edwards *Mature Women Students: Separating or Connecting Family and Education*, Taylor and Francis, 1993 and M.E. David, R. Edwards, M. Hughes and J. Ribbens *Mothers and Education Inside Out? Exploring Family-Education Policy and Experience*, London, Macmillan, 1993.

Chapter Five

1. E.J. Thompson, 'The growth of Greater London', *Quarterly Bulletin of the Research and Intelligence Unit GLC*, no. 8, September, 1969.
2. M.C. Borer, *The City of London: A history*, 1977.
3. F. Sheppard, *London 1808–1870: The Infernal Wen*, 1971, p. 19.
4. J.F.B. Firth, *Municipal London; or, London government as it is, and London under a municipal council*, 1876, pp 98–9.
5. S. Webb and B. Webb, *English Local Government. The Manor and the Borough*, 1908, pp 569–79.
6. D. Owen (R. MacLeod ed.), *The Government of Victorian London 1855–1889* Cambridge, Mass., 1982, p. 255.

7. J. Lang, *City and Guilds of London Institute, 1878–1978. An Historical Commentary*, 1978, p. 13.
8. W. Carew Hazlitt, *The Livery Companies of the City of London. Their Origin, Character Development and Social and Political Importance*, 1892, p. 35.
9. ibid., p. 32.
10. L.B. Sebastian, *The City Livery Companies and Their Corporate Properties*, 1885.
11. I.G. Doolittle, *The City of London and its Livery Companies*, Dorchester, 1982 p. 5.
12. J.K. Melling, *Discovering London's Guilds and Liveries*, 3rd ed., 1981.
13. J.R. Kellett, 'The breakdown of Guild and Corporation control over the handicraft and related trade in London', *Economic History Review*, X, 1957–8.
14. Doolittle, op. cit., p. 89.
15. *Second Report of the Commissioners appointed to inquire into the Municipal Corporations in England and Wales (London and Southwark, City Companies)*, Cmd. 239, 1837, XXV.
16. Owen, op. cit., p. 239.
17. Doolittle, op. cit., p. 25.
18. Sheppard, op. cit., p. 150.
19. W.L. Rowland, 'Royal Commissions and Commissions of Enquiry touching the Corporation of London', *Transactions of the Guildhall Historical Association*, III, 1963.
20. *Report of the Select Committee on London Corporation (Charges of Malversation)*, PP., 1887, X, 161.
21. Owen, op. cit., p. 228.
22. *Royal Commission on the State of the City Corporation*, XXVI, 1772.
23. ibid., pp. XXVI, XXVII – XXVIII.
24. Owen, op. cit., p. 228.
25. The new authority for London will exclude the City thus honouring a long established tradition.
26. Royston Lambert, *Sir John Simon, 1816–1904, and English Social Administration*, 1963.
27. Owen, op. cit., Chapter three.
28. W.A. Robson, *The Government and Misgovernment of London*, 1939, p. 41.
29. J. Simon, *The Social Origins of English Education*, 1970: Nicholas Hals, *New Trends in Education in the Eighteenth Century*, 1951, pp 63–81.
30. P. Earle, *A city full of people. Men and women of London, 1650–1750*, 1984
31. N. Harte and J. North, *The World of University College London, 1828–1990*, 1991.
32. Hals, op. cit., pp 82–116.

33. Borer, op. cit.
34. R. O'Day, *Education and Society 1500–1800. The Social Foundation of Education in Early Modern Britain*, 1982.
35. W.K. Jordan, *The Charities of London, 1480–1660*, 1960.
36. W.J. Reader, *Professional Men. The Rise of the Professional Classes in Nineteenth Century England*, 1966.
37. R.C. Michie, *The City of London. Continuity and Change, 1850–1990*, 1992.
38. D.J. Olsen, *The Growth of Victorian London*, 1976, p. 123.
39. R. Price Williams, 'The Population of London, 1801–1881', *Journal of the Royal Statistical Society*, 48, 3, 1885; Shannon, op. cit.
40. *Royal Commission on State of the City Corporation*, 1854, XXVI, minutes of evidence.
41. J. Summerson, 'The Victorian re-building of the City of London', *The London Journal*, III, 1977.
42. Sheppard, op. cit., p. 47.
43. J.R. Kellett, *The Impact of Railways on Victorian London*, 1969.
44. Michie, op. cit.
45. D. Kynaston, *The City of London. Volume I. A World of its Own, 1815–1890*, 1994.
46. P. Stevens, *City and Guilds of London Institute. A Short History 1878–1992*, 1993
47. G. Smalley, *The Life of Sir Sydney Waterlow Bt. London Apprentice, Lord Mayor, Captain of Industry, and Philanthropist*, 1909.
48. idem, p. 213.
49. J.F.C. Harrison. *A history of the Working Men's College 1854–1951*, 1954.
50. Records of City and Guilds of London Institution. Guildhall Library. Minute Books. MS 22,000.
51. ibid. MS 21,813 and MS 21,812 for records of formal proceedings.
52. Smalley, op. cit.
53. Stevens, op. cit., p. 14.
54. ibid.
55. Report of a speech given at a Prize Distribution at Greenwich on 11 November 1875. *The Times*, 12 November 1875.
56. Presidential Address, Society of Arts, 3 December 1875.
57. Quoted by Lang, op. cit., 1978, p. 15.
58. Quoted in F. Johnson, 'Evening Education in England with special reference to London', Ph.D., London University, 1937, p. 91.
59. Smalley, op. cit., pp 213–4.
60. Stevens, op. cit., p. 17.
61. Guildhall Library, Minutes of the Executive Sub-Committee. MS 21,813.
62. Guildhall Library, Minutes of the General Committee for the purpose of preparing a scheme for a national system of Technical Education, 1877–8. MS 21,812.

63. Stevens, op. cit., p. 18.
64. Lang, op. cit., 1978, p. 13.
65. See *The Times*, 18 October 1881, for comments on Magnus: Frank Foden, *Philip Magnus. Victorian Educational Pioneer*, 1970.
66. Stevens, op. cit., p. 33.
67. Smalley, op. cit., p. 220.
68. Lang, op. cit., p. 46.
69. Guildhall Library. MS 21,861.
70. Guildhall Library. MS 21,870 Correspondence with the Corporation of London: MS 21,871 Correspondence with the Livery Companies.
71. Stevens, op. cit., p. 64.
72. ibid, 56.
73. ibid, 60.
74. W. Gilbert, *The City, An Inquiry into the Corporation, its Livery Companies, and the Administration of their Charities and Endowments*, 1877.
75. *Report of the Royal Commission on the City of London Livery Companies*, Cmd. 4073, 1884.
76. Owen, op. cit., p. 255.
77. *Report of the Select Committee on London Corporation (Charges of Malversation)*, 1887.
78. ibid., XXXIX, Owen, op. cit., p. 157.
79. Cmd. 4073, 1884, p. 30.
80. Letter to *The Times*, 30 June 1869, signed 'Civis'.
81. Belcher, op. cit., p. 9.
82. PD, CLXXX, 705–7.
83. Belcher, op. cit., p. 22.
84. *Royal Commission appointed to inquire into the condition and administration of the Parochial Charities in the City of London*, 1880. C. 2522 XX I
85. *Dictionary of National Biography:* H.A.L. Fisher, *James Bryce (Viscount of Dechmont)*, 1927.
86. *Report from the Select Committee on Parochial Charities (London) Bill and London Parochial Charities Bill*, PP., 1882, XII.
87. Belcher, op. cit., p. 52.
88. W. Fishman, *East End 1888. A Year in a London Borough among the Labouring Poor*, 1988.
89. Doolittle, op. cit., p. 86.
90. Belcher, op. cit., p. 57.
91. *Charity Record*, 4 August 1887, p. 249.
92. *Royal Commission on Technical Instruction. Second Report*, 1884. C. 3981
93. G. Stedman Jones, *Outcast London. A Study of the Relationship between Classes in Victorian Society*, 1976.
94. Johnson, op. cit., p. 162.

95. C.H. Dudley and C.B. Spencer, *The Unconventional Civil Servant: Sir Henry H. Cunynghame*, 1938.
96. *Return of certain Objectives and Suggestions received by the Charity Commissioners . . . and of certain Memoranda and Reports prepared by the Charity Commissioners*, PP., 1890, LV, pp 72–112.
97. E. M. Wood, *A History of the Polytechnic*, 1965, p. 135.
98. *Return of Certain Objectives . .* op. cit., pp 112–216; see also *The Times*, 3 October 1887 for a statement of the intentions of the Commissioners.
99. Johnson, op. cit., pp 162.
100. Wood, op. cit., p. 19–23.
101. ibid., p. 25.
102. ibid., p. 54.
103. G.P. Moss and M.V. Saville, *From Palace to College: An Illustrated Account of Queen Mary College*, 1985.
104. ibid., p. 21.
105. *The Times* 3rd October 1887, p. 4.
106. D. Richards, *Offspring of the Vic. A history of Morley College*, 1958, p. 81.
107. Belcher, op. cit., p. 62.
108. ibid., p. 64.
109. A.G.B. Atkinson, *St Botolph Aldgate: The Story of a City Parish*, 1898.
110. S.J. Farthing, 'Sir John Cass and his School', *Transactions of the London and Middlesex Archeological Society*, 1910.
111. Owen, op. cit., p. 294: Belcher, op. cit., p. 64.
112. *The Times*, 26 September 1889, p. 13.
113. Belcher, op. cit., p. 72.
114. *41st Report of the Charity Commissioners*. PP., 1894. XXVIII, pp 33–37.
115. Belcher, op. cit., p. 120.
116. ibid., p. 121.
117. A. Saint, 'Technical Education and the early LCC', in A. Saint (ed.) *Politics and the People of London. The LCC 1889–1965*, 1989; E.J.T. Brennan, *Education for National Efficiency. The Contribution of Sidney and Beatrice Webb*, 1975.
118. *London Polytechnic Council. Minute Books 1894-1907*, vol. II, pp 4–5.
119. K. Young, *London Politics and the Rise of Party*, 1975.
120. *Royal Commission on the Amalgamation of the City and County of London*. Cmd. 7493, 1894.
121. P. Thompson, *Socialists, Liberals and Labour. The struggle for London, 1885–1914*, 1967.
122. Kynaston, op. cit., vol.I, p. 22.
123. Caroline Bingham, *The History of Royal Holloway College 1886–1986*, 1987.

124. ibid., p. 32.
125. Kynaston, op. cit., p. 84.
126. ibid., p. 202.
127. H. Perkin, *The Rise of Professional Society: England since 1800*, 1989.
128. Hudson, op. cit., p. 7.
129. ibid., p. 52.
130. J. Bryce, 'Commercial Education', *North American Review*, June 1899.
131. *The Times*, 10th August 1887.
132. S. Webb, *London Education 1904*, p. 100.
133. K. Lysons, *A Passport to Employment. A History of the London Chamber of Commerce and Industry Education Scheme 1887–1987*, 1988.
134. ibid., p. 33.
135. R. Dahrendorf, *LSE. A History of the London School of Economics and Political Science 1895–1995*, 1995.
136. LCC. Technical Education Board. *Report of the Special Sub-Committee on Commercial Education. Adopted by the TEB, 20th February, 1899*, TEB, 1899.
137. ibid., p. 74.

Chapter Six

1. W.E. Jackson, *Achievement: A Short History of the LCC* (London: Longman, Green & Co. Ltd., 1963), p. 3.
2. S. Webb, *The London Programme* (London: Sonnenschein, cheap edition, 1892), p. 17.
3. R.M. MacLeod, 'Education: Scientific and Technical' in *Education* (Dublin: Irish University Press, 1977), ed. Gillian Sutherland and others, p. 212.
4. A.M. McBriar, 'Sidney Webb and the LCC' in *The Webbs and their Work* (Hassocks: The Harvester Press Ltd. 1974), ed. Margaret Cole, p. 87.
5. LCC Minutes of Proceedings, Jan-Jun, 1891, p. 29.
6. ibid., p. 153.
7. ibid., p. 155.
8. ibid., p. 156.
9. ibid., p. 32.
10. *The London Programme*, Preface.
11. ibid., p. 16.
12. Beatrice Webb, *Our Partnership*, ed. by B. Drake and M.I. Cole, 2nd ed. (Cambridge: Cambridge University Press, 1975), p. 76.
13. *The London Programme*, p. 175.
14. LCC Minutes of Proceedings, Jan-Jun, 1892, p. 328.
15. ibid., p. 392.

16. *Our partnership*, p. 78.
17. A.H.C. Acland, H. Llewellyn Smith, *Technical Education in England and Wales* (London: National Association for the Promotion of Technical and Secondary Education, 1889), p. 135.
18. H. Llewellyn Smith, *Report to the Special Committee on Technical Education (LCC: London, 1892), pp 5–6*.
19. ibid., p. 10.
20. ibid., p. 11.
21. ibid., p. 9.
22. ibid., p. 18.
23. ibid., p. 25.
24. ibid., p. 71.
25. ibid., p. 78.
26. LCC Minutes of Proceedings, Jan-Jun, 1893, p. 133.
27. *Education for National Efficency: the Contribution of Sidney and Beatrice Webb* (London: Athlone Press of the University of London, 1975), ed. E.J.T. Brennan, p. 27.
28. Technical Education Board Annual Report, 1893–94, p. 4.
29. Ibid., p. 6.
30. ibid., p. 17.
31. *Our partnership*, p. 102.
32. Sidney Webb, *London Education* (London: Longmans, 1904), p. 170.
33. TEB Annual Report, 1893–94, p. 25.
34. W.A. Devereux, *Adult Education in Inner London 1870–1980* (London: Inner London Education Authority, 1982), p. 33.
35. B.M. Allen, *William Garnett, a memoir* (Cambridge: Heffer, 1933), pp. 78–79.
36. *Fabian News*, June 1899, quoted in L. Radice, *Beatrice and Sidney Webb: Fabian Socialists* (London: Macmillan, 1984), p. 151.
37. *London Education Service* (London: London County Council, 1939).
38. Ibid., p. 49.
39. Ibid., p. 42.
40. S. Maclure, *A History of Education in London 1870–1990* (London: Allen Lane, The Penguin Press, 2nd ed. 1990), p. 181.
41. *Review of the London Scheme of Further Education 1949* (LCC: Education Committee, 1951) ed. 779.
42. *A History of Education in London 1870–1990, p. 230*.

Chapter Seven

1. D. Owen, *English Philanthropy 1660–1960,* Oxford University Press, London, 1965, p. 59 and *Everyman's Encyclopaedia*, J.M. Dent & Sons, London, 1978, vol. III p. 284.
2. S. Webb, *London Education*, Longman, Green and Co., London, 1904, p. 138.

3. V. Belcher, *The City Parochial Fund 1891–1991*, Scholar Press, Aldershot, 1991, p. 62.
4. *Mansion House Speech 1888*, Surrey University Archives.
5. *Spicer Papers*, S.U.A.
6. Belcher, op. cit., p. 110.
7. T. Hinde, *An Illustrated History of the University of Greenwich*, James & James (Publishers) Ltd., London, 1996, pp. 12–13.
8. Ibid., p. 16.
9. *Burdett-Coutts Papers*, Westminster College Archives.
10. Owen, op. cit., p. 415.
11. Ibid., p. 419.
12. Ibid., p. 417.
13. *Burdett-Coutts Papers*, Westminster College Archives.
14. Owen, op. cit., p. 395.
15. Ibid., p. 397.
16. Ibid., p. 398.
17. Belcher, op. cit., p. 97.
18. Ibid., p. 120.
19. Ibid., p. 121.
20. *Mansion House Speech 1888*, Surrey University Archives.
21. Belcher, op. cit., p. 63.
22. Ibid., p. 62.
23. *Spicer Papers*, Surrey University Archives.
24. *Original Printed List of Donations*, Surrey University Archives.
25. Belcher, op. cit., p. 127.
26. Webb, op. cit., p. 139.
27. Belcher, op. cit., p. 61.
28. Ibid., p. 148.
29. M. E. Bryant, *The London Experience of Secondary Education*, The Athlone Press, London, 1986, p. 402.
30. Belcher, op. cit., p. 131.
31. *Poster and Report on Bazaar 1889*, Surrey University Archives.
32. Belcher, op. cit., p. 130.
33. Ibid., p. 131.
34 Ibid, p. 141
35. S.J. Curtis, *History of Education in Britain, 7th Edition*, University Tutorial Press, London, 1967, p. 497.
36. Ibid., p. 497 and Belcher, op. cit., p. 123.
37. Webb, op. cit., p. 143.
38. Ibid., p. 144.
39. Curtis, op. cit., p. 499.
40. London County Council, *Technical Education Board Report 1893–94*.
41. J. Lawson and H. Silver, *A Social History of Education in England*, Methuen., London, 1973, p. 347 and Curtis, op. cit., p. 495.

42. M. E Bryant, op. cit., pp 403–04.
43. *Battersea Polytechnic Principal's Report 1896*, Surrey University Archives.
44. Belcher, op. cit., p. 143.
45. London County Council, 1904, *Reports of Technical Education Board 1893–1903*.
46. *Staff Register 1890 onwards*, Alleyn's School Archives.
47. *Battersea Polytechnic Institute Prospectus 1894–95*, Westminster College Archives.
48. *Headmaster's Report 1906*, Alleyn's School Archives.

Chapter Eight

1. Extract from a Letter of Quintin Hogg published in *The Polytechnic Magazine* in May 1880. Hogg published this magazine regularly and wrote most of its contents himself.
2. Ragged Schools were set up as early as 1835 to provide schooling and food for the very poorest children in London, Bristol and Norwich. By 1844 a Ragged School Union was set up and within 20 years provided material help to some 200 such schools. Among their many offshoots was the Boys' Shoeblack Brigade which kept many an urchin out of the workhouse. Once education became compulsory, the ragged schools were phased out – but the union continued for some considerable time to provide poor youngsters with employment.
3. The French *Ecoles Polytechniques* – *Les Grandes Ecoles* – grew not only in size but in stature and reputation. They are highly selective, admitting only the *crème de la crème* of *baccalaureat* holders who then also have to sit and pass a stiff entrance examination. These institutions were (and still are) considered of a higher standard than even the best universities. Shortly before British polytechnics took on university titles, French *polytechniques* were advised by their own umbrella body not to confuse polytechnics with *polytechniques* and not to enter into any academic agreements with them.
4. The swimming bath in the basement is still to be seen – and used – today.
5. E.M. Wood *The Polytechnic and its Founder Quintin Hogg* (1932), quoted in V. Belcher's *The City Parochial Foundation 1891–1991* (1991), p. 59.
6. C.H. Dudley Ward and C.B. Spencer *The Unconventional Civil Servant: Sir Henry H Cunynghame* (1938).
7. Victor Belcher *The City Parochial Foundation 1891–1991* (1991).
8. John Major, Prime Minister of a Conservative Government, to the House of Commons in May, 1991, at the launch of the White Paper which led to the Further and Higher Education Acts (March 1992).
9. On 6 March 1992, the Queen signed the Royal Assent to the Further

and Higher Education Acts (England and Wales) and ten days later, on 16 March, the equivalent Act (Scotland), that cleared the way to university title and status.

10. V. Belcher *The City Parochial Foundation 1891–1991*, p. 62.
11. Ibid.
12. V. Belcher *The City Parochial Foundation 1891–1991*, p. 62.
13. C. T. Millis *Technical Education: Its Development and Aims* (1925) p. 81.
14. Annual Report Northern Polytechnic Institute, 1896; University of North London archives.
15. V. Belcher, *The City Parochial Foundation 1891–1991*, p. 121.
16. Ibid., p. 121.
17. This article appeared in *The Islington Gazette*, 24 September 1889, but was a verbatim copy of a leader written and published four days earlier in the *Evening News and Post*.
18. The letter was first published in *The Times*, 21 September 1889. It was reprinted in *The Morning Post* two days later on 23 September.
19. *London Evening News*, 24 September 1889.
20. This long and involved report in *The Times*, dated 26 September 1889, was by-lined 'From a Correspondent'.
21. Report in *The Mercury*, 9 November 1889.
22. The report of the meeting and contents of Mr Fearon's letter were published in the *Daily Chronicle* and also reported in the *Daily News* and *The Standard*, all dated 16 November 1889.
23. This item appeared in *The Daily Telegraph*, 23 November 1889.
24. A full and detailed account of the Caledonian Road meeting was publishned in the *Islington Gazette*, 25 November 1889.
25. The meeting was reported in *The Echo*, 6 December 1889.
26. University of North London archives.
27. Various newspaper cuttings; North Western Polytechnic archives.
28. University of North London, Annual Report, 1897.
29. *Northern Polytechnic Institute Prospectus 1903–1904*.
30. *Northern Polytechnic Institute Prospectus 1904–1905*.
31. *Principal's Report*, 1913–14.
32. *Principal's Report*, 1915–16.
33. *University of North London Principal's Report*, 1916–17.
34. *Principal's Report*, 1930–31 Northern Polytechnic.
35. It was later to become Highbury Grove School for Boys.
36. *Principal's Report, Northern Polytechnic for the Session 1930–31*, p. 5.
37. Victor Belcher, *The City Parochial Foundation 1891–1991* (1991), pp. 61–2.
38. Colleges of Advanced Technology, designated in 1956, were given university status in 1963–4. They included the City of London Northampton College (one of the old 'polys') which became City

University. Others became the universities of Aston in Birmingham, Bath, Brunel, Bradford, Loughborough, Salford, Surrey and the University of Wales Institute of Science and Technology.

39. The CNAA – a body which was awarded its own royal charter in 1964 (another Robbins recommendation) to validate courses and award degrees *outside* the university sector. The CNAA was wound up a few months after the New Polytechnics became New Universities.

40. The other London polytechnics had also new titles: City of London Polytechnic (its wish to call itself City of London University was rejected as it could be confused with City University) became London Guildhall University; Polytechnic of East London became the University of East London; Kingston Polytechnic became Kingston University; Middlesex Polytechnic – Middlesex University; Polytechnic of North London – University of North London; South Bank Polytechnic – South Bank University; Thames Polytechnic – University of Greenwich; Polytechnic of West London – Thames Valley University.

41. From a Letter of Quintin Hogg published in *The Polytechnic Magazine* in May 1880.

Chapter Nine

1. N. Harte, *The University of London, 1836–1986* (London: Athlone Press, 1986), p. 25.
2. F.M.G. Willson, *Our Minerva: the Men and Politics of the University of London, 1836–1858* (London: The Athlone Press, 1995), p. 41.
3. R. Aldrich, 'The Evolution of Teacher Education', in N.J. Graves, *Initial Teacher Education Policies and Progress* (London: Kogan Page and Institute of Education, University of London, 1990), p. 13.
4. R.W. Rich, *The Training of Teachers in England and Wales during the Nineteenth Century* (Cambridge: Cambridge University Press, 1933), p. 5.
5. British and Foreign School Society, Annual Report, 1814, p. 3, quoted in R.W. Rich, *The Training of Teachers in England and Wales during the Nineteenth Century* (Cambridge: Cambridge University Press, 1933), pp 7–8.
6. G.F. Bartle, *A History of Borough Road College* (London: Dalkeith Press, 1976), p. 9.
7. G.F. Bartle, *A History of Borough Road College* (London: Dalkeith Press, 1976), pp 45–6.
8. N. Whitbread, *The Evolution of the Nursery-Infant School: A History of Infant and Nursery Education in Britain, 1800–1970* (London: Routledge & Kegan Paul, 1972), pp 21–2.
9. Quoted in M. Cole, *'Be Like Daisies': John Ruskin and the Culti-*

vation of Beauty at Whitelands College (London: Bentham Press), p. 3.

10. J. Kay-Shuttleworth, *Four Periods of Public Education* (1862), p. 399, quoted in R.W. Rich, *The Training of Teachers in England and Wales during the Nineteenth Century* (Cambridge: Cambridge University Press, 1933), p. 65. For Kay-Shuttleworth see R.J.W. Selleck, *James Kay-Shuttleworth, Journey of an Outsider* (London: Woburn Press, 1994); for Battersea see T. Adkins, *The History of St. John's College, Battersea* (London: National Society, 1906).

11. J. Kay-Shuttleworth, *Four Periods of Public Education* (1862), pp 404–5, quoted in R.W. Rich, *The Training of Teachers in England and Wales during the Nineteenth Century* (Cambridge: Cambridge University Press, 1933), p. 69.

12. R.W. Rich, *The Training of Teachers in England and Wales during the Nineteenth Century* (Cambridge: Cambridge University Press, 1933), p. 75.

13. H.C. Dent, *The Training of Teachers in England and Wales, 1800–1975* (London: Hodder and Stoughton, 1977), p. 12.

14. D. Coleridge, *The Teachers of the People* (1862), p. 37, quoted in R.W. Rich, *The Training of Teachers in England and Wales during the Nineteenth Century* (Cambridge: Cambridge University Press, 1933), p. 88.

15. R. Aldrich, 'The Evolution of Teacher Education', in N.J. Graves, *Initial Teacher Education Policies and Progress* (London: Kogan Page and Institute of Education, University of London, 1990), pp 18–20.

16. G. Handley, *The College of All Saints: An Informal History of One Hundred Years* (London: College of All Saints, 1978), p. 3.

17. F.M.G. Willson, *Our Minerva: the Men and Politics of the University of London, 1836–1858* (London: The Athlone Press, 1995), p. 319.

18. T.H. Simms, *Homerton College, 1695–1978* (Cambridge: Homerton College, 1979), p. 24.

19. T.H. Simms, *Homerton College, 1695–1978* (Cambridge: Homerton College, 1979), p. 34.

20. G.F. Bartle, *A History of Borough Road College* (London: Dalkeith Press, 1976), p. 55.

21. G.F. Bartle, *A History of Borough Road College* (London: Dalkeith Press, 1976), p. 69.

22. I.M. Lilley, *Maria Grey College 1878–1976* (npp: np, 1981), pp 20–1.

23. A. Pomfret, *Dartford College, 1885–1985* (London: Thames Polytechnic, 1985), p. 12.

24. N. Whitbread, *The Evolution of the Nursery-Infant School: A History of Infant and Nursery Education in Britain, 1800–1970* (London: Routledge & Kegan Paul, 1972), pp 36–7.

25. G. Handley, *The College of All Saints: an Informal History of One Hundred Years* (London: College of All Saints, 1978), pp 30–39.

26. H.C. Dent, *The Training of Teachers in England and Wales, 1800–1975* (London: Hodder and Stoughton, 1977), p. 26.

27. R.W. Rich, *The Training of Teachers in England and Wales during the Nineteenth Century* (Cambridge: Cambridge University Press, 1933), p. 237.

28. H. Chester, *The Proper Limits of the State's Interference in Education* (1861), quoted in R.W. Rich, *The Training of Teachers in England and Wales during the Nineteenth Century* (Cambridge: Cambridge University Press, 1933), p. 220.

29. M. Argles, *South Kensington to Robbins: an Account of English Technical and Scientific Education since 1851* (London: Longmans, 1964), pp 52–3.

30. City and Guilds of London Institute, *City and Guilds of London Institute: A Short History, 1878–1992* (London: City and Guilds of London Institute, 1993), p. 18.

31. Quoted in S.F. Cotgrove, *Technical Education and Social Change* (London: George Allen and Unwin, 1958), p. 33.

32. R. Aldrich, *School and Society in Victorian Britain: Joseph Payne and the New World of Education* (New York: Garland; Epping: College of Preceptors, 1995), pp 166, 172–3.

33. W. Taylor, 'Education', in F.M.L. Thompson (ed.), *The University of London and the World of Learning, 1836–1986* (London: Hambledon Press, 1990), pp 228, 230.

34. H.C. Barnard, 'John William Adamson (1857–1947)', *British Journal of Educational Studies*, 1961, X(1), pp 20–2.

35. F.J.C. Hearnshaw, *The Centenary History of King's College London 1828–1928* (London: Harrap, 1929), p. 510.

36. F.J.C. Hearnshaw, *The Centenary History of King's College London 1828–1928* (London: Harrap, 1929), pp 369, 511; H. Hale Bellot, *University College London, 1826–1926* (London: University of London Press, 1929), p. 386.

37. M.J. Tuke, *A History of Bedford College For Women, 1849–1937* (London: Oxford University Press, 1939), p. 259, Chart 1.

38. Robert R. Rusk, 'Sir John Adams: 1857–1934', *British Journal of Educational Studies*, 1961, X(1), pp. 49–50.

39. J.W. Tibble, 'Sir Percy Nunn: 1870–1944', *British Journal of Educational Studies*, 1961, X(1), p. 67.

40. Quoted in P. Gardner, 'Higher Education and Teacher Training: a Century of Progress and Promise' in J. Furlong and R. Smith (eds), *The Role of Higher Education in Initial Teacher Training* (London: Kogan Page, 1996), p. 38.

41. F.J.C. Hearnshaw, *The Centenary History of King's College London, 1828–1928* (London: Harrap, 1929), p. 512.

42. M.J. Tuke, *A History of Bedford College For Women, 1849–1937* (London: Oxford University Press, 1939), p. 259.

43. M.V. Boyd, *The Church of England Colleges, 1890–1944: An Administrative Study* (Leeds: Museum of the History of Education, University of Leeds, 1984), p. 5.
44. S. Maclure, *One Hundred Years of London Education, 1870–1970* (London: Allen Lane, 1970), p. 91.
45. University of London Institute of Education, *Jubilee Lectures* (London: Institute of Education, 1952), p. 25.
46. Quoted in A.E. Firth, *Goldsmiths' College: A Centenary Account* (London: The Athlone Press, 1991), p. 25.
47. A.E. Firth, *Goldsmiths' College: A Centenary Account*, (London: The Athlone Press, 1991), p. 33.
48. D. Dymond (ed.), *The Forge: The History of Goldsmiths' College, 1905–1955* (London: Methuen, 1955), pp 10–14.
49. D. Shorney, *Teachers in Training 1906–1985: A History of Avery Hill College* (London: Thames Polytechnic, 1989), pp 53–9.
50. University of London Institute of Education, *Jubilee Lectures* (London: Institute of Education, 1952), p. 24.
51. S. Webb, 'London Education', *The Nineteenth Century*, October 1903, printed in E.J.T. Brennan (ed.), *Education for National Efficiency: The Contribution of Sidney and Beatrice Webb* (London: The Athlone Press, 1975), p. 112.
52. University of London Institute of Education, *Jubilee Lectures* (London: Institute of Education, 1952), pp 28–30.
53. J. Vincent Chapman, *Professional Roots: The College of Preceptors in British Society* (Epping: Theydon Bois Publications, 1985), pp 102–3.

Chapter Ten

1. N. Harte, *The University of London 1836–1986: An Illustrated History*. London: The Athlone Press, 1986, 48.
2. A.R. Hall, *Science for Industry: A Short History of the Imperial College of Science and Technology and its Antecedents*, London: Imperial College, 1982, 1.
3. T. Claxton, *Hints to Mechanics, on Self-education and Mutual Instruction*. London: Taylor & Walton, 1839.
4. *Star*, 12 November 1823.
5. *Bell's Weekly Messenger*, 16 November 1823.
6. For the history of Birkbeck College and its antecedents the London Mechanics' Institution and the Birkbeck Literary and Scientific Institution, see C. Delisle Burns, *A Short History of Birkbeck College (University of London)*. London: University of London Press, 1924.
7. Open letter by R.T. Stothard, 1839. Birkbeck College Archives, quoted in Burns.
8. H.G. Wells, *Experiment in Autobiography: Discussions and Conclusions of a Very Ordinary Brain (since 1866)*, London: Gollancz, Cresset Press, 1934.

9. A. Desmond, *Huxley: The Devil's Disciple*. London: Michael Joseph, 1994; R.W. Clark, *The Huxleys*. London: Heinemann, 1968.
10. Hall, 21–2.
11. H.E. Armstrong, *H.E. Armstrong and the Teaching of Science, 1880–1930*; ed. W.H. Brock. Cambridge: Cambridge University Press, 1973; H.E. Armstrong, *H.E. Armstrong and Science Education: Selections from 'The Teaching of Scientific Method' and other Papers on Education*; ed. G. Van Praagh. London: John Murray, 1973; J. Vargas Eyre, *Henry Edward Armstrong, 1848–1937: The Doyen of British Chemists and Pioneer of Technical Education.* London: Butterworths, 1958.
12. Department of Science and Art, *Reports*. London: Eyre & Spottiswoode, 1853–99.
13. Department of Science and Art, *First Report*. London: Eyre & Spottiswoode, 1854. Appendix C.
14. M.T. Lockyer and W.L. Lockyer, *Life and Work of Sir Norman Lockyer*, London: Macmillan, 1928; A.J. Meadows, *Science and Controversy: A Biography of Norman Lockyer*, London: Macmillan, 1972.
15. Burns, 74–7 and 116.
16. Select Committee on Scientific Instruction, *Report*. London: HMSO, 1867–8.
17. Royal Commission on Scientific Instruction and the Advancement of Science, *Report*. London: HMSO, 1871–4, 4 v.
18. Gresham University Commission, *Report & Minutes of Evidence.* London: HMSO, 1894, 2 v.
19. Select Committee on Museums of the Science and Art Department, *Reports*. London: HMSO, 1897–8, 2 v.
20. For the history of Imperial College and its various antecedents, see Hall, and also R.G. Williams and A. Barrett, *Imperial College: An Illustrated History*. London: Imperial College Archives, 1988.
21. For Haldane, see R. Burdon, Haldane: *An Autobiography*. London: Hodder & Stoughton, 1929, 2 v.; Sir F. Maurice, *Haldane: The Life of Viscount Haldane of Cloan*. London, Faber, 1937–9, 2 v.; D. Sommer, *Haldane of Cloan: His Life and Times, 1856–1928*, London: Allen and Unwin, 1960; E. Ashby and M. Anderson, *Portrait of Haldane at Work on Education*, London, Faber: 1956.

Chapter Eleven

1. Sir J. Reynolds, *Discourses on Art*, ed. R. Wark, Huntingdon Library, San Marino, California, 1959; First Discourse (1769), p. 13.
2. S. Macdonald, *The History and Philosophy of Art Education*, London, 1971, p. 38.
3. B.R. Haydon, *The Autobiography and Memoirs of Benjamin Robert*

Haydon, ed. Tom Taylor, new ed. (Intr. A. Huxley), Peter Davies, London, vol. II, p. 572.

4. Haydon,op. cit., p. 573.
5. Q. Bell, *The Schools of Design*, London, 1963, pp 57–60.
6. T.S.R. Boase, 'The decoration of the Palace of Westminster', *The Journal of the Warburg and Courtauld Institutes*, 1954, pp 319–58.
7. Bell, op. cit., p. 256.
8. S. Macdonald, *The History and Philosophy of Art Education*, University of London Press, 1971, Appendix A.
9. J. Ruskin, *The Laws of Fesole*, 1879; reprinted in *The Complete Works of John Ruskin*, ed. E.T. Cooke and J. Wedderburn, George Allen and Unwin, 1904, vol. XV, p. 344.
10. M. Richardson, *Architects of the Arts and Crafts Movement*, Trefoil Press, London, 1983, p. 8.
11. O. Garnett, Shearer West 'England, XV. Art Education' in *The Dictionary of Art*, ed. J. Turner, Macmillan, London, 1994, vol. X, p. 373.
12. M. Swenarton, *Artisans and Architects: The Ruskinian Tradition in Architectural Thought*, Macmillan Press, London, 1989, pp 96–108.
13. G. Stedman-Jones, *Outcast London. A Study in the Relationships between Classes in Victorian Society*, Oxford, 1971; Harmondsworth, 1976, pp. 19–32.
14. A. Saint, *The Image of the Architect*, Yale University Press, London and New Haven, 1983, pp 51–6.
15. J. Summerson, *A New Description of the Sir John Soane Museum*, Sir John Soane Museum, London, 1955, p. 7.
16. Saint, op. cit., p. 61.
17. Report by Webb to the TEB, February 1996. Quoted in Swenarton, op.cit., p. 114.
18. Swenarton, op.cit., p. 118.
19. Quoted in Swenarton, op. cit., p. 121.
20. J.A. Barnes (Forward) *City and Guilds of London Institute: A Short History 1878–1992*, London, 1993, p. 12.
21. The acquisition of the Lambeth school is dealt with in Chapter five.
22. J. Lang *City and Guilds of London Institute Centenary, 1878–1978*, London, 1978, p. 90.
23. Lang, op. cit., p. 91.
24. G. Hassell, *Camberwell – A Brief History*, London, 1962.
25. D. Dymond(ed.), *The Forge. The History of Goldsmith's College, 1905–1955*, Methuen, London, 1955, p. 2.
26. quoted in *The Forge*, op. cit., p. 3.
27. *The Forge*, op. cit., p. 5.
28. B. Laughton, *The Slade. 1871–1971. A Centenary Exhibition*, Royal Academy of Arts, London, 1971, p. 5.
29. S. Webb, *London Education*, London, 1904, p. 162.

Index